Kantianism, Liberalism, and Feminism

Kantianism, Liberalism, and Feminism
Resisting Oppression

Carol Hay
University of Massachusetts Lowell, USA

© Carol Hay 2013

Softcover reprint of the hardcover 1st edition 2013 978-1-137-00389-8

All rights reserved. No reproduction, copy or transmission of this publication may be made without written permission.

No portion of this publication may be reproduced, copied or transmitted save with written permission or in accordance with the provisions of the Copyright, Designs and Patents Act 1988, or under the terms of any licence permitting limited copying issued by the Copyright Licensing Agency, Saffron House, 6–10 Kirby Street, London EC1N 8TS.

Any person who does any unauthorized act in relation to this publication may be liable to criminal prosecution and civil claims for damages.

The author has asserted her right to be identified as the author of this work in accordance with the Copyright, Designs and Patents Act 1988.

First published 2013 by
PALGRAVE MACMILLAN

Palgrave Macmillan in the UK is an imprint of Macmillan Publishers Limited, registered in England, company number 785998, of Houndmills, Basingstoke, Hampshire RG21 6XS.

Palgrave Macmillan in the US is a division of St Martin's Press LLC, 175 Fifth Avenue, New York, NY 10010.

Palgrave Macmillan is the global academic imprint of the above companies and has companies and representatives throughout the world.

Palgrave® and Macmillan® are registered trademarks in the United States, the United Kingdom, Europe and other countries

ISBN 978-1-349-43445-9   ISBN 978-1-137-00390-4 (eBook)
DOI 10.1057/9781137003904

This book is printed on paper suitable for recycling and made from fully managed and sustained forest sources. Logging, pulping and manufacturing processes are expected to conform to the environmental regulations of the country of origin.

A catalogue record for this book is available from the British Library.

A catalog record for this book is available from the Library of Congress.

For Becca, whose welcome arrival didn't help the completion of this book. And for John, who surely did.

"So if I noticed or I didn't, why does it have to be my deal? What, because there's assholes in the world I don't get to ride on The Zipper? I don't get to ever spin?" ...

"Assholes are just assholes. What's getting hot and bothered going to do about it except keep me from getting to have fun?" ...

"[You] might ought to try just climbing on and spinning and ignoring assholes and saying Fuck 'em. That's pretty much all you can do with assholes."

– David Foster Wallace

"To let oneself be insulted without reprisal is already a diminution of one's own worth. The man who lets himself be trampled underfoot, shows himself to be a worm, a bee without a sting. He displays a want of forcefulness, whereas his duty is to stand opposed to all attacks on his personality. If he wishes others to have respect for his person, he must likewise hold fast to it, and show that he respects himself. He must at least bring the offending party to the point of an apology, so that he may be forgiven."

– Immanuel Kant (*Lectures on Ethics* 27: 606-607)

Contents

Preface viii

Acknowledgements xii

1 Liberalism & Oppression 1
2 A Feminist Defence of Kant 50
3 The Obligation to Resist Sexual Harassment 89
4 The Obligation to Resist Oppression 117
5 Respect-Worthiness and Dignity 158

Selected Bibliography 186

Index 197

Preface

What does the philosophy of a bunch of dead white men have to tell us about oppression? Rather a lot, I will argue.

This is a book about the harms of oppression, and about addressing these harms using the resources of liberalism and Kantianism. Its central thesis is that people who are oppressed are bound by the duty of self-respect to resist their own oppression. In it, I argue that it is only through liberal and Kantian principles that contemporary feminists can adequately describe and counteract the harms of oppression. And I argue that it is only by paying proper attention to the treatment of oppressed groups that Kantian liberalism can realize its promise. I have found that attempting to make sense of the harms of oppression using the resources of mainstream philosophy has the potential to pit me against two different camps of philosophers: those mainstream philosophers who do not seem to care much about the problems of oppression, on the one hand, and those philosophers who care quite a lot about oppression but reject both liberalism and Kantianism, on the other. My hopes here are to convince mainstream philosophers that the problems of oppression are real, and that they matter, and also to convince those who know very well what these problems are that the traditional canon of Western ethics and social and political philosophy has a great deal to offer in their analysis and resolution.

My analysis defends the importance of certain core ideals, specifically autonomy, the intrinsic and inalienable dignity of the individual, the importance of rationality, and the duty of self-respect. I make the case – a case that is explicitly Kantian – that these ideals are pivotal in both understanding and counteracting oppression. I acknowledge, and discuss in detail, the dangers of adopting this strategy, dangers that have been routinely described by theorists who worry that Kant's emphasis on autonomy as the locus of moral value fails to describe the full spectrum of ethical life, and that liberalism's historical failure to address oppression in any systematic way is a constitutive, not accidental, feature of the tradition. These dangers are real, but they are not unavoidable.

This book is divided into two sections. The first section is a detailed defence of the possibility of using both the liberal and Kantian theoretical frameworks to address feminist concerns. These expansions of liberalism and Kantianism amount to a significant revision and redeployment of what are now regarded by many philosophers interested in issues of social justice as antiquated and outmoded moral and social theories. The second section applies these two frameworks to a particular practical and theoretical concern: the question of whether people who are oppressed have an obligation to resist their oppression. I argue that if we take seriously certain central tenets of Kantian liberalism – those defending the fundamental importance of rationality, autonomy, and self-respect – then it follows that people who are oppressed have an obligation to themselves to resist their own oppression. My analysis throughout focuses primarily on sexist oppression, but for the most part I take my arguments and conclusions to apply, *mutatis mutandis*, to other forms of oppression as well.

Chapter 1 lays out the theoretical groundwork that is necessary for understanding the arguments that follow in the rest of the book. In it, I attempt to head off a number of misconceptions about what both oppression and liberalism are. I begin by offering a definition of oppression that says that an individual is oppressed if and only if (i) she is unjustly harmed in a group-specific way, and, (ii) this harm is part of a structural and systemic network of social institutions. I then synthesize what I think are the most incisive criticisms of the liberal tradition's inability to accommodate the reality of oppressive social circumstances, cataloguing along the way how contemporary liberals are responding to these criticisms. I argue that many of these criticisms are not without merit, but that contemporary liberals can and do have responses here, that liberalism is an evolving doctrine whose contemporary manifestations are compatible with feminist, anti-racist, and anti-colonialist concerns. The version of feminist liberalism that I ultimately defend, however, requires a commitment to certain objective, transcultural moral ideals; this makes it a liberalism that that many liberals will reject as too comprehensive and many radicals will reject as imperialism in disguise.

Chapter 2 defends these moral ideals on Kantian grounds. I have found this to be a rather unpopular proposal. Kant is regarded by many as deeply hostile to the feminist goal of counteracting oppression. In this chapter, I defend the Kantian moral framework from two related criticisms, both of which claim that this framework is unsuitable for feminist purposes. One of these criticisms focuses on Kant's privileging the rational over the animal; the other focuses on his privileging the rational over the emotional. While I admit that there is much to be learned from these two criticisms, I deny that the oversights and inadequacies they highlight are necessary consequences of adopting the Kantian view. Kantianism has the resources within it, I claim, to both show us the full extent of the psychological harms that people can experience when they live under oppressive social conditions, and to suggest novel ways to ameliorate these harms, that we might otherwise not see. I caution that if we reject the Kantian framework because of the sorts of considerations emphasized by these criticisms we risk, in effect, throwing the baby out with the bathwater. I argue that Kantianism is uniquely able to capture the fundamental moral importance of self-respect, and thus is uniquely able to explain what is wrong with the gendered norms of self-sacrifice that have historically exploited women.

Chapter 3 is where I begin to use the liberal and Kantian frameworks to establish my claim that there is an obligation to resist oppression. The preliminary attempt in this chapter restricts its focus to the narrower question of whether women have an obligation to confront the men who sexually harass them. I argue that women's obligation to protect their autonomy from the harms of sexist oppression translates into a general obligation to confront harassers. A reluctance to be guilty of blaming the victims of sexual harassment, coupled with other practical and normative considerations that tell in favour of the unfairness of this obligation, might make us think that women never have an obligation to confront their harassers. But I argue that the fact that women are oppressed is not usually sufficient to relieve them of their moral obligation to resist that oppression by confronting the men who sexually harass them. Normative considerations of fairness do not remove this obligation, even if we are willing to recognize that it is not fair that women are burdened by extra moral obligations as a result of their oppression. We can recognize that women's oppression leaves them with an unfair share of obligations and still be justified in saying that they have further obligations to resist their oppression. I argue that the fact that patriarchy harms women by burdening them with unfair obligations is just one more reason it must be eradicated. I then take up an objection that attempts to undermine the obligation to resist sexist oppression by pointing out that its harms are almost never severe enough to completely destroy women's autonomy; answering this charge, I argue, requires a proper understanding of the relationship between autonomy and responsibility in general. I close the chapter with a preliminary analysis of the possibility that there can be many different ways to resist oppression.

In Chapter 4, I move on to my central argument in favour of a general obligation to resist oppression. This is an obligation that people have to themselves, I argue, which is grounded in a Kantian duty of self-respect. I begin by presenting a Kantian account of the obligation to resist one's oppression as an obligation that oppressed people have to protect their rational nature. I defend this Kantian account by considering some of the many ways oppression can harm people's rational nature, arguing that this harm is evidenced by a number of practical irrationalities to which oppressed people are particularly susceptible. I consider four objections that reject the obligation to resist oppression as too demanding – because it can be too dangerous; because requiring it amounts to blaming the victim; because it can be impossible and thus flouts the rule of ought implies can; and because it is only ever supererogatory – and respond by arguing that the obligation is not as onerous as it might initially appear to be because it is best thought of as an imperfect duty. This means there are many different forms that resistance to oppression can take, some of which I enumerate. I go on to argue that, because the fundamental duty here is one of self-respect, even in cases where external resistance is imprudent or impossible, an oppressed person can still recognize that something is wrong with her situation and that she deserves better. This, I argue, is profoundly better than nothing.

In Chapter 5 I take up what I consider to be the most pressing unresolved objection to my argument, the concern that it follows from the terms of this account that failing to fulfill the obligation to resist oppression might actually vitiate future instances of this obligation. The thought here is that if oppression harms rational nature, and if the value of rational nature is what grounds the obligation to resist oppression, then a person whose rational nature has been harmed by oppression will at some point no longer be obligated to resist it. Another way to think about this problem is that because someone who fails to fulfill the objection to resist her oppression has behaved immorally, and because it is someone's moral agency that gives her the sort of value that makes her worthy of moral respect, then being immoral might affect her respect-worthiness. And if someone is not worthy of respect, then it looks like she has no obligation to respect herself, and thus no obligation to resist her oppression. I respond to this dilemma by defending a novel interpretation of Kant's views on the relationship between the value we have and the respect we are owed. I argue, contra the received view among Kant scholars, that the feature in virtue of which someone has unconditional and incomparable value is not the same feature in virtue of which she is owed the respect that constrains how she may be treated. So, even though someone who fails to attempt to protect her rational nature fails to respect herself in the right way, and even though this moral failing does make her lose a certain kind of value, her obligations to respect herself do not go away.

Acknowledgements

I gratefully acknowledge permission to reprint various parts of my previously published works. This project began its life as my doctoral dissertation, "Rationality and Oppression: A Defence of the Obligation to Resist Oppression" (2008). It has changed a great deal since then. Some of the defences of liberalism in Chapter 1 were published, to very different ends, in my "Consonances between Liberalism and Pragmatism," *The Transactions of the C. S. Peirce Society* 48 (2012): 141–168 and "Justice and Objectivity for Pragmatists: Cosmopolitanism in the Work of Martha Nussbaum and Jane Addams," *The Pluralist* 7 (2012): 86–95. A very early version of the discussion in Chapter 3 was published as "On Whether to Ignore Them and Spin: Moral Obligations to Resist Sexual Harassment," *Hypatia* 20 (2005): 94–108. Earlier versions of the arguments in Chapter 4 and Chapter 5 were published as "The Obligation to Resist Oppression," *Journal of Social Philosophy* 42 (2011): 21–45, and "Respect-Worthiness and Dignity," *Dialogue: Canadian Philosophical Review* 51 (2012): 587–612 respectively.

The development of the ideas expressed in this book has benefited a great deal from the philosophical discussions I have had at a number of professional venues. Versions of the arguments defending liberalism that I develop in Chapter 1 were presented at a meeting of the Summer Institute in American Philosophy in 2011, a meeting of the Society for the Advancement of American Philosophy in 2011, a meeting of the Northern New England Philosophical Association in 2010, a Midwest Division meeting of the Society for Women in Philosophy in 2009, and a Pacific Division meeting of the American Philosophical Association in 2009. Parts of the feminist defence of Kant that I develop in Chapter 2 were presented at a Pacific Division meeting of the Society for Women in Philosophy in 2010. Some of the arguments in Chapter 3 were presented at a Society for Value Inquiry conference in 2005 and a Society for Analytical Feminism conference in 2004. Versions of the arguments in Chapter 4 were presented at the MIT Workshop on Gender and Philosophy in 2009, a Society for Analytical Feminism conference in 2008, and the University of Dayton's Richard R. Baker Colloquium on the topic of "Building Coalitions Across Difference" in 2008.

For their constructive feedback on this work in its many different stages, my sincerest thanks are owed to Louise Antony, Amy Baehr, Zac

Cogley, Ann Cudd, Robin Dillon, Jean Harvey, Sally Haslanger, Bob Innis, John Kaag, José Mendoza, Charles Mills, Susanne Sreedhar, Anita Superson, Timothy Schroeder, Sigrún Svavarsdóttir, Amelia Wirts, the participants of WOGAP, and several anonymous reviewers. Thanks to my family for their love and support. And thanks most of all to my partner, John Kaag, for making the writing of this book, and just about everything else in life, not only possible but wonderful.

1
Liberalism & Oppression

This chapter lays the groundwork for the remainder of this book. Because I do not assume that my reader has an expert knowledge of the theories of liberalism or of oppression, my goal here is to acquaint parties from each camp with the lessons of the other. I begin by articulating a definition of oppression that synthesizes the ideas of theorists as far back as J.S. Mill. I then summarize what I take to be the four most trenchant critiques of the liberal tradition's inability to accommodate the reality of oppressive social circumstances, cataloguing along the way the various ways that liberals are responding to these critiques. The literature in contemporary liberalism is vast, so I do not pretend to provide a completely comprehensive survey here. Instead this chapter should be read as a set of orienting remarks that set the stage for the subsequent discussions of Kantianism, liberalism, and oppression.

Liberalism has become extremely unpopular in some academic disciplines – particularly those disciplines that focus on the pernicious historical role liberal ideals have played in causing and justifying imperialism and colonialism, and those disciplines that aim to solve the problems involved in defining and negotiating the diverse multicultural ways of life that characterize our contemporary world. In a time when economic and political hegemonies threaten local traditions and populations, liberalism is now frequently viewed as the intellectual handmaid of homogenization, colonization, and marginalization. Critics of liberalism have argued that (1) because it relies on suspect notions of autonomy and liberty; (2) because it is overly individualistic; (3) because it is overly abstract; and (4) because of its commitment to either universalism or pluralism, liberalism is incapable of properly conceptualizing, much less ameliorating, the harms of oppression. I respond to each of these accusations in turn, admitting that in many cases these charges were almost certainly true of liberalism's historical incarnations. There is no denying that liberalism has historically failed to address oppression in any systematic way. But I will argue that because these failures are not the necessary result of liberalism's core tenets, they are not inevitable. We will see that contemporary liberal theorists can and do take these lessons on board. There is a radical potential in liberalism, a potential to use the resources of liberalism to respond to the realities of oppression, that many of its current critics overlook. Realizing this potential, however, requires assenting to a conclusion that neither all liberal theorists nor all anti-oppression theorists will be happy to accept. I conclude the chapter by arguing that anyone interested in social justice must be committed to certain objective, transcultural moral ideals.

A definition of oppression

Almost 150 years ago, in his 1869 *The Subjection of Women,* John Stuart Mill articulated what was probably the first liberal theory of oppression.[1] According to this account, oppression is a denial of equal liberty, which, for Mill, is tantamount to a denial of the opportunity to develop one's rational capacities for thought and action. Mill's central concern in *The Subjection of Women* was to establish that "the legal subordination of one sex to the other...is wrong in itself, and...one of the chief hindrances to human improvement."[2] Establishing this required, Mill thought, undermining the "almost universal opinion" that the subordination of women to men in his society was natural and therefore just.[3] To undermine this opinion, he addressed the question of why women in his society appeared to submit voluntarily to their oppression. His answer had three parts. First, Mill showed how women were made to be inferior, or allegedly inferior, to men by being coerced and by not having equal opportunities to develop their talents. The mechanisms that were used to manufacture and entrench women's inferiority included both social roles, such as motherhood, and legal institutions, such as marriage and property. Second, he showed how these real or perceived inferiorities were used to justify women's inequalities; women were seen as not fit for the public sphere because of their fragile and flighty natures and inferior mental faculties. Finally, he showed how, unlike other oppressed groups, women were made, not just to *obey* their oppressors, but to *want* to obey them:

> All men...desire to have, in the woman most nearly connected with them, not a forced slave but a willing one, not a slave merely, but a

favourite. They have therefore put everything in practice to enslave their minds.... All women are brought up from the very earliest years in the belief that their ideal of character is the very opposite to that of men; not self-will, and government by self-control, but submission, and yielding to the control of others.[4]

Women were raised to be content with their situation and to believe that their inferiority made their subordination to men natural. Women's beliefs and desires were manipulated by the oppressive social situations in which they lived so that they appeared to consent to these oppressive situations voluntarily. But women's choice to acquiesce in their oppression was hollow, Mill argued, because it took place in the absence of meaningful alternatives – the choice was between "that or none."[5]

Mill's account of the forces that conspired to oppress the women of his time was comprehensive and thorough; while it focused primarily on women's lack of legal rights, it also included economic, political, social, and psychological elements. The account that follows owes a great debt to this founding liberal thinker. This account of oppression has two conditions that are both individually necessary and jointly sufficient. According to this account, *an individual is oppressed if and only if (i) she is unjustly harmed in a group-specific way, and, (ii) this harm is part of a structural and systemic network of social institutions.* We will consider these two conditions in turn.

Unjust group-specific harm

Unlike non-oppressive harms, oppressive harms are directed at individuals in virtue of their membership in a group of people (and not every group of people will count as one whose members can be subject to oppression). This means that, for example, when in a case of oppression a woman is picked out as an individual who deserves harmful treatment, this treatment is directed at her not solely as an individual with particular handicaps or failures, but also as a member of a group – the group comprised of all women – whose members are considered collectively deserving of such treatment. Because oppressive harms come about as a result of judgements that concern the qualities that all members of a group are presumed to share, or that concern what such people are presumed to deserve, a harm counts as oppressive only if it results from the recognition that the individual in question is a member of a certain group or category of people. This is the first condition of oppression – that oppressive harms apply *in virtue of group membership*.

This condition has to do with how one becomes a candidate for being subject to oppressive harms. An individual is harmed in this group-specific way if and only if:

(i) she is harmed in virtue of being a member of a group, G; and,
(ii) on balance, members of G have a relative lack of social esteem, power, or authority; and,
(iii) on balance, members of another group, G*, benefit from her being harmed; and,
(iv) this harm is unfair, unearned, or illegitimate in some other way.

Because oppression is, fundamentally, a form of injustice that concerns groups, individual people are oppressed if and only if they are subject to injustice because they are members of a particular group. Sexist oppression harms people, then, in virtue of the fact that they are (or are taken to be) women. Racist oppression harms people in virtue of the fact that they are (or are taken to be) members of a particular race. And so on. But we need to ask, what *kind* of group of people we are talking about here. Do oppressed groups share certain specific features in virtue of their oppression? Iris Marion Young has argued that, because of the wide range of social and historical contexts in which the members of different oppressed groups live, it is not possible to come up with a single set of criteria capable of accounting for all the different conditions of oppression. She argues instead that different forms of oppression share only a family resemblance.[6] While Young is right to avoid an overly narrow definition of oppression – lest the account leave out some groups that should count as oppressed or leave out some of the ways that members of different groups are oppressed – there is reason to be wary of an account of oppression being *too* nonspecific. After all, if a definition ends up including groups that we do not intuitively think *should* count as oppressed, we risk not taking completely seriously the ways in which the harms of oppression are uniquely damaging. Taking account of the many different ways that oppression can be manifested is important, but it is also important that the concept not be diluted to the point where a charge of oppression carries little normative weight.

Also, there simply is more that can be said about the commonalities between different kinds of oppressed groups. This is where the second subcondition of this condition of oppression comes in: one characteristic that is shared by all oppressed groups is the *relative lack of social esteem* that is accorded them. Members of oppressed groups live in societies where their interests are widely seen as not as important as those of non-oppressed groups. This lack of social esteem means that the members of groups that are oppressed have *less power* and *less authority* than the rest of people in society. Oppressed people are more likely to be both politically disenfranchised (by, say, being forbidden or discouraged from voting or holding political office, or by having restricted access to other positions of political power and influence) and economically disenfranchised (by, say, being forbidden or discouraged from working, or by having restricted access to the best jobs, or by not being permitted to own property).

These disparities in esteem, power, and authority result not only in many unfair restrictions on the members of groups that are oppressed, but also in correspondingly unearned privileges for the members of groups that are not oppressed. To count as oppressive, the harms faced by the members of oppressed groups must also, on balance, serve the interests of the members of another group. This is the third subcondition of this condition of oppression: the members of another group must ultimately *benefit* from the harms experienced by the members of an oppressed group for these harms to be instances of oppression. This subcondition might seem strange, until one realizes that *relative advantage* can count as a benefit. If members of one group face systematic hardships that members of a second group do not, then members of the second group will be in a better position than members of the first group to compete for limited resources. Not having to compete on fair terms with members of oppressed groups is thus an unearned privilege that members of non-oppressed groups benefit from.[7] This subcondition rules out the possibility that everyone is equally oppressed. The harms of oppression are not inevitabilities like aging, disease, or death; oppression is not a necessary aspect of the human condition. This condition also explains why many of the harms members of non-oppressed groups experience in virtue of their membership in a group do not count as instances of oppression – because these harms ultimately do not benefit the members of oppressed groups.[8]

There are, however, some situations where the members of one group benefit from the harms experienced by the members of another group, and where the members of the latter group suffer from a relative lack of social esteem that results in a lack of power and authority, and yet these harms do not count as instances of oppression. For example, the systematic restrictions that prisoners face serve the interests of another group – the group consisting of law-abiding members of society at large. And prisoners make up a group of people that is generally looked down upon by society at large, and this relative lack of social esteem results in a lack of power and authority. Were meeting either of these two conditions not merely necessary but also sufficient for someone counting as oppressed, then prisoners would count as oppressed. But surely it is uncontentious to assume that a theory of just punishment can account for at least some restrictions on prisoners' agency, at least some of the time. When prisoners have earned the restrictions on their agency, these restrictions are legitimate and therefore not oppressive. The legitimacy of a harm – in this case, because it is deserved – should, intuitively, rule out the possibility of it being oppressive. This means that both facing harms that serve the interests of another group, and facing a lack of social status and a resulting lack of power and authority, are necessary but not sufficient conditions for someone to count as oppressed.

This point leads us to the final necessary subcondition: an oppressive harm or restriction must be unfair, unearned, or illegitimate in some other way. Harms that are deserved (say, because they are the result of just punishment) are not oppressive. As we have just seen, prisoners, for example, are harmed in virtue of their membership in a group but they do not count as oppressed just in virtue of their imprisonment. Assuming that a prisoner's incarceration is just, he or she has earned the restrictions on his or her agency and so he or she deserves this harm. Usually, restrictions count as unfair only when they are undeserved or unearned.[9] Only when a harm or restriction is *unfair*, then, is it a candidate for being an oppressive harm.

To recap: the first condition of our definition of oppression tells us that someone is oppressed only if she has undergone an unjust harm to which she is subject in virtue of her membership in a group or category of people. More specifically, an individual is harmed in this group-specific way if and only if (i) she is harmed in virtue of being a member of a group, G; (ii) on balance, members of G have a relative lack of social esteem, power, or authority; (iii) on balance, members of another group, G*, benefit from her being harmed; and, (iv) this harm is unfair, unearned, or illegitimate in some other way. These four subconditions are individually necessary and jointly sufficient for an individual to count as harmed in this group-specific way.

Structural and systemic harm

Unlike non-oppressive harms, which are more often the result of the intentional actions of a few people, or perhaps the result of a few isolated social policies, oppressive harms are more often the unintentional result of certain social norms and assumptions, the legitimacy of which typically goes unquestioned. Because of the role of these publicly shared assumptions, oppressive harms are rarely fully explainable by appealing solely to the actions or intentions of the particular person or the particular policy that might be directly responsible for them. In other words, oppressive harms are part of a *structural* and *systemic* network of social institutions. This is the second condition of oppression.

The systematicity of oppression has been most famously explained by Marilyn Frye, who illustrates the systematic nature of sexist oppression by analogy to a birdcage.[10] Frye points out that if you only ever look at a birdcage one wire at a time you will never see how such a structure could limit the mobility of its occupant. You will just assume that the bird could pick itself up, dust itself off, and fly around the wire in its way. But, if you were to step back and look at all of the wires of a birdcage together, you would see an interconnected system of barriers that function collectively to restrict the bird's freedom. Analogously, it can be hard to recognize people's oppression if you focus exclusively on any particular social, political, or economic institution or even if you focus exclusively on any particular restriction or frustration or instance of harm. Taken by themselves, these sorts of things can seem innocuous – not really capable of limiting someone's freedom in terribly profound or important ways. You will just assume that any given person should be able to pick herself up, dust herself off, and get on with her life in just the way anyone unlucky enough to be faced with a random setback would. Frye's metaphor suggests that it is only when you step back and look at the system of social, political, and economic institutions as a whole that you can see how it functions to oppress people.

Oppression thus needs to be understood from a macroscopic point of view, taking into account how economic, political, social, and psychological factors function in concert to negatively affect the life prospects of members of oppressed groups. This explains why oppressive harms can be overlooked – or explained away as individual slights or innocuous inconveniences or minor annoyances – unless we are careful to pay attention to the ways that these harms function systematically. That oppression is systemic means that the detrimental effects of oppression are usually only fully evident from a perspective that takes into account all their effects on a person's life prospects.

Because it is perpetuated primarily through social institutions, rather than the isolated actions of individual agents, a common (though not necessary) feature of oppression is that its harms are very often invisible and unintentional. Young describes this characteristic of oppression in terms of "the vast and deep injustices [members of] some groups suffer as a consequence of often unconscious assumptions and reactions of well-meaning people in ordinary interactions, media and cultural stereotypes, and structural features of bureaucratic hierarchies and market mechanisms – in short, the normal processes of everyday life."[11] The systematicity of oppression means that an oppressive harm need not be intended to be oppressive in order to be oppressive nor, even, need it be intended as a *harm*. The norms and assumptions responsible for the creation and maintenance of the institutions that are oppressive in societies like ours – institutions like the workplace, the family, the academy, religion, popular culture, and the media – very often function far beneath the level of the conscious intentions of the people taking part in these institutions. Oppression is thus fundamentally a social phenomenon that does not require individual people as oppressors. To be sure, oppression can take place when one individual person intentionally performs an action that harms another. But this is not the only, nor even the most common, kind of oppressive harm. Most oppressive harms tend not to be the result of the intentional actions of an individual person, but are more often the unintentional result of an interrelated system of social norms and institutions.[12] The existence of this latter kind of oppression means that even if everyone were well-intentioned, people could still be oppressed because many of the structural barriers of oppression function below the level of what people consciously intend.

Because the harms of oppression are, very commonly, not the result of the intentional actions of a single agent, notice what this means for the sense in which an oppressed person is "picked out" for harmful treatment in virtue of her membership in a social group. The language of "picking out" implies that there is an individual who does this picking, but in many of the most common cases of oppression this is not how things work. Sally Haslanger explains what goes on instead:

> In the context of oppression, certain properties of individuals are socially meaningful. This is to say that the properties play a role in a broadly accepted (though usually not fully explicit) representation of the world that functions to justify and motivate particular forms of social intercourse. The significant properties in question – in the cases at hand, assumed or actual properties of the body – mark you 'for application of oppressive pressures' insofar as the attribution of these properties is interpreted as adequate, in light of this background representation, to explain and/or justify your social position in a structure of oppressive social relations. In the case of women, the idea is that societies are guided by representations that link being female with other facts that have implications for how one should be

viewed and treated; insofar as we structure our social life to accommodate the cultural meanings of the female (and male) body, females occupy an oppressed social position.[13]

When an oppressed person is harmed in virtue of being a member of a group, it is not usually the case that this harm is the result of an individual saying to himself, "Ah, she's a member of the social group comprised of women! People who are women deserve to be treated in this harmful way!" This (or something like it) does happen sometimes. But in the more usual case, oppressive harms are not the result of the intentional actions of an individual person. Instead, they are the unintentional result of an interrelated system of social norms and institutions, or of the implicit biases held even by those individuals who consider themselves to be egalitarian.[14]

In addition to oppressive harms being unusual in that they are often not the intended result of a single intentional agent, they are also unusual in that they often involve the participation of those who suffer them. Oppressed people often actually participate in their own oppression. We saw Mill troubling over this phenomenon above, but he argued that this participation was only ever apparent – he was convinced that no one would actually voluntarily consent to being oppressed. Apparent consent was to be explained away as the result of coercion or ignorance. Many contemporary theorists of oppression are no longer this optimistic.

Instead, some argue that oppressed people face incentive structures that give them reason to actually participate in their own oppression. In these sorts of cases, labelled "oppression by choice" by Ann Cudd, "the oppressed are co-opted through their own short-run rational choices to reinforce the long-run oppression of their social group."[15] Successfully resisting oppression, for Cudd, emerges as a kind of collective action problem whereby it is individually rational for a person to support the oppression of her social group and thus, by extension, herself. She outlines the motivational forces that oppressed people face – both material forces (including violence and economic necessity) and psychological forces – and shows how the short-term payoffs of acquiescing to these forces can outweigh the long-term payoffs of attempting to resist oppression. Oppressed people thereby frequently find themselves in situations where it seems to be rational to acquiesce in their own oppression.

Another explanation for this acquiescence comes from the recognition that internalized oppression can damage people's sense of self-worth. This results in a phenomenon that the liberal tradition, with its emphases on individualism and autonomy, has a surprisingly difficult time dealing with. Part of respecting someone as an autonomous agent seems to require respecting her as the ultimate author of, and authority over, who she is, what she believes, what she desires, and what she values. But it is clearly the case that social forces can influence what desires we come to have. Anyone who has suffered the self-imposed indignity of enduring an evening wearing an excruciatingly uncomfortable but unbelievably stylish pair of shoes can attest to this. Social forces can make us want things that we almost certainly would not want in the absence of these forces. Still, often this kind of influence on us does not strike us as a particularly bad thing. We are, after all, social creatures, so we should expect a great deal of who we are, and what we want, to be shaped by the society in which we live. Recognizing that these things are often greatly affected by factors that are out of one's control seems to threaten the liberal ideal of autonomous agency. This problem is compounded when we recognize that social forces are capable of making people desire things that are patently not in their best interest, or fail to desire things that are in their best interest. Impractical shoes are one thing; choices that threaten one's actual well-being are quite another. Famously, the economist Amartya Sen has shown that, in conditions of prolonged scarcity, women and other oppressed people can actually fail to desire basic human goods when they become habituated to their absence and socialized to believe that expectations of receiving such goods are inappropriate for people like them.[16] In such cases, people can actually stop preferring to live otherwise, even when their quality of life is demonstrably below that which they need to survive. And, as we will see below, many feminists have argued that patriarchy causes many women to desire to fulfil stereotypical sex roles that actually severely restrict both the kind and the quality of choices that are open to them. This phenomenon, when people come to have preferences that are inimical to their best interests because of the effects of oppressive social forces, has come to be known as the problem of *adaptive preferences*. Examining the implications of this problem further will be a central focus of mine in the chapters that follow.

The system of oppressive social norms and institutions has *economic, political, social, and psychological* components, all of which are interrelated. The *economic* component of oppression is that people who are oppressed are economically disenfranchised. Historically (even currently, in some countries), this has meant that people who were oppressed were not permitted to own property. Currently, this means that people who are oppressed, on average, earn less money than non-oppressed people. The *political* component of oppression is that people who are oppressed are politically disenfranchised. Historically (and currently, in some countries), this has meant that people who were oppressed were not permitted to vote. Currently, this means that people who are oppressed tend not to occupy positions of political power and influence, either in politics proper or in the business world more generally. The *social* component of oppression is that the harms of oppression run much deeper than mere economic and political inequality. Some of the most powerful mechanisms of oppression are also the most mundane, because they have to do with ubiquitous social norms and roles, the legitimacy of which is often taken for granted. These social norms and roles define different standards of appropriateness for both oppressed and non-oppressed people for everything from behaviours and mannerisms to aspirations, values, interests, and terms of success. These social norms and roles function in concert to determine what it is possible for people to achieve, and the possibilities for people who are oppressed are much worse than they are for people who are not oppressed. The *psychological* component of oppression refers to the fact that the effects of oppression affect the inner lives of people who are oppressed. The psychological effects of oppression range from fear and trauma to humiliation, shame, and low self-esteem. Each of these effects harm people who are oppressed by depriving them of the psychological means necessary to compete with those who are not oppressed and to protect themselves from further harm. The structural and systemic nature of oppression means that each of these components of oppression – the economic, political, social, and psychological components – interacts with the others to harm people who are oppressed.

It is this system of interrelated harms that liberalism stands accused of being unable to address. Critics of liberalism argue that because it relies on suspect notions of autonomy and liberty, because it is overly individualistic, because it is overly abstract, and because of its commitment to pluralism, liberalism is incapable of properly conceptualizing, much less ameliorating, the harms of oppression. We will consider each of these objections to liberalism below. But first, it is worth getting clearer on exactly what the target is.

A definition of liberalism

What, exactly, is liberalism? Let me start with some platitudes. Liberals, most obviously, agree that *liberty* is the most important political value.

They agree that the best possible state is one that secures the greatest amount of liberty for each individual that is compatible with like liberty for all. They agree that this politically important liberty should give individuals freedoms such as freedom from the unwanted interferences of others, freedom to live the life of one's choosing, and freedom to choose one's own conception of the good. They agree that the role of the liberal state is to support the freedom and equality of its citizens, and that the best way of doing this is in the context of a democracy. They agree that the rights and interests of the individual, not those of the larger social group, are both the justification of and the limiting condition on the power and authority of the liberal state. They agree that the legitimacy of the liberal state depends on whether it can be justified to its members, and that this justification must proceed via a certain conception of reason.

But it turns out that liberals disagree about almost as many things as they agree on. They disagree about how best to mediate the conflicts that arise between the interests of the individual and the interests of the group. They disagree about how best to understand what these interests even are. They disagree about whether individuals are always the best judge of what their interests are (or even whether they should always at least be treated as if they are). They disagree about how groups should determine what their collective interests are. They disagree about the ontological status of both individuals and social groups. They disagree about what social institutions are required by a liberal state. They disagree about how much and what kind of market regulation economic justice requires – with libertarians defending complete *laissez-faire* non-interference and egalitarians defending sometimes significant regulation in the name of fairness. They disagree about the value and role of religion in public life. They disagree about whether utilitarianism, contractarianism, or some other framework should ground a society's foundational moral views. These disagreements can be both practical and theoretical, and they are seemingly endless.

This diversity of liberal perspectives is responsible for a number of misconceptions or confusions about what liberalism actually amounts to. These misconceptions have made liberalism extremely unpopular in some academic disciplines, particularly those disciplines that focus on the pernicious historical role liberal ideals have played in causing and justifying imperialism and colonialism, and those disciplines that aim to solve the problems involved in negotiating the diverse multicultural ways of life that characterize our contemporary world. These concerns are not without merit, and I fear that merely appealing to broad platitudes ultimately does little to undermine misconceptions of what liberalism is, or what it can be.

Perhaps a better way to understand what liberalism is, then, is to consider what it is *not*. That is, perhaps liberalism can be best understood by examining how it is characterized by its critics. Many of the most trenchant contemporary critiques of liberalism fall into two broad and overlapping categories: those from radicals and those from communitarians.

Radical critiques of liberalism generally focus on power and the way it functions in the social, political, economic, and legal institutions that individuals must navigate.[17] Individuals are not merely molded by power, they argue, but actually produced by it. Radicals affirm Marx's contention that we can develop into individuals only within a society and portray liberalism as erroneously pretending that the individual is ontologically prior to society. They argue that liberalism is committed to an individualistic social ontology that is incapable of accommodating the realities of nonvoluntary social groups; this makes liberalism, as they understand it, incapable of understanding (much less addressing) the injustices of oppression, which affect people in virtue of their membership in social groups they have not chosen. Furthermore, radicals argue, liberalism overlooks important differences between individuals in favour of a purportedly abstract and generalized conception of the self that is, in fact, a particular self in a position of power; liberalism's ideals are therefore developed and applied erroneously, operating as if all individuals have no interests and concerns other than those of bourgeois white men. According to radicals, then, what is liberalism? It is a political framework committed to a social ontology whose individualism and abstraction fundamentally misrepresents the sorts of beings we are and thus fails to address the worst injustices of oppression. But, as we will see, at least some contemporary liberals can and do escape these charges.

Communitarian critiques of liberalism generally focus on the importance of tradition and social context for moral and political theorizing, about the social nature of the self, and about the value of community.[18] Some communitarians reject liberalism's claim to a universally applicable conception of justice, arguing that because the standards of justice necessarily come from the forms of life and traditions of particular societies, they will vary between contexts. Others reject liberalism's overly individualistic conception of the self, arguing that our selves are not (as liberals would have it) constituted by the pursuit of our individual life projects but by our attachments to certain communal affiliations (for example, to our families or religious traditions). And others reject liberalism on practical grounds, arguing that liberal institutions and practices either contribute to, or are impotent in the face of, the realities of alienation and fragmentation that characterize modern life. According to communitarians, then, what is liberalism? It is a political framework that is committed to a homogenizing moral universalism that overlooks difference. It is one that fundamentally misunderstands the rich interconnectedness of human experience, portraying individuals instead as self-sufficient and mutually disinterested bargainers. And it is one that is committed to protecting the selfish interests of the individual at all costs, even at the expense of the communities that sustain that individual. But, as we will see, very few contemporary liberals would be happy with these characterizations of their commitments.

Some of these radical and communitarian critics are directly concerned with liberalism's purported inability to accommodate a reality in which oppression exists. Others have different axes to grind, but level charges against liberalism that are then taken up by theorists who are explicitly interested in combating oppression. I believe these various critics are correct to point out that, despite the promising start offered by Mill, liberalism has historically failed to address oppression in any systematic way. But I contend that this failure is not a necessary consequence of liberalism's core tenets, and it is therefore not inevitable. Instead, I will argue that there is a radical potential in liberalism that is overlooked when it is simply equated with, or reduced to, conservative neoliberalism or libertarianism or capitalism.

With other liberals who are concerned with social justice, I argue that liberalism's blind spots can be attributed to the historical fact that the political philosophers and theorists who have developed its dominant strains have, almost without exception, come from a particular social group.[19] Because liberal theorists have historically been almost exclusively bourgeois white males, the theory they have developed has tended to reflect their group's interests and reproduce their group's privileges. Oppression has not been on their radar because their social situation shields them from experiencing its negative effects. These theorists' lack of empathetic imagination – their failure to recognize the unearned privileges afforded to them by their social position and concomitant failure to admit that most people do not enjoy these privileges – has resulted in stunted developments and blinkered applications of liberalism's ideals. The solution to this problem, however, is not to reject liberalism, but rather to apply its ideals fairly and develop them so that they reflect and can respond to the lives of *all* people, not just a privileged few. Liberalism's critics are quite right to caution us about the risk of these errors occurring, but wrong about their inevitability. These rejections of liberalism rely on an unfounded pessimism about the possibility of using liberal concepts for liberatory purposes. From the contingent historical fact that the people who have articulated and applied liberal concepts have sometimes failed to live up to the ideals of justice that liberalism espouses, these critics draw the unsupported conclusion that this failure is necessary.

The oppression-related charges against liberalism can be grouped into four interrelated and overlapping categories: (i) that liberalism relies on suspect notions of autonomy and liberty; (ii) that liberalism is overly individualistic; (iii) that liberalism is overly abstract; and (iv) that liberalism is problematically committed to either universalism or pluralism. We will now consider these critiques in detail.

Autonomy and liberty

The concept of autonomy is central to liberal moral and political philosophy. At the core of this ideal is the notion of the self-determining individual who has the right to author his or her own life free from the coercive influence of others.

Critiques of autonomy

A number of the most trenchant critiques of autonomy have come from feminist theorists. Some feminists criticize autonomy as irredeemably androcentric, characterizing it as nothing more than a masculine obsession that has been dressed up with moral and political legitimacy.[20] Some argue that detachedness is a characteristically masculine trait and interpret autonomy as nothing more than a valourization of this masculine behaviour. They contrast this detachedness with the interconnectedness that is supposedly observed in women and argue in favour of some other, more "feminine" moral ideal.[21] Others take issue with the notion of the self implicit in the traditional conception of autonomy, arguing that it misrepresents the thoroughly social nature of the self;[22] that it erroneously portrays the self as fundamentally independent, self-interested, and free of caring relationships with dependent others;[23] that it exaggerates the extent to which the self is transparently self-aware;[24] or that it overemphasizes the importance of rationality in what should be considered the self's authentic decisions.[25] Other feminists do not necessarily advocate a wholesale rejection of autonomy, but argue that liberal moral and political theory's preoccupation with this concept passes over other important aspects of our social lives. They argue that while autonomy might be useful for understanding voluntary bargaining between nonintimate equals who are capable of reciprocity, or perhaps contractual or institutional relationships in the public sphere more generally, it is far less useful when applied to relationships between intimates or nonequals that are characterized by dependence and vulnerability; they charge that liberalism's obsession with autonomy leads it to functionally ignore the domestic, familial, private sphere.[26]

Poststructuralist critiques of autonomy accuse liberalism of mistakenly presuming the existence of a unified, coherent subject with a stable identity.[27] The rational, autonomous individual who expresses or reveals her preferences through the choices she makes is derided as a fiction, and autonomy's goal of being in control of one's life is derided as a pathological compulsion. Their point here is not merely that the self is socially constructed; their point is rather that there is no core self that exists beneath the contingent social roles, that who we are is always fragmented, shifting, and incomplete. This makes the goal of autonomy an impossible ideal that can itself function as a mechanism of power and oppression. Pretending that people have the ability to choose who they are or what kind of life they want to live, an ability that is entirely independent of the contingencies of social circumstance, imposes an unfair responsibility for the forces that structure one's life. When liberals act as if the issue is as simple as whether people are living their own lives or whether they are living lives dictated by others, they do a disservice to the messiness and intricacy of life as it is actually lived. Poststructuralists thus believe that autonomy, even as an ideal, is the wrong goal.[28]

Some communitarians take issue with the valourization of a certain kind of independence that they think follows inevitably from the liberal ideal of autonomy. They contend that this ideal conceives of an individual's identity as being formed independently of the communities to which she belongs, mistakenly pretending that it is possible to "stand back from any and every situation in which one is involved, from any and every characteristic that one may possess, and to pass judgment on it from a purely universal and abstract point of view that is totally detached from all social particularity."[29] This mischaracterization of the human condition ignores and devalues the fact that who we are and what we value is inevitably dependent on traditions, social practices, and social institutions. As we will see below, this charge is also picked up by feminists who advocate replacing or supplementing liberalism's individualism with a relational conception of autonomy and selfhood.

The Marxist critique of autonomy focuses on how liberals understand human freedom.[30] Proponents of this critique argue that liberals' focus on *formal* freedom (the legally recognized power to make decisions) obscures the material conditions that prevent people from achieving *real* freedom (the ability to pursue the ends one has set for oneself). The concern here is that focusing on autonomy only with respect to a particular set of decisions leads liberals to overlook the structural forces that shape the background social conditions within which decisions are actually made.[31] These critics argue that the mere absence of external constraints is not a sufficient condition for freedom in any morally meaningful sense. This negative view of freedom – where freedom is nothing more than the absence of intentional constraints on an individual's ability to pursue his or her ends – is socially, ethically, and politically impoverished. Instead, what is really valuable about freedom for an individual is not merely the negative absence of interference but the positive power of self-determination. When we attend to the background social conditions in which an individual exists – conditions that include her race, gender, socioeconomic class, religion, sexual orientation, and so on – we begin to see that answering the question of whether or not this person is meaningfully free requires more than simply knowing whether she has the legal right to do something or whether she is currently being subjected to direct, unwelcome coercion. This is because when people are oppressed they face incentive structures that influence their available options in ways that affect both the quantity and quality of their choices.

Proponents of this critique are right to emphasize the paucity of merely negative freedom as a moral or political ideal. And they are right to criticize the various historical incarnations of liberalism for pretending otherwise. This distinction between positive and negative liberty did not originate with these critics, however; the thought that there are both positive and negative conceptions of liberty goes back at least as far as Kant. While both defenders and critics of liberalism have been grappling with the implications of this distinction for centuries, it was in the 1950s and '60s, beginning with Isaiah Berlin's "Two Concepts of Liberty," that social and political philosophers started examining the concepts in earnest.[32] Berlin's argument is that the concepts of positive and negative liberty are best thought of as incompatible ways of understanding what the political ideal of liberty really amounts to. Defenders of negative liberty (such as Berlin himself) argue that defending liberty amounts to defending the right of individuals to be free of state intervention; defenders of positive liberty argue that defending liberty amounts to defending the right of individuals to self-realize, self-actualize, or self-determine, the achievement of which will often require more state intervention than defenders of negative liberty will usually be comfortable with. Defenders of negative liberty are motivated by the conviction that the state must remain neutral with respect to any particular conception of the good; this motivation stems from a recognition that state attempts to support or entrench a particular conception of the good have, historically, tended to go very badly, leading to civil strife or unjust forms of authoritarianism. Defenders of positive liberty are motivated by the conviction that true liberty requires the social, material, and psychological resources to actually be able to make meaningful decisions about one's life; they believe that assuring the fair distribution of these resources will often require state interventions such as programs that redistribute wealth, or programs that ensure access to education and other mechanisms that assure the possibility of social mobility.

Defences of autonomy

Contemporary liberals have responses to each of these critiques of autonomy. In fact, a large amount of the scholarship in contemporary liberalism can be interpreted as the attempt to grapple with their implications. For example, according to the standard way of carving things up, defenders of liberalism will be proponents of the negative conception of liberty, while critics of liberalism will be proponents of the positive conception of liberty. This picture was probably true of liberalism and its critics in their historical incarnations. But things have changed. Many contemporary defenders of liberalism now recognize that negative liberty is, by itself, usually insufficient for meaningful autonomy. Most liberal thinkers now recognize that people need *freedom to*, not merely *freedom from*, if they are to count as meaningfully free, and most attempt to incorporate this positive understanding of liberty into their conceptions of autonomy. Contemporary liberals now recognize the tension between classical liberalism's negative understanding of liberty as the absence of constraints and a more robust, positive, understanding of liberty as self-determination. Few, if any, claim to have fully dissolved this tension. But almost everyone recognizes it, and yet they do not see it as a reason to reject liberalism outright.

A great number of contemporary liberal philosophers also take up the issue of what autonomy ultimately amounts to, with some arguing that the concept is most profitably conceived of as something as minimal as the bare capacity to set and pursue ends, and others arguing that the concept cannot be meaningfully understood without incorporating a robust account of the social and material conditions necessary to exercise this capacity. In light of this debate, liberals have articulated a number of different accounts of what autonomy consists of: the capacity to govern oneself; the actual condition of self-government; the feature of persons that should prevent paternalistic interventions; the independence from external manipulation; a set of rights that express one's sovereignty over oneself; or some combination of all these factors.[33] Others ask whether autonomy is a relatively thin ideal that requires merely that agents have freedom of choice, or whether it is a thicker ideal that requires that the choices that agents are free to make must be in some sense worthwhile or valuable; those who defend the latter conception of autonomy hold that a state has both a negative duty to respect its citizens' autonomy and a positive duty to foster the social conditions that make this autonomy possible.[34] Other liberals concern themselves with the question of whether a person needs to be able to alter the factors that guide her life in order to count as autonomous.[35] And many more are concerned with articulating precisely what social and material conditions need to be in place in order for an autonomous person to be able to engage in the reflective endorsement that is necessary for autonomy.[36]

There is also an extensive body of literature that focuses on understanding how oppressive social conditions complicate and problematize conventional understandings of the concept of autonomy. Some defend autonomy as a concept that allows us to understand and critique oppressive social conditions.[37] As we saw above, others take up the problem of adaptive preferences, which moves from the recognition that people's preferences can be influenced by oppressive background social conditions to considering questions such as when we might be justified in criticizing or ignoring the preferences people actually have in favour of other norms or principles when we are deciding certain fundamental issues of social choice.[38] Some engage with the puzzle of whether it is legitimate to say that people may autonomously choose to live nonautonomous lives.[39] Others argue that, even though it is impossible to distinguish which values an individual has legitimately adopted through a process of autonomous reflection and which have been illegitimately absorbed from the restricted set of those culturally available to her, it is politically important that people are treated as if they are fully autonomous beings.[40]

Abstraction

Liberals use methods of abstraction to arrive at characterizations of the human condition that are supposed to be general, impartial, and universal. This is necessary, liberals think, because, in order to determine what social arrangements are just, we need to be able to transcend the particularities of any given social context and evaluate these arrangements according to standards that are applicable to all. What is perhaps the most well-known and influential example of liberal abstraction is Rawls's original position, a thought experiment which models the impartiality and rationality required by fairness when constructing the principles of justice for a society by having us imagine ourselves behind a hypothetical veil of ignorance that obscures from us information about our personal characteristics and social status.[41]

Critiques of abstraction

We just saw how liberalism is criticized for its abstraction in its conception of autonomy. The argument, in effect, is that when liberalism abstracts the individual from his or her social context it is likely to emphasize the importance of negative liberty over more robust, positive, conceptions of liberty that recognize that meaningful human agency requires more than mere absence of external constraint. Liberals' concern with formal equality thereby abstracts from actual power asymmetries. This is a serious concern, and, as we have seen, it has been taken up by many contemporary liberals who know full well that equality of opportunity cannot be achieved without attending to background inequalities. Adding the insights of other theorists to this concern, however, yields an even more trenchant critique of liberalism's methods of abstraction.

Proponents of this radical critique point out that any method of abstraction necessarily involves bracketing certain features in favour of focusing on others.[42] But, they argue, deciding which features to bracket, and which to focus on, are not decisions that can be entirely impartial or neutral. And, because those with the most power are usually the ones making these decisions, they argue that these decisions will tend to both reflect and serve the interests of those with this power. Liberalism's supposedly abstract and impartial ideals are thus actually particular and biased, and they function to entrench an unjust status quo. Ignoring the differences between people perpetuates oppression because it allows the ideals of the majority to be presented as neutral and universal. Liberal abstraction becomes functionally assimilationist, presenting the ideals and concerns of those in power as if they were the ideals and concerns of everyone. When the voices of oppressed minorities are heard at all, their difference from those in the majority leads them to be written off as deviant, inferior, or as "selfish special interests that deviate from the impartial general interest."[43] Because the privileged majority presents its ideals as universal, claims that it treats all people impartially in reality serve to mask and entrench oppression. Proponents of this critique suggest that these mistakes are somewhere between *very likely* and *inevitable*, and thus contend that liberalism is incapable of achieving social justice in the context of oppression.

Defences of abstraction

Clearly, not all theorists interested in social justice have viewed this critique as a reason to reject liberalism outright.[44] Instead, they argue that not only is liberalism capable of accommodating these concerns, but also that the liberal method of abstraction scrutinized by radicals is actually the most promising strategy for achieving liberatory goals. They defend liberalism's abstraction by arguing that the extent to which its supposedly abstract and impartial ideals have actually reflected the particular interests and perspectives of those in power is not a problem that is inherent to liberalism itself. Rather, when this has occurred, it has been because the liberal theorists in question have failed to properly apply liberalism's own ideals. When male-biased, class-biased, race-biased (and so on) liberal theorists are guilty of taking rich white men's experiences as the norm, and of ignoring the interests of all others, they are guilty not of *too much* abstraction but rather of *not enough*. They are guilty of unjust forms of particularity and favouritism. But none of this is fundamental to liberalism, which, these theorists remind us, is committed to the view that all of us possess "equal dignity and worth," the primary source of which is our "power of moral choice...that consists in the ability to plan a life in accordance with one's own evaluations of ends."[45] Women are every bit as capable of this as men, people of colour are just as capable of this as people who are white, people of limited economic means are just as capable of this as people who are wealthy, and so on. These oppressed people are therefore every bit as morally valuable. Insofar as all people are of equal dignity and worth, enshrining the interests of a privileged few at the expense of the interests of everyone else is really at odds with the deepest tenets of liberalism. Therefore, the "[a]pparent internal conceptual/normative barriers to an emancipatory liberalism can be successfully negotiated by drawing on the conceptual/normative resources of liberalism itself."[46] These defenders of liberalism are not pretending that a depressing number of theorists in the liberal tradition have not gotten this wrong. They are arguing that the solution is not to reject liberalism's ideals, but to actually apply them properly.

Other liberals defend the suitability of liberal methods of abstraction for dealing with the particular problems that arise under oppression.

Some defend an ideal of liberation from oppression that requires eliminating group-based differences; the ideally non-oppressive society, they argue, would be one where group-based differences such as race and sex would be the functional equivalent of eye colour in our current society, affecting neither one's identity, nor one's political rights or obligations, nor one's social benefits.[47] Such an ideal would put the lie to the purported naturalness and necessity of these group-based differences, providing a clear and unambiguous standard of equality and justice and maximizing the choices open to individuals who would find themselves unconstrained by group-specific social norms.

Others have defended Rawls's original position as a solution to the problem of adaptive preferences.[48] As we saw, this problem arises when internalized oppression cripples an oppressed person's sense of worth, leaving her with no sense of what she is justly entitled to. In the original position, when designing principles of justice for a society without knowledge of one's particular personal characteristics or status within that society, the abstraction imposed by the veil of ignorance forces one to take account of as many voices as possible and to be particularly concerned with those who are least well off. Rather than relying on reports of subjective preferences (which are subject to the problem of adaptive preferences), or the reports of a culture's leaders or other "well-socialized" members (which are likely to rationalize a status quo from which they consider themselves to benefit), the original position is an abstract perspective that permits both oppressors and the oppressed, both insiders and outsiders, to evaluate the legitimacy of cultural practices.

> What Moslem man is likely to take the chance of spending his life in seclusion and dependency, sweltering in head-to-toe black clothing? What prerevolutionary Chinese man would cast his vote for the breaking of toes and hobbling through life, if he well might be the one with the toes and the crippled life? What man would endorse gross genital mutilation, not knowing *whose* genitals?[49]

In these sorts of cases, abstraction grants the critical distance from which to evaluate the justice of oppressive social practices, a distance not provided by those critics of liberalism whose reverence for the integrity of cultures boils down to a relativistic and exoticizing "worship of difference."[50] Rawls himself was slow to recognize the possibility of using his abstract theoretical apparatus for anti-oppressive purposes, but did, late in life and in response to those who criticized him for failing to include gender and race as things about which those behind the veil of ignorance were ignorant, appear to come to just this realization: "in a well-ordered society under favourable conditions, with the equal basic liberties and fair equality of opportunity secured, gender and race would not specify relevant points of view."[51,52]

Individualism

Liberalism's individualism is inseparable from its abstraction and its commitment to autonomy. Liberal conceptions of the self characterize us as beings who are fundamentally rational, autonomous, and individual. While liberals acknowledge that we exist, probably necessarily, in larger social groups, they remain committed to the view that the individual is both the basic unit of social reality and the fundamental locus of value.

Critiques of individualism

Most critiques of liberal individualism focus on how liberals are purported to understand the self. Proponents of these critiques argue that the social relations an individual claims – and those relations that claim an individual – are not merely *additive*, but are, rather, *constitutive* of selfhood. There is no core or hidden self upon which social relations are layered to constitute an individual's identity, they argue. Instead, we are born into particular social relations, and claim a variety of relations for our own, and these relations define *who we are* as individuals. By denying that the self and its desires are constituted by, not separate from, the society in which they exist, liberalism is committed to an incoherent conception of the self. This critique is advanced primarily by poststructuralist and communitarian critics of liberalism.[53] A related critique comes from radical theorists who criticize liberalism's ontology of social groups, arguing that, insofar as liberalism recognizes the existence of social groups at all, it conceives of them solely as voluntary associations; this obviously does not accommodate the reality of class, race, and gender memberships, none of which are chosen and all of which fundamentally affect an individual's life prospects and experiences in both negative and positive ways.[54] Another critique attacks liberalism's individualism for feeding a "privatizing, withdrawlist conception of citizenship" that is at odds with fostering solidarity between members of oppressed groups.[55]

Yet another related critique has been picked up by those who articulate and defend relational conceptions of autonomy and selfhood. Relational theorists advocate a shift away from the individualism they see underlying traditional liberal conceptions of autonomy and the self, toward a conception that recognizes that the interests of the individual are inseparable from the interests of others.[56] They criticize the liberal conception of the person for underemphasizing how factors such as one's gender, race, ethnicity, or religion actually constitute one's identity; failing to recognize this, these critics argue, puts liberals at risk of wrongly assuming that people can separate themselves from all their cultural commitments.[57]

Another critique of liberal individualism put forward by radical critics focuses on liberalism's purported methods of identifying oppression.[58] Liberalism is not likely to be able to identify oppressive harms, this argument claims, because it would have us focus exclusively on individual people's experiences rather than on the commonalities of experience shared by people who are oppressed. The harms of oppression, however, are often only fully evident from a more macroscopic perspective. Liberalism's insistence on focusing on individual people's experiences, rather than on the experiences people share in virtue of the social contexts in which they find themselves, makes it likelier to write off as 'personal' phenomena that are actually *political*. Radical methods of identifying oppression, on the other hand, differ from liberal methods in their explicit focus on the perspective of the oppressed. Liberal methods of identifying oppression instead abstract away from the details of people's lives and focus on people primarily as generic individuals rather than as members of particular social groups. The best liberals can do to attempt to identify oppressive injustices is to ask questions such as whether one's preferences are satisfied, whether one has been subject to treatment that runs afoul of the harm principle, or whether one's rights have been violated. Liberal methods like these take a person's gender, race, or class as incidental to the question of whether he or she has been subjected to injustice. Radical strategies, in contrast, put these considerations at the centre of the analysis. Instead of asking whether people have been subject to various generic harms that have nothing to do with their social group, these theorists have us ask people themselves about their experiences under oppression.

Defences of individualism

But these, too, are all lessons that have been taken on board by a great number of contemporary liberals. Some liberals argue, for example, that liberalism is not committed to requiring that an individual be able to define herself in a way that is entirely separate from her relations, connections, and commitments; all that liberalism requires, they argue, is that no single one of these factors is beyond review.[59] Other contemporary liberals defend classical liberalism's attachment to a relatively individualistic conception of identity and autonomy by arguing that liberalism's core ideal of *self-government* remains a laudable moral aim, particularly given that one of the greatest injustices many people continue to face is a restriction of the quality and quantity of choices that are open to them. These theorists argue that we can accommodate many of the points made by those who are critical of the liberal tradition – that people's decisions are influenced by values that are largely determined by interpersonal relations; that these interpersonal relations are not just inevitable, but also valuable; that the interests of the individual are not cleanly separable from the interests of others – without giving up on the liberal idea that it is important that, ultimately, people be free to make their own choices and promote their self-interest.[60]

Other liberals take a slightly different tack in defending individualism, arguing that the liberal strategy of focusing on people primarily as individuals with interests of their own is superior to non-liberal strategies that focus on people, and their interests, primarily in terms of the interests of the larger social groups of which they are members – groups such as communities, religions, and families.[61] Liberalism can (and, indeed, must) recognize that membership in these groups plays a constitutive role in people's lives. But liberalism also focuses on the commonalities, the "core of rational and moral personhood," that people share across groups.[62] And thus these liberals argue that the locus of value is always the individual person, not the larger social group in which individuals find themselves. When liberals (and others) have gone wrong on this front, it has been because they have not been individualistic enough: they have pretended that the interests of the group were more important than the interests of the individual people who make up that group.

Finally, liberals have defended liberalism's ability to identify oppressive harms. According to this radical critique, remember, because liberalism focuses on people first and foremost as individuals it will miss the common forms of oppression people experience as members of the same oppressed group, whereas radicalism's method of focusing on people first and foremost as members of oppressed groups will help us discover that apparently localized individual experiences are in fact shared with others. But it is unclear here what it means to *focus on* individuals or groups. Insofar as liberalism focuses on individuals rather than groups it is not telling us that we should ignore (or even avoid looking for) how people's experiences are shared with other members of their oppressed group. It is saying that the only reason we should care about how the group is doing is that it is comprised of individual people who are the locus of value. It is, in other words, rejecting communitarianism. It is not denying that people's interests often coincide with the interests of their communities, their religions, or even their families; it is saying that when the interests of the individual conflict with the interests of these larger groups, the interests of the individual must trump. It is saying that if the interests of the organic whole matter at all, it is because the individual people who make up the organic whole need the organic whole to thrive. But what has value, ultimately, are the individual people who make up the organic whole. And there is no reason liberals cannot agree with radicals that these harms will be difficult to identify if we do not focus on the commonalities of experience shared by members of their social groups. Liberalism's commitment to individualism need not require a rejection of more radical methods of identifying oppression. *What this commitment amounts to is an ontological claim about what is the basic unit of social reality and a metaethical claim about what is the fundamental locus of value (that is, the individual person, not the community or group), as well as an ethical claim about the importance of fairly attributing this value (and the abilities of moral choice that give people this value) to all people in an unbiased way.*[63] Neither of these claims rules out the possibility of adopting radical methods of identifying and ameliorating oppression.

Universalism and pluralism

Liberalism, we have seen, is committed to the universal ideals of liberty and equality. Respecting people as free and equal means liberalism is committed to respecting people as the authors of their lives, as their own best judges of what kind of life they want to lead. Liberal universalism thus translates into a pluralism that requires the state to be neutral with respect to competing conceptions of the good.

Critiques of universalism and pluralism

Contemporary liberals strive to find a middle ground between contradicting critiques that charge it with being either too universalistic or too relativistic. Those who take issue with liberalism's universalism argue that its ideals ineliminably reflect, and therefore reproduce, its history of patriarchalism, racism, imperialism, and colonialism. They argue that attempts to articulate abstract, general, transcultural normative standards will only ever entrench the ideals of the privileged status quo. They argue that because people make sense of the ideals that guide their lives always from particular social contexts, we cannot abstract away from these ways of life when evaluating these ideals. And they argue that critiques of social practices and institutions must always derive from, and make sense within, the contexts in which people actually live, and not be imposed by others from without. Those who take issue with liberalism's pluralism, on the other hand, argue that it collapses into a relativism that masquerades as cultural sensitivity and toleration, but in fact it leaves us impotent to criticize atrocity.

Some of the most influential critics of liberal pluralism have been certain feminists who, as we will see in more detail below, argue that liberalism can be too quick to accommodate cultural diversity. The effect of this, they argue, is the uncritical acceptance of the legitimacy of claims for cultural autonomy made by sexist religious traditions. Pluralism – or multiculturalism, in the terms of the relevant debate – thus functions to perpetuate women's oppression. The other major category of critiques of liberal pluralism come from civic republicans, who reject classical liberalism's commitment to neutrality with respect to conceptions of the good, instead defending a positive conception of liberty that requires that people have the capacity to be self-governing and that they are not subject to domination.[64] Because they insist that meaningful liberty is only possible if the state takes active steps to cultivate in its citizens the qualities of character that are required for self-government, civic republicans characterize liberalism as committed to a morally pernicious relativism that threatens to undermine the state's ability to properly facilitate the possibility of its citizens living good lives. But, for whatever reason, civic republicans have not tended to be interested in issues of oppression, and so their arguments will not occupy my central focus here.

More commonly than being criticized for its pluralism, however, liberalism is criticized for its universalism. Communitarian and anti-colonialist critics point out that liberalism's ideals have been implemented historically in ways that consistently ignore the experiences of the oppressed members of society. Justice requires transforming social institutions so they address the needs and concerns of these most vulnerable people, and this is possible only if we listen to them to discover what their needs and concerns actually are. This means that anti-oppressive social movements must be bottom-up, must come from within, and must attend to the voices of the most marginalized.[65] Attending to these voices is the only means we have to determine whether the customs and mores of the prevailing social order are ethically acceptable. Because dominant members of society benefit from their participation in the status quo they lack the critical perspective from which to evaluate which customs and mores are ethically acceptable and which are not. Oppressed members of society have this critical perspective because they do not benefit from the status quo.[66]

There are both metaphysical and epistemic points to be emphasized about this anti-universalist critique. The metaphysical point is that this critique permits both more and less relativist interpretations. Some versions of this critique affirm that there are objective moral standards against which we can judge the customs and mores of different societies, arguing that liberalism's core ideals of liberty and equality *are* universally correct although they have often not been applied fairly.[67] The more common version of this critique takes a more relativist line, however, arguing that, because ideals of justice always come from within the practices and institutions of particular cultures, liberalism's commitment to universal cross-cultural ideals makes it politically and morally incoherent.[68] The epistemic point to be emphasized here is that all versions of this anti-universalist critique caution that our epistemic access to the ideals of justice is prone to biases born of hubris and power that can be overcome only by attending to those who do not share in, nor benefit from, this power. The very societies that have historically thought themselves to have direct access to these standards have been the ones most likely to err, these critics point out. Since the Enlightenment, liberal societies have claimed that their use of reason has given them privileged access to objective ethical ideals; these same societies have been responsible for the horrors of slavery, colonialism, and imperialism.

Defences of universalism and pluralism

In light of these critiques many liberals now argue that liberalism is best thought of as a "political" rather than a "comprehensive" doctrine. This discussion, like so many others, began with Rawls, who, in his later work, defended a political liberalism that remains neutral with respect to questions of value, ethics, epistemology, and the metaphysics of the person and society.[69] Insofar as modern societies exhibit a "reasonable pluralism" with respect to these questions, Rawls argues that the liberal's role is to avoid adding yet another comprehensive doctrine to the mix, and instead to provide an overarching political framework that is neutral between a society's competing comprehensive doctrines. Liberalism should abandon truth as the standard of correctness for political justice, replacing it with the standard of reasonableness, where a doctrine qualifies as reasonable if its principles and standards can be agreed to as fair terms for cooperation by people with competing (but not unreasonable) comprehensive doctrines. In the wake of Rawls'ss influence, most contemporary liberals now situate their theories on a continuum between the minimal and the substantive, with those who are closer to the minimal side tending to argue that liberals should focus on specifying the procedures by which people's preferences will be aggregated in a society and on minimizing the constraints on people's actions,[70] and those who are closer to the substantive side tending to argue that liberals must embrace comprehensive theories of value and endorse some conceptions of the good over others.[71]

A related way that contemporary liberals talk about these issues can be found in the debate between perfectionism and proceduralism. Some contemporary liberals challenge the idea that liberalism must be committed to normative neutrality when formulating and applying political principles. These liberals defend *perfectionist* accounts that claim that there are certain objective values that an individual or a society *should* accept or endorse, even if the individual or population does not endorse them.[72] Some liberals who defend perfectionist accounts do so because they are concerned to rule out the possibility of attributing autonomy to people in oppressive and overly restrictive life situations.[73] Others do so because they argue that improving the quality of life and social standing of members of oppressed groups requires being able to evaluate the choices that these people actually make, and only a concrete set of perfectionist principles permits this kind of evaluation.[74] Many other liberals defend *proceduralist* accounts that deny there are objective values that individuals or societies should endorse, instead claiming that liberals' focus should be on ensuring that certain material and political conditions are in place so that people are free to engage in the reflective endorsement necessary for autonomous decision-making.[75]

On the question of how a liberal society should engage with another non-liberal society, many liberals advocate tolerating, rather than intervening in, the practices of other non-liberal cultures. They argue that because the self-conceptions of the members of a non-liberal culture are based, at least in part, on their participation in these practices, these people would be harmed by the imposition of liberal principles, even if many of their liberties are denied by their non-liberal cultures.[76] Rawls himself distinguishes between "decent" and "outlaw" non-liberal societies and argues that, while the failure of outlaw states to respect human rights should not be tolerated, decent illiberal states should not be coercively forced to be liberal.[77] The issue of toleration is more complex when it comes to non-liberal groups within a liberal society, but for the most part the existence of a viable exit option is taken to be sufficient evidence that individuals who remain members of a group that appears to be illiberal are at least tacitly consenting to its practices.[78] The issue becomes more vexed when it comes to the case of children, who are, by definition, not capable of voluntarily consenting to their membership in such a group, but many liberals still oppose intervention on the grounds that it is never the role of the state to arbitrate between competing comprehensive doctrines.[79] Some liberals, however, do favour intervention in these cases, in the name of protecting the autonomy or "open futures" of these vulnerable people.[80] Rawls proposes a middle ground that permits parents to educate their children as they wish, so long as they are educated in a way that prepares them to be fully cooperating and self-supporting members of society who are aware of both their civic rights and the fact that they are political equals, even if they are treated unequally in their particular comprehensive doctrine.[81]

The danger of failing to intervene in these cases is illustrated in a debate that was initiated by Susan Moller Okin.[82] Okin underscored the tensions between multiculturalism and feminism, cautioning liberals against responding to the existence of competing conceptions of the good by too quickly defending a group's right to decide these issues for itself. The issue here boils down to a concern that protecting group rights can come at the expense of protecting the rights of individual women (and other vulnerable people) within a group. "Too often, ... group rights are used to subordinate women. Group rights may appear fair in the abstract but in fact they often mean giving rights to the particular leaders of these groups; when these leaders are men with a traditional view of the world, as they often are, then it is hardly surprising, though certainly disturbing, that group rights are often used to oppress women."[83] There is a danger in treating a group (or its leaders or dominant members) as a proxy for its individual members, because the individuals in every group will inevitably have both shared and divergent interests. A group's leaders and more privileged members will have the power to ensure that it is their interests that take priority in cases of conflict, at the expense of the interests of the less privileged members of that group. Group rights can thereby threaten the individual rights of those who are most vulnerable.[84]

Okin argues that when a group's ideals and practices are inegalitarian, we should be more concerned about the well-being of the oppressed members of that group than the well-being of the group itself. She points out that it is very often women who bear the brunt of the traditional cultural practices that defenders of group rights are at pains to protect: it is women who wear veils; undergo clitoridectomies; die in honour-killings; are the multiple spouses of polygamy; are disadvantaged by traditional marriage, divorce, and child custody laws; are both raped and then denied justice afterward; and are responsible for unpaid domestic labour. Defending group rights, or deferring to cultural tradition, thus often amounts to defending the reproduction of men's power over women.

Following Okin's lead, I will argue next that moving too far in the direction of minimalism or proceduralism is a mistake, that at least some comprehensive doctrines cannot be discarded if the harms of oppression are to be addressed fully. Specifically, I argue that combating oppression requires an objective account of what counts as harm and flourishing for human beings. The liberalism that results leaves room for pluralism, but not relativism: there might be many different right ways to live a life, but there are also some wrong ones.

Social justice, objectivity, and comprehensive liberalism

Many social theorists reject the tenability of, or the need for, objective standards of justice, arguing that any attempt to defend objective values only ends up enshrining the values of a privileged few. In the place of objective ideals, many theorists attempt to answer the question of whether a person's life is going well or badly by appealing to the standards of that person's community, appealing to ever-wider communities if necessary. The problem with this approach, however, is that it is far too easy to find historical and contemporary examples of communities that are committed to morally unacceptable (for example, sexist or racist) ideals *all the way up*. The most deeply entrenched problems of social justice do not tend to occur because a relatively small community is committed to unacceptable moral ideals that can be checked against the better ideals of a larger social group. Rather, these problems occur because the largest social groups are themselves committed to morally unacceptable ideals. Many theorists argue that adopting objective standards always ends up imposing a particular conception of the good onto people who might have legitimately different views on the matter. The problem with this approach, however, is that improving the quality of life and social standing of members of oppressed groups requires being able to evaluate the choices that these people actually make, and only a concrete set of objective moral standards permits this kind of evaluation.

Social justice demands that we be able to recognize when individuals are and are not doing well – and this means *all* individuals, regardless of the social and cultural contexts in which they are found. We must admit that we cannot necessarily trust our own judgement on this matter, because we can be (and have been) mistaken; our Western history of colonialism and imperialism abounds with examples of paternalistic interventions in the lives of others, performed with perhaps the best of intentions but to catastrophic ends. Nor can we necessarily simply trust the subjective reports made by individuals themselves, because the problem of adaptive preferences shows that people can and do internalize beliefs that rationalize and normalize their oppression, leading them to accept conditions that are manifestly not in their best interests. We must, somehow, be able to make judgements about human flourishing not just by our own, or others', lights but by universal standards that everyone can (or at least should) agree to, regardless of their particular culture. But we must also remain vigilantly aware that it is precisely this move – the appeal to standards that are supposed to be universal – that was used to justify imperialistic chauvinism in the past.

We have seen how the problem of adaptive preferences presents a difficulty for what would otherwise be the best liberal response when people seem to consent to oppressive social practices. We cannot simply appeal to people's subjective preferences – what people choose for themselves – when internalized oppression has undermined their sense of what they are entitled to. We need a way to respect people's right to decide their own conception of the good without collapsing into moral relativism. Okin encapsulates the liberal activist's goal here as that of

> reconciling women's full equality with men...while recognizing the centrality of religion or culture in defining most women's identities and deeply held values.... [The goal is] to increase women's sense of entitlement to treatment as full human beings without undermining their most fundamental sense of who they are.[85]

What is perhaps the most promising liberal response to this issue is found in the work of Martha Nussbaum and Amartya Sen, who defend a view they call the *capabilities approach*.[86] The capabilities approach has us ask people the following question:

> What activities characteristically performed by human beings are so central that they seem definitive of a life that is truly human? In other words, what are the functions without which...we would regard a life as not, or not fully, human?[87]

The list of capabilities that results from this inquiry is both empirical and open-ended, because it summarizes the "empirical findings of a broad and ongoing cross-cultural inquiry."[88] It is also deliberately general, because it attempts "to put forward something that people from many different traditions...can agree on, as the necessary basis for pursuing their good life."[89] And it is incredibly varied, addressing aspects of our lives ranging from our "mortality," our "embodiment (including the need for food and drink, need for shelter, sexual desire, capacity for mobility)," our "capacity for pleasure and pain," our "distinctive cognitive capabilities," our "prolonged neoteny," our "capacity for and exercise of practical reason," our "capacity and desire for affiliation with other human beings," our "relatedness to other species and to nature," our "capacity for humour and play," and our "separateness."[90] The goal of this list is more than mere survival; its goal is human *flourishing*. A life that lacks any one of these capabilities will be judged to "fall short of a good human life."[91] So, when we are assessing the quality of life in a country and trying to figure out which public policies to implement, the most important question this approach has us ask is whether those policies help people achieve these capacities.

The methodology used to produce this list of capabilities is explicitly Aristotelian. Aristotle determines what constitutes flourishing for human beings by looking for our distinctive functions, that is, what differentiates us from all other species. This turns out to be reason (understood, roughly, as the ability to set ends or purposes for ourselves) and so he claims that the good human life is one organized around this understanding of reason. This is the universalist move here: Nussbaum admits that we recognize that reason plays this distinctive role only because we have already accepted a normatively loaded conception of human nature. That is, we do not recognize the importance of reason from an external, non-normative point of view. If we did not already think that our capacity to set our own ends was so valuable, we would not see it as the thing that is distinctive about us. Now, Nussbaum and Sen are hardly alone in characterizing us as fundamentally rational animals, but this move is still not uncontroversial. Their commitment to this conception of human nature leaves their account open to the critique of chauvinism they are at pains to avoid – for imposing a particular culture's conception of human flourishing onto others who might have legitimately different views on the matter.

They respond to this line of critique by emphasizing where the concrete details of this list of capabilities actually comes from: an extensive *empirical* and *cross-cultural* inquiry. The list of capabilities was most adamantly not generated from a philosopher's armchair, and it is thus much harder to write it off simply as the expression of the ideals of a dominant culture that are meant to be imposed on the unfortunates from dominated cultures. (To the critic who doubts this, note the number of capabilities on the list that many of us in the West would probably find strange. Most of us, for example, would not say that a life without humour or play, or one without the opportunity for relationships with other species and with nature, would "fall short of a good human life.") The list is the result of going out into the world and talking to people – not just Western people, not just privileged people, not just powerful people, but as many people from as many walks of life as possible – about how they experience their life and what they find most valuable about it. The resulting list of capabilities represents these theorists' best attempt at articulating not merely an overlap but a synthesis of humanity's ideals: they admit that they are using a normatively loaded conception of human nature in compiling this list, but they claim that these ideals really are there to be found, in one form or another, in the beliefs and ideals of virtually everyone they talk to. (Nussbaum, for example, writes movingly about how, if you actually ask oppressed Indian women – not the patriarchal leaders of their communities, not their husbands or fathers, but the women themselves – if they want to be free to live lives of their own choosing, they answer overwhelmingly in the affirmative.)

Nussbaum repeatedly insists that the capabilities approach is intended as a political, rather than a comprehensive, liberalism.[92] It is not clear to me that this move is ultimately successful,[93] but unlike many of her critics (and Nussbaum herself) I do not take this to be a problem. Nussbaum is concerned that requiring the state to endorse a comprehensive liberalism would require demanding that individuals "drop their own doctrine in favour of our own,"[94] that it would show insufficient respect for people and their diverse conceptions of the good,[95] and that it would fail to respect the inegalitarian, but nevertheless reasonable, conceptions of the good held by some people who do not champion the values of equality and autonomy.[96] The question here boils down to how inegalitarian a conception of the good can be and still count as reasonable. Remember, the principles and standards of reasonable doctrines are those that can be agreed to as fair terms of cooperation by people with competing (but not unreasonable) comprehensive doctrines; it is not clear why Nussbaum thinks that reasonable people would agree to inegalitarianism, particularly if we avail ourselves of Rawls's earlier metaphor and think of them as deciding matters behind the veil of ignorance. In any case, there are better and worse comprehensive doctrines, and Nussbaum's – a comprehensive doctrine that is quite minimal and thin; that can thereby accommodate as many different ways of life as possible; that is drawn from the beliefs and ideals of many of the world's cultures; and that is just as quick to condemn the unjust practices that occur in liberal societies as in others – is significantly harder to charge with Western arrogance or imperialism. This is not to deny that there will be cultural practices that are condemned by the capabilities approach, but to demand otherwise amounts to abandoning the possibility of acting in the face of atrocity. Nussbaum slips around on this issue – emphasizing the empirical and cross-cultural elements of the capabilities approach here, and the importance of the liberal ideals of respect, autonomy, reason, human dignity, equality, and the inviolability of the person there – but at the end of the day I think her liberal commitment to human dignity, and her feminist commitment to women's equality, should override her reticence to admit that she endorses a partly comprehensive liberalism.

Okin, too, resists being labeled as a comprehensive liberal.[97] This repudiation, however, is in explicit response to a characterization of comprehensive liberalism as being necessarily committed to endorsing the significant use of state power to enforce certain conceptions of the good. Rawls himself seems to endorse this understanding of the distinction between political and comprehensive liberalism when he argues that "reasonable persons will think it unreasonable to use political power, should they possess it, to repress comprehensive views that are not unreasonable, though different from their own."[98] However, Ruth Abbey argues that there is no reason to think that intrusiveness is a necessary component of all comprehensive liberalisms. As Samantha Brennan puts it, "one can pursue philosophical questions about the kind of life it is best to lead without believing that it would be legitimate for the state to enforce one's conclusions,"[99] thus there is no reason for Okin (or anyone else) to resist the label.[100] But I will argue next that condemning oppressive injustices requires going one step further, actually requiring state intervention in certain cases.

Liberal states are already supposed to be committed to ensuring that no individual's conception of the good infringes upon another's; this by itself will rule out the legitimacy of a good number of oppressive comprehensive doctrines. Liberalism has long had the resources to respond to situations where one person's conception of the good threatens the well-being of another; Mill's harm principle famously establishes that your right to swing your fist ends at my nose. If I am right, responding to oppression requires moving beyond this, to actively endorsing some comprehensive doctrines over others. Notice that most liberal states already do noncoercively encourage the adoption of some conceptions of the good over others; they incentivize those that robustly encourage respecting the free and equal status of all individuals, for example, by implementing policies that ensure access to publicly-funded education that includes regular exposure to the truth that all individuals are free and equal and provides the skills (such as literacy) required for full participation as a free and equal citizen. Having the state sanction such policies amounts to endorsing some conceptions of the good over others, but virtually no one criticizes them as illiberal. Rawls defends many such policies as required by the standards of reasonableness.[101] I contend that accommodating the realities of oppression requires supporting and expanding policies like these. When it comes to cases where an individual adopts a conception that is at odds with her own status as a free and equal citizen – for example, women whose religious beliefs lead them to adopt traditional sexist roles – I contend that the liberal state has an obligation to ensure that she has viable exit options (while recognizing the differential exit potential that women face as a result of sexist oppression),[102] and to ensure that she is not staying because of coercion or fear, and only then to respect her autonomous right to decide this for herself. When it comes to the children of adults whose traditional beliefs would threaten their children's future status as free and equal citizens – for example, by inculcating the belief that girls are inferior and appropriately subservient – I contend that the liberal state has an obligation to ensure that these children are not abused or mistreated while in their parents' care, and to ensure that they have viable future exit options (again, recognizing differential exit potentials). All of these arguments require the state to endorse a comprehensive doctrine that is at least robust enough to affirm the fundamental truth that all people are free and equal and worthy of being treated as such.

It should be clear that I am defending a feminist liberalism that is more comprehensive than many other liberal feminists seem completely comfortable with. The question is whether it is tenable to defend this comprehensive liberalism without falling prey to liberalism's historic chauvinism. The liberal feminist with whom this goal resonates most closely is Jean Hampton, who offers what I take to be an entirely convincing defence of the possibility of liberalism providing a theoretical framework for addressing the problems of oppression. Hampton argues that liberals can, and should, endorse certain comprehensive doctrines, thereby paving the way for addressing the concerns that arise in navigating the tensions of pluralism without collapsing into relativism.

In "The Common Faith of Liberalism," Hampton endorses a comprehensive liberalism that she traces back to the Enlightenment, thereby setting herself at odds with Rawls.[103] Because Enlightenment liberalism is a partly comprehensive view – because it makes certain moral commitments that not everyone will agree to (specifically, that people are free and equal) – Rawls rejects it in favour of his political liberalism, which purports to make no such commitments. He does affirm the ideals of freedom and equality, but claims that these are political, rather than ethical ideals for him – they just happen to be ideals we buy into, so they are useful starting points in determining our conception of justice. Hampton rejects this move. Rawls would make the ideals of freedom and equality merely politically convenient starting points, but Hampton contends that treating these ideals as if they are temporary, contingent, and subject to revision or replacement undermines Rawls'ss (and our) goal of a permanent and just solution to the problem of pluralism. Furthermore, Hampton argues that it is implausible to claim that it is the Rawlsian conceptions of freedom and equality that are the ones we happen to accept. His conception of autonomy, for example, presupposes a certain conception of human nature; one according to which we have two moral powers ("a capacity for a sense of justice and for a conception of the good"), and certain powers of reason ("judgement, thought, and inference connected with these powers").[104] This picture of human agency is not particularly robust or detailed, but it is robust enough that not everyone will agree to it. This means that Rawls is committed to far more robust conceptions of freedom and equality than he would like to admit. This puts him in the same boat as the Enlightenment liberals he is trying to distance himself from.

Where Rawls would probably claim to be set apart, however, is in his view of the role these ideals play. This is because he takes himself to be rejecting the Enlightenment view that reason will (eventually) reveal the truth about justice. His public reason is concerned only with achieving an overlapping consensus, whereas traditional liberals think reason will show us the truth. Again, Hampton is not convinced; she argues that, insofar as Rawls thinks the overlapping consensus cannot just be any random combination of views (that is, insofar as he thinks there is good reasoning and bad reasoning), he is committed to the Enlightenment conception of reason, whether he cares to admit it or not. In a similar fashion, she argues that Rawls's burdens of judgement argument about the inevitability of the plurality of moral, religious, and political views itself rests on reasoning that is itself not subject to plurality. Rawls argues that reasonable people can correctly disagree about many things, and this is why we should be tolerant, but he is thereby committed to the view that this argument for tolerance is not something about which reasonable people can disagree. Hence, he is as much a defender of reason as Enlightenment liberals are. Hampton argues that reasonableness plays basically the same role for Rawls as reason does for Enlightenment liberals: it shows a faith in a particular process of engaging with others as the best way to resolve conflicts and secure political stability. Thus,

> [c]ontrary to appearances, Rawls does not abandon the traditional liberal commitment to the idea that reason is universal enough and powerful enough to allow us to make progress on the right kind of social structure in which (free and equal) individuals flourish.... [Furthermore,] Rawls'ss implicit commitment to this notion of reason is as much a function of the fact that Rawls is a *philosopher* as it is a function of the fact that he is a liberal. Philosophizing is an Enlightenment project.... No philosopher who *argues* for his conception of liberalism can claim to be renouncing a commitment to the Enlightenment notion of reason in his political philosophizing.[105]

Hampton thereby demonstrates how all liberals must be committed to a conception of reason that rejects the relativism that would refuse to rule out the legitimacy of oppressive ways of life. She defends this commitment to reason as arising out of the liberal commitment to the intrinsic value of the individual. "To be committed to persuading by rational argument is...to be committed to respecting the individual, not necessarily as a virtuous person, or as a smart person, or as a person satisfying some normative ideal, but as a human being who, like you, can and should choose what he believes in his life."[106] Hampton's comprehensive liberalism gives us a universalism that demands a respect for the freedom and equality of each individual person. But because this is only a partly comprehensive liberalism – because it is committed to a relatively thin comprehensive doctrine that does not insist on much beyond this basic respect for the intrinsic value of the individual – it maintains a pluralism that respects as many different competing ways of life as possible. Liberals thus need not shy away from either universalism or pluralism, Hampton shows.

In opening up the space for a comprehensive, not purely political, liberalism, Hampton provides the grounds for addressing the feminist concerns raised by Okin. By showing how the liberal commitment to respecting the individual's right to his or her own conception of the good need not be at odds with the feminist concern for social justice, she achieves something that Rawls could, or would, not. She strikes a balance between universalism and pluralism that corrects liberalism's historical mistakes without losing the ability to address the realities of oppression. Hampton shows why those conceptions of the good that conflict with the basic liberal commitment to the freedom and equality of all individuals do not deserve accommodation or respect.

Just as I side with Hampton over Nussbaum in endorsing a partly comprehensive, rather than purely political, liberalism to address the problems of oppression, I also side with Hampton in the foundational theoretical framework I favour; where Nussbaum prefers Aristotle, Hampton and I turn to Kant.[107,108] Central to the Kantian framework is the idea that human beings have intrinsic worth in virtue of our rational capacities to set and pursue ends for ourselves. As we have seen, this conception of human nature has been dismissed as Enlightenment dogma, criticized for its abstraction, its individualism, its masculinism, and its dependence on rationalism. In this chapter I have shown how liberals can and do respond to these various critiques. In the next chapter I will explore the prospects for Kantian feminism on moral, rather than political, grounds.

Notes

1. John Stuart Mill, "The Subjection of Women," in J.S. Mill and Harriet Taylor Mill, *Essays on Sex Equality*, Rossi (ed.) (Chicago: University of Chicago Press, 1970 [1869]).
2. Mill, "The Subjection of Women," 125.
3. Mill, "The Subjection of Women," 126.
4. Mill, "The Subjection of Women," 141.
5. Mill, "The Subjection of Women," 156.
6. Young does, however, admit that at the most abstract level there are some experiences shared by all oppressed people. Specifically, she claims that oppressed people experience an "inhibition of their ability to develop and exercise their capacities and express their needs, thoughts, and feelings." See Iris Marion Young, *Justice and the Politics of Difference* (Princeton: Princeton University Press, 1990), 40.
7. A concrete example of this kind of relative advantage is the benefits that accrue to men as a result of women's disproportionate risk of being subject to sexual violence. This disproportionate risk results in a "male protection racket," whereby men in general benefit from the immoral actions of a specific few men who actually assault women. The idea of the male protection racket was first introduced by Susan Brownmiller. See Susan Brownmiller, *Against Our Will: Men, Women and Rape* (New York: Simon and Schuster, 1975). The climate of fear of sexual violence against women gives men an opportunity to benefit from being seen as "nice guys" – by walking

a woman to her car late at night, for example – because women feel vulnerable and dependent. This is, of course, not to suggest that men who walk women to their cars late at night, or do whatever else they can to make women feel safe, are in some way intending to exploit women. Nor is it to suggest that men should *not* do these things. It is just to point out that the opportunities men have to perform these courtesies both result from and ultimately help strengthen oppressive structures that systematically benefit men at women's expense. Men also benefit from women's disproportionate risk of sexual violence because it effectively reduces women's competition with them for certain jobs. These sorts of harms that women undergo as members of a group count as oppressive because the existence of these harms ultimately serves the interests of men as a group.

8. For example, Marilyn Frye has argued that, when a white person is unable safely to walk the streets of a racial ghetto, this restriction on his or her agency is not an oppressive one, because ultimately this sort of ghetto benefits white people at the expense of those who are ghettoized. Its purpose is to keep non-white people *in* its borders; that it also functions to keep white people *out* might indeed be a harm that white people must endure, but being made to endure this harm is not a case of oppression because it does not on balance benefit those in the ghetto. See Marilyn Frye, "Oppression," *The Politics of Reality* (Freedom, CA: The Crossing Press, 1983).

9. An exception to this might be, for example, certain privileges or restrictions that, as a matter of good or bad luck, result from a person's physical characteristics. A tall person has an easier time reaching something off a high shelf; a shorter person has an easier time fitting comfortably into an airplane seat. These sorts of restrictions and privileges are not really deserved (in the sense that one has not done anything to earn them), but they are not unfair. I do not, however, take the existence of these sorts of exceptions to undermine the general egalitarian point here, that undeserved restrictions and unearned privileges are usually unfair.

10. Frye, *The Politics of Reality*, 4–5.
11. Young, *Justice and the Politics of Difference*, 41.
12. Sally Haslanger's distinction between *agent* and *structural* oppression also captures these two distinct kinds of oppression. See Sally Haslanger, "Oppressions: Racial and Other," *Racism, Philosophy and Mind: Philosophical Explanations of Racism and Its Implications*, Levine and Pataki (eds) (Ithaca: Cornell University Press, 2007), 100.
13. Sally Haslanger, "Gender and Race: (What) Are They? (What) Do We Want Them To Be?" *Nous* 34 (2000): 39.
14. See, for example, Elizabeth Anderson, "Epistemic Justice as a Virtue of Social Institutions," *Social Epistemology* 26 (2012): 163–173; Lawrence Blum, "Stereotypes and Stereotyping: A Moral Analysis," *Philosophical Papers* 33 (2004): 251–290; Samantha Brennan, "Feminist Ethics and Everyday Inequalities," *Hypatia* 24 (2009): 141–159; Sally Haslanger, "Changing the Ideology and Culture of Philosophy: Not by Reason (Alone)," *Hypatia* 23 (2008): 210–222; and Alexis Shotwell, *Knowing Otherwise: Race, Gender, and Implicit Understanding* (University Park: Pennsylvania University Press, 2011).
15. Ann Cudd, *Analyzing Oppression* (New York: Oxford University Press, 2006), 22. Also see her "Strikes, Housework, and the Moral Obligation to Resist,"

Journal of Social Philosophy 29 (1998): 20–36; and her "Oppression by Choice," *Journal of Social Philosophy* 25 (1994): 22–44.
16. See, for example, Amartya Sen, "Gender Inequality and Theories of Justice," *Women, Culture, and Development*, Glover and Nussbaum (eds) (New York: Oxford University Press, 1995), 259–274, and "Rights and Capabilities," *Resources, Values, and Development* (Oxford and Cambridge: Blackwell and MIT Press, 1984), 307–324.
17. This categorization of radical critiques of liberalism relies heavily on one provided by Charles Mills. See Charles Mills, "Occupy Liberalism! Or, Ten Reasons Why Liberalism Cannot be Retrieved for Radicalism (And Why They're All Wrong)," *Radical Philosophy Review* 15 (2012): 305–323.
18. This categorization of communitarian critiques of liberalism relies heavily on one provided by Daniel Bell. See Daniel Bell, *Communitarianism and Its Critics* (Oxford: Clarendon Press, 1993).
19. See, for example, Mills, "Occupy Liberalism!," Cudd, *Analyzing Oppression*; and Martha Nussbaum, *Sex and Social Justice* (New York: Oxford University Press, 1999).
20. See, for example, Kathryn Pyne Addelson, *Moral Passages: Toward a Collectivist Moral Theory* (New York: Routledge, 1994); Seyla Benhabib, "The Generalized and the Concrete Other," *Women and Moral Theory*, Kittay and Meyers (eds) (Totowa: Rowman & Littlefield, 1987); Claudia Card, *The Unnatural Lottery: Character and Moral Luck* (Philadelphia: Temple University Press, 1996); Lorraine Code, *What Can She Know? Feminist Theory and the Construction of Knowledge* (Ithaca: Cornell University Press, 1991); Susan Hekman, *Moral Voices, Moral Selves* (University Park: Pennsylvania State University Press, 1995); Sarah Hoagland, "Some Thoughts about 'Caring'," *Feminist Ethics*, Card (ed.) (Lawrence: University Press of Kansas, 1991); Alison Jaggar, *Feminist Politics and Human Nature* (Totowa: Roman and Allanheld, 1983); Jean Keller, "Autonomy, Relationality, and Feminist Ethics," *Hypatia* 12 (1997): 152–164; Jennifer Nedelsky, "Reconceiving Autonomy: Sources, Thoughts, and Possibilities," *Yale Journal of Law and Feminism* 1 (1989): 7–36.
21. See, for example, Code, *What Can She Know?*; Elizabeth Fox-Genovese, *Feminism Without Illusions: A Critique of Individualism* (University of North Carolina Press, 1991); Carol Gilligan, *In a Different Voice: Psychological Theory and Women's Development* (Cambridge: Harvard University Press, 1982); Virginia Held, *Feminist Morality: Transforming Culture, Society, and Politics* (Chicago: University of Chicago Press, 1993); Nel Noddings, *Caring: A Feminine Approach to Ethics and Moral Education* (Los Angeles: University of California Press, 1984); Carole Pateman, *The Sexual Contract* (Stanford: Stanford University Press, 1988).
22. See, for example, Benhabib, "The Generalized and the Concrete Other"; Code, *What Can She Know?*; Hoagland, "Some Thoughts about 'Caring'"; Keller, "Autonomy, Relationality, and Feminist Ethics"; and Nedelsky, "Reconceiving Autonomy: Sources, Thoughts, and Possibilities."
23. See, for example, Wendy Brown, *States of Injury: Power and Freedom in Late Modernity* (Princeton: Princeton University Press, 1995); Eva Feder Kittay, *Love's Labor: Essays on Women, Equality, and Dependency* (New York: Routledge, 1998); Noddings, *Caring*.

24. See, for example, Jean Grimshaw, "Autonomy and Identity in Feminist Thinking," *Feminist Perspectives in Philosophy*, Griffiths and Whitford (eds) (Bloomington: Indiana University Press, 1988): 90–108.
25. See, for example, Code, *What Can She Know?*
26. See, for example, Annette Baier, "What Do Women Want in a Moral Theory?," *Nous* 19 (1985): 53–63, "The Need for More than Justice," *Science, Morality and Feminist Theory*, Hanen and Nielsen (eds) (Calgary: University of Calgary Press, 1987), and *Moral Prejudices* (Cambridge: Harvard University Press, 1995); Benhabib, "The Generalized and the Concrete Other"; Code, *What Can She Know?*; Robin Dillon, "Care and Respect," *Explorations in Feminist Ethics: Theory and Practice*, Cole and Coultrap-McQuin (eds) (Bloomington: Indiana University Press, 1992); Fox-Genovese, *Feminism Without Illusions*; Grimshaw, "Autonomy and Identity in Feminist Thinking"; Virginia Held, "Feminism and Moral Theory," *Women and Moral Theory*, Kittay and Meyers (eds) (Totowa: Rowman and Littlefield, 1987), 111–128; Kittay, *Love's Labor*; Susan Moller Okin, *Justice, Gender, and the Family* (New York: Basic Books, 1989); Pateman, *The Sexual Contract*; Sara Ruddick, *Maternal Thinking: Towards a Politics of Peace* (Boston: Beacon Press, 1989); Naomi Scheman, *Engenderings: Constructions of Knowledge, Authority, and Privilege* (New York: Routledge, 1993); Joan Tronto, *Moral Boundaries: A Political Argument for an Ethic of Care* (New York: Routledge, 1993); Margaret Urban Walker, *Moral Understandings: A Feminist Study in Ethics*, 2nd Edition (New York: Oxford University Press, 2007).
27. See, for example, Judith Butler, *Gender Trouble: Feminism and the Subversion of Identity* (New York: Routledge, 1990).
28. See Ann Phillips, "Feminism and Liberalism Revisited: Has Martha Nussbaum Got it Right?," *Constellations* 8 (2001): 249–266.
29. Alasdair Macintyre, *Dependent Rational Animals* (Illinois: Carus Publishing, 1999), 42.
30. Karl Marx, *Grundrisse*, Nicolaus (trans.) (Harmondsworth: Penguin Books, 1973).
31. See, for example, Louis Althusser, *Essays in Self-Critique*, Lock (trans.) (London: New Left Books, 1976); Alain Badiou, *The Meaning of Sarkozy*, Fernbach (trans.) (London: Verso, 2008); and Peter Hallward, "The Will of the People: Notes Towards A Dialectical Voluntarism," *Radical Philosophy* 155 (2009): 17–29.
32. Isaiah Berlin, "Two Concepts of Liberty," *Four Essays on Liberty* (London: Oxford University Press, 1969), 118–172.
33. See, for example, Gerald Dworkin, *The Theory and Practice of Autonomy* (New York: Cambridge University Press, 1988), and "The Concept of Autonomy," *The Inner Citadel: Essays on Individual Autonomy*, Christman (ed.) (New York: Oxford University Press, 1989), 54–62; and Joel Feinberg, "Autonomy," *The Inner Citadel: Essays on Individual Autonomy*, Christman (ed.) (New York: Oxford University Press, 1989), 27–53.
34. See, for example, Joseph Raz, *The Morality of Freedom* (Oxford: Clarendon Press, 1986).
35. See, for example, Dworkin, *The Theory and Practice of Autonomy*; and Alfred R. Mele, *Autonomous Agents: From Self-Control to Autonomy* (New York: Oxford University Press, 1995).

36. See, for example, Drucilla Cornell, *At the Heart of Freedom* (Princeton: Princeton University Press, 1998); Cudd, *Analyzing Oppression*; Alfred R. Mele, *Autonomous Agents: From Self-Control to Autonomy* (New York: Oxford University Press, 1995); Diana T. Meyers, *Self, Society, and Personal Choice* (New York: Columbia University Press, 1989), "Feminism and Women's Autonomy: The Challenge of Female Genital Cutting," *Metaphilosophy* 31 (2000): 469–491, and *Being Yourself: Essays on Identity, Action, and Social Life* (Lanham: Rowman and Littlefield, 2004); and Susan Moller Okin, "Justice and Gender: An Unfinished Debate," *Fordham Law Review* 72 (2003): 1537–1546.
37. See, for example, Cornell, *At the Heart of Freedom*; Cudd, *Analyzing Oppression*; Marilyn Friedman, "Autonomy and Social Relationships: Rethinking the Feminist Critique," *Feminists Rethink the Self*, Meyers (ed.) (Boulder: Westview Press, 1997), 40–61, and *Autonomy, Gender, Politics* (New York: Oxford University Press, 2003); Jean Hampton, "Feminist Contractarianism," *A Mind of One's Own: Feminist Essays on Reason and Objectivity*, Antony and Witt (eds) (Boulder: Westview Press, 1993); Andrew Kernohan, *Liberalism, Equality, and Cultural Oppression* (New York: Cambridge University Press, 1999); Diana T. Meyers, "Personal Autonomy and the Paradox of Feminine Socialization," *Journal of Philosophy* 84 (1987): 619–628; and Susan Wolf, *Freedom and Reason* (New York: Oxford University Press, 1990).
38. See, for example, Cudd, *Analyzing Oppression*; Martha Nussbaum, *Women and Human Development: The Capabilities Approach* (Cambridge: Cambridge University Press, 2000); Sen, "Gender Inequality and Theories of Justice," and "Rights and Capabilities"; Anita Superson, "Deformed Desires and Informed Desire Tests," *Hypatia* 20 (2005): 109–112; and Kimberly Yuracko, *Perfectionism and Contemporary Feminist Values* (Bloomington: University of Indiana Press, 2003).
39. See, for example, Ruth Abbey, "Persuasive Universalism and Political Liberalism," *The Return of Feminist Liberalism* (Montreal and Kingston: McGill-Queen's University Press, 2011), 226–247.
40. This is a common theme in many of the articles in *Varieties of Feminist Liberalism*, including Anita Allen's "Coercing Privacy," Drucilla Cornell's "Freed Up: Privacy, Sexual Freedom, and Liberty of Conscience," and Ann Cudd's "The Paradox of Liberal Feminism: Preference, Rationality, and Oppression." See *Varieties of Feminist Liberalism*, Baehr (ed.) (Lanham: Rowman and Littlefield, 2004).
41. John Rawls, *A Theory of Justice* (Cambridge: Belknap Press, 1971), and *Justice as Fairness: A Restatement* (Cambridge: Belknap Press, 2001).
42. See, for example, Susan Babbitt, *Impossible Dreams: Rationality, Integrity, and Moral Imagination* (Boulder: Westview Press, 1996); Kittay, *Love's Labor*; Catharine MacKinnon, *Feminism Unmodified: Discourses on Life and Law* (Cambridge: Harvard University Press, 1987), and *Toward a Feminist Theory of State* (Cambridge: Harvard University Press, 1991); Lisa Schwartzman, *Challenging Liberalism: Feminism as Political Critique* (University Park: Pennsylvania State University Press, 2006), and "Non-Ideal Theorizing, Social Groups, and Knowledge of Oppression: A Response," *Hypatia* 24 (2009): 177–188; and Young, *Justice and the Politics of Difference*.
43. Young, *Justice and the Politics of Difference*, 116.

44. See, for example, Elizabeth Anderson, *Value in Ethics and Economics* (Cambridge: Harvard University Press, 1993); Mills, "Occupy Liberalism!" and "Schwartzman vs. Okin: Some Comments on Challenging Liberalism," *Hypatia* 24 (2009): 164–177; and Nussbaum, *Sex and Social Justice*.
45. Nussbaum, *Sex and Social Justice*, 57.
46. Mills, "Occupy Liberalism!," 309.
47. Richard Wasserstrom, "On Racism and Sexism," *Philosophy and Social Issues* (Notre Dame: Notre Dame University Press, 1980).
48. See, for example, Susan Moller Okin, "Gender Inequality and Cultural Differences," *Political Theory* 22 (1994): 5–24.
49. Okin, "Gender Inequality and Cultural Differences," 19–20.
50. See, for example, Okin, "Gender Inequality and Cultural Differences"; and Martha Nussbaum, "Human Functioning and Social Justice," *Political Theory* 20 (1992): 202–246.
51. Rawls, *Justice as Fairness*, 66.
52. Some defenders of Rawls do not concede that Rawls himself was actually concerned about gender or racial injustice, but argue instead that these concerns can be addressed as a matter of corrective justice, using the non-ideal aspects of Rawlsian theory. See, for example, Charles Mills's chapters in Carole Pateman and Charles Mills, *Contract and Domination* (Malden: Polity Press, 2007) and Mills, "Schwartzman vs. Okin: Some Comments on Challenging Liberalism."
53. See, for example, Butler, *Gender Trouble*; Charles Taylor, *Philosophical Papers, vol. I: Human Agency and Language; vol. II: Philosophical Sources of the Self: The Making of Modern Identity* (Cambridge: Harvard University Press, 1989); Michael Sandel, *Liberalism and the Limits of Justice* (Cambridge: Cambridge University Press, 1981); and Schwartzman, *Challenging Liberalism* and "Non-Ideal Theorizing, Social Groups, and Knowledge of Oppression."
54. See, for example, Bernard Boxill, *Blacks and Social Justice* (Totowa: Rowman and Allanheld, 1984); Cudd, *Analyzing Oppression*; Fox-Genovese, *Feminism Without Illusions*; Martha Minow, *Making All the Difference* (Ithaca: Cornell University Press, 1990); Young, *Justice and the Politics of Difference*.
55. Bonnie Honig, "'My Culture Made Me Do It'," *Is Multiculturalism Bad for Women*? Cohen, Howard, and Nussbaum (eds) (Princeton: Princeton University Press, 1999), 39.
56. See, for example, Code, *What Can She Know?*; John Christman, "Relational Autonomy, Liberal Individualism, and the Social Constitution of Selves," *Philosophical Studies* 117 (2004): 143–164; Jaggar, *Feminist Politics and Human Nature*; Nedelsky, "Reconceiving Autonomy: Sources, Thoughts and Possibilities"; Naomi Scheman, "Individualism and the Objects of Psychology," *Discovering Reality: Feminist Perspectives on Epistemology, Metaphysics, Methodology, and Philosophy of Science*, Harding and Hintikka (eds) (Dordrecht, Holland: D. Reidel, 1983); Susan Sherwin, "A Relational Approach to Autonomy in Health Care," *The Politics of Women's Health: Exploring Agency and Autonomy*, Sherwin and the Feminist Health Care Ethics Research Network (eds) (Philadelphia: Temple University Press, 1998); Catriona Mackenzie and Natalie Stoljar (eds), *Relational Autonomy: Feminist Perspectives on Autonomy, Agency, and the Social Self* (New York: Oxford University Press, 2000); and Andrea Westlund, "Rethinking Relational Autonomy," *Hypatia* 24 (2009): 26–49.

57. See, for example, Diana Meyers, "Intersectional Identity and the Authentic Self: Opposites Attract," *Relational Autonomy: Feminist Perspectives on Autonomy, Agency, and the Social Self*, MacKenzie and Stoljar (eds) (New York: Oxford University Press, 2000), 151–180; Uma Narayan, "Minds of Their Own: Choices, Autonomy, Cultural Practices, and Other Women," *A Mind of One's Own: Feminist Essays on Reason and Objectivity*, 2nd edition, Antony and Witt (eds) (Boulder: Westview Press, 2002), 418–432.
58. See, for example, MacKinnon, *Feminism Unmodified* and *Toward a Feminist Theory of State*; Pateman, *The Sexual Contract*; Schwartzman, *Challenging Liberalism*, and "Non-Ideal Theorizing, Social Groups, and Knowledge of Oppression."
59. See, for example, Will Kymlicka, *Liberalism, Community and Culture* (Oxford: Clarendon Press, 1989), and "Liberal Complacencies," *Is Multiculturalism Bad for Women?* Cohen, Howard, and Nussbaum (eds) (Princeton: Princeton University Press, 1999), 31–34.
60. See, for example, John Christman, "Feminism and Autonomy," *Nagging Questions: Feminist Ethics in Everyday Life*, Bushnell (ed.) (Savage: Rowman and Littlefield, 1995), 17–39; and Friedman, "Autonomy and Social Relationships", and *Autonomy, Gender, Politics*.
61. See, for example, Susan Moller Okin and Brooke Ackerly, "Feminist Social Critique and the International Movement for Women's Rights as Human Rights," *Democracy's Edges*, Shapiro and Hacker-Cordon (eds) (Cambridge: Cambridge University Press, 1999), 134–162; and Nussbaum, *Sex and Social Justice*.
62. Nussbaum, *Sex and Social Justice*, 70.
63. See, for example, Elizabeth Anderson, "Toward a Non-Ideal, Relational Methodology for Political Philosophy: Comments on Schwartzman's Challenging Liberalism," *Hypatia* 24 (2009): 130–145; Chandran Kukathas, "Liberalism, Multiculturalism and Oppression, *Political Theory: Tradition and Diversity* (Cambridge: Cambridge University Press, 1997), 132–153, and "Is Feminism Bad for Multiculturalism?," *Public Affairs Quarterly* 15 (2001): 83–98; and Nussbaum, *Sex and Social Justice*.
64. See, for example, Philip Pettit, "Freedom as Antipower," *Ethics* 106 (1996): 576–604, *Republicanism: A Theory of Freedom and Government* (Oxford: Clarendon Press, 1997), *A Theory of Freedom: From the Psychology to the Politics of Agency* (Oxford: Oxford University Press, 2001), "Agency-Freedom and Option-Freedom," *Journal of Theoretical Politics* 15 (2003): 387–403, and "Freedom and Probability: A Comment on Goodin and Jackson," *Philosophy and Public Affairs* 36 (2008): 206–220; and Sandel, *Liberalism and the Limits of Justice*, "The Procedural Republic and the Unencumbered Self," *Political Theory* 12 (1984): 81–96, and *Democracy's Discontent: America in Search of a Public Philosophy* (Cambridge: Harvard University Press, 1996).
65. See, for example, Enrique Dussel, *Twenty Theses on Politics*, Ciccariello-Maher (trans.) (Durham: Duke University Press, 2008); MacKinnon, *Feminism Unmodified* and *Toward a Feminist Theory of State*; Pateman, *The Sexual Contract*; Pateman and Mills, *Contract and Domination*; Schwartzman, *Challenging Liberalism*; Michael Walzer, *Spheres of Justice: A Defense of Pluralism and Equality* (New York: Basic Books, 1983); and Young, *Justice and the Politics of Difference*.

66. See, for example, Enrique Dussel, *Ethics and Community*, Knoll (trans.) (New York: Orbis Books, 1988).
67. See, for example, Dussel, *Twenty Theses on Politics* and *Ethics and Community*.
68. See, for example, Seyla Benhabib, *Situating the Self: Gender, Community and Postmodernism in Contemporary Ethics* (Cambridge: Polity Press, 1992); Alasdair MacIntyre, *Against the Self-Images of the Age* (Notre Dame: University of Notre Dame Press, 1978), and *Whose Justice? Which Rationality?* (Notre Dame: University of Notre Dame Press, 1988); and Taylor, *Philosophical Papers*, vols. I & II.
69. See John Rawls, *Political Liberalism* (New York: Columbia University Press, 1993), and *Justice as Fairness: A Restatement*.
70. Mill's utilitarian liberalism falls near the minimal end of the continuum. Contemporary liberals who embrace relatively minimal theories include, for example, Elizabeth Brake, Ann Cudd, David Gauthier, and Robert Nozick. See Elizabeth Brake, "Rawls and Feminism: What Should Feminists Make of Liberal Neutrality?," *Journal of Moral Philosophy* 1 (2004): 293–309; Cudd, "The Paradox of Liberal Feminism"; David Gauthier, *Morals By Agreement* (New York: Oxford University Press, 1987); and Robert Nozick, *Anarchy, State, and Utopia*, (USA: Basic Books, 1974).
71. Kant's deontological liberalism falls near the substantive end of the continuum. Contemporary liberals who embrace relatively substantive theories include, for example, Jean Hampton, Martha Nussbaum, Susan Moller Okin, and Joseph Raz. See Jean Hampton, "Should Political Philosophy be Done without Metaphysics?," *Ethics* 99 (1989): 791–814; Nussbaum, *Sex and Social Justice*; Susan Moller Okin, "Feminism and Multiculturalism: Some Tensions," *Ethics* 108 (1998): 661–684, and "Is Multiculturalism Bad for Women?"; and Joseph Raz, "Facing Diversity: The Case of Epistemic Abstinence," *Philosophy & Public Affairs* 19 (1990): 3–46.
72. See, for example, Thomas Hurka, *Perfectionism* (New York: Oxford University Press, 1993); Kymlicka, *Liberalism, Community and Culture*; Joseph Raz, *The Morality of Freedom* (Oxford: Clarendon Press, 1986); George Sher, *Beyond Neutrality: Perfectionism and Politics* (Cambridge: Cambridge University Press, 1997); L.W. Sumner, *Welfare, Happiness and Ethics* (New York: Oxford University Press, 1996); and Steven Wall, *Liberalism, Perfectionism and Restraint* (New York: Cambridge University Press, 1998).
73. See, for example, Paul Benson, "Freedom and Value," *Journal of Philosophy* 84 (1987): 465–486; and Bernard Berofsky, *Liberation from Self* (New York: Cambridge University Press, 1995).
74. See, for example, Yuracko, *Perfectionism and Contemporary Feminist Values*; and Linda Hirshman, *Get to Work: A Manifesto for Women of the World* (New York: Viking Penguin, 2006).
75. See, for example, John Christman, "Liberalism and Individual Positive Freedom," *Ethics* 101 (1991): 343–359; Ronald Dworkin, *Sovereign Virtue* (Cambridge: Harvard University Press, 2000); Gauthier, *Morals By Agreement*; and Rawls, *A Theory of Justice*, *Political Liberalism*, and *Justice as Fairness*.
76. See, for example, Chandran Kukathas, *The Liberal Archipelago* (Oxford: Oxford University Press, 2003); Raz, "Facing Diversity: The Case of Epistemic

Abstinence"; and Yael Tamir, *Liberal Nationalism* (Princeton: Princeton University Press, 1993).
77. John Rawls, *The Law of Peoples* (Cambridge: Harvard University Press, 2001), 63–70.
78. See, for example, Jeff Spinner-Halev, "Feminism, Multiculturalism, Oppression and the State," *Ethics* 112 (2001): 84–115.
79. See, for example, Harry Brighouse, "Civic Education and Liberal Legitimacy," *Ethics* 108 (1998): 719–745; William Galston, "Two Concepts of Liberalism," *Ethics* 105 (1995): 516–534; Nomi Stolzenberg, "He Drew a Circle That Shut Me Out: Assimilation, Indoctrination, and the Paradox of Liberal Education," *Harvard Law Review* 106 (1993): 581–667.
80. See, for example, Joel Feinberg, "The Child's Right to an Open Future," *Whose Child? Children's Rights, Parental Authority, and State Power*, Aiken and LaFollette (eds) (Totowa: Rowman and Littlefield, 1980); Stephen Macedo, "Liberal Civic Education and Religious Fundamentalism: The Case of God v. John Rawls?," *Ethics* 105 (1995): 468–96; Susan Moller Okin, "Mistresses of Their Own Destiny: Group Rights, Gender, and Realistic Rights of Exit," *Ethics* 112 (2002): 205–230.
81. Rawls, *Political Liberalism*, 199.
82. Susan Moller Okin, "Feminism and Multiculturalism: Some Tensions," *Ethics* 108 (1998): 661–684, "Is Multiculturalism Bad for Women?," and "Multiculturalism and Feminism: No Simple Question, No Simple Answers," *Minorities within Minorities: Equality, Rights and Diversity* (Cambridge: Cambridge University Press, 2005), 67–89.
83. Spinner-Halev, "Feminism, Multiculturalism, Oppression, and the State," 84.
84. See, for example, Friedman, *Autonomy, Gender, Politics*; Tracy Higgins, "Gender, Why Feminists Can't (Or Shouldn't) be Liberals," *Fordham Law Review* 72 (2004): 1629–1641; Chandran Kukathas, "Is Feminism Bad for Multiculturalism?"; Ayelet Shachar, *Multicultural Jurisdictions: Cultural Differences and Women's Rights* (Cambridge: Cambridge University Press, 2001); and Spinner-Halev, "Feminism, Multiculturalism, Oppression, and the State."
85. Susan Moller Okin, "Recognizing Women's Rights as Human Rights," *American Philosophical Association Newsletter on Philosophy and Law* 97 (1998): 99–102.
86. See, for example, Amartya Sen, "Rights and Capabilities," *The Standard of Living* (Cambridge: Cambridge University Press, 1989), *Inequality Reexamined* (Cambridge: Harvard University Press, 1992), and *Commodities and Capabilities* (Oxford: Oxford University Press, 1999), *The Quality of Life*, Nussbaum and Glover (eds) (New York: Oxford University Press, 1993), and *Women, Culture, and Development* (New York: Oxford University Press, 1995); and Martha Nussbaum, *Sex and Social Justice, Women and Human Development: The Capabilities Approach, Frontiers of Justice: Disability, Nationality, and Species Membership* (Cambridge: Belknap Press, 2007), and *Creating Capabilities: The Human Development Approach* (Cambridge: Belknap Press, 2011).
87. Nussbaum, *Sex and Social Justice*, 39
88. Nussbaum, *Sex and Social Justice*, 40.
89. Nussbaum, *Sex and Social Justice*, 40.
90. Nussbaum, *Sex and Social Justice*, 41.

91. Nussbaum, *Sex and Social Justice*, 42.
92. See, for example, Martha Nussbaum, "Public Philosophy and International Feminism," *Ethics* 108 (1998): 762–796; *Women and Human Development: The Capabilities Approach*, 5, 8, 180; "Aristotle, Politics and Human Capabilities: A Response to Antony, Arneson, Charlesworth and Mulgan," *Ethics* 111 (2000): 124, "Aristotelian Social Democracy," *Liberalism and the Good*, Douglass, Mara, and Richardson (eds) (New York: Routledge, 1990), 203–252, and *Creating Capabilities* 79, 89–93, 182.
93. Louise Antony, for example, charges that it must, ultimately, be Nussbaum's antecedent normative commitments that do the justificatory work in the capabilities approach. See Louise Antony, "Natures and Norms," *Ethics* 111 (2000): 5–36. Linda Barclay contends that Nussbaum's admission that "there is no consensus on her list of capabilities and it is most certainly not developed from ideas implicit in the public political culture of those democracies," along with her whole-hearted endorsement of the ideal of autonomy, rule out the possibility of the capabilities approach qualifying as a truly political liberalism. See Linda Barclay, "What Kind of Liberal is Martha Nussbaum?" *SATS – Nordic Journal of Philosophy* 4 (2003): 12. Jane Flax also argues that the capabilities approach is built on a metaphysically robust conception of human nature and a comprehensive conception of the good. See Jane Flax, "A Constructionist Despite Herself? On Capacities and their Discontents," *Controversies in Feminism*, Sterba (ed.) (Lanham: Rowman and Littlefield, 2001), 47–57. Ruth Abbey provides a comprehensive summary of the debate over how best to categorize Nussbaum's liberalism, also concluding that Nussbaum is committed to a less political version of liberalism than she is willing to admit. See Ruth Abbey, *The Return of Feminist Liberalism* (Montreal and Kingston: McGill-Queen's University Press, 2011).
94. Martha Nussbaum, "Political Liberalism and Respect: A Response to Linda Barclay," *SATS – Nordic Journal of Philosophy* 4 (2003): 27.
95. Nussbaum, "Aristotle, Politics and Human Capabilities," 129, and *Creating Capabilities*, 89–93.
96. Nussbaum, "Political Liberalism and Respect," 36, 41, and *Creating Capabilities*, 89–93.
97. Susan Moller Okin, "Reply," *Is Multiculturalism Bad for Women?* Cohen, Howard, and Nussbaum (eds) (Princeton: Princeton University Press, 1999), 129.
98. Rawls, *Political Liberalism*, 60.
99. Samantha Brennan, "The Liberal Rights of Feminist Liberalism," *Varieties of Feminist Liberalism*, Baehr (ed.) (Lanham: Rowman and Littlefield, 2004), 87.
100. Ruth Abbey, "Back toward a Comprehensive Liberalism? Justice as Fairness, Gender, and Families," *Political Theory* 35 (2007) 5–28.
101. Rawls, *Political Liberalism*, 195–200.
102. See, for example, Partha Dasgupta, *An Inquiry into Well-being and Destitution* (Oxford: Clarendon Press, 1993); Susan Moller Okin, *Justice, Gender, and the Family*, "Gender Inequality and Cultural Differences," and "Mistresses of Their Own Destiny"; and Amartya Sen, "Gender and Co-operative

Conflicts," *Women and World Development*, Tinker (ed.) (New York: Oxford University Press, 1990).
103. Jean Hampton, "The Common Faith of Liberalism," *The Intrinsic Worth of Persons: Contractarianism in Moral and Political Philosophy* (New York: Cambridge University Press, 2007).
104. Hampton, "The Common Faith of Liberalism," 165.
105. Hampton, "The Common Faith of Liberalism," 183.
106. Hampton, "The Common Faith of Liberalism," 161. Also see Hampton, "Should Political Philosophy be Done without Metaphysics?."
107. Nussbaum herself has recognized the importance of Kant, particularly his insistence that "social welfare should never be pursued in a way that violates people's fundamental entitlements," in formulating the capabilities approach. Nussbaum, *Creating Capabilities*, 94. Also see Martha Nussbaum, "Interview," *Key Philosophers in Conversation*, Pyle (ed.) (London: Routledge, 1999), 239–256.
108. For Hampton's defences of Kant, see her "Contract and Consent," *A Companion to Contemporary Political Philosophy* 2 (1993): 478–492, and "Feminist Contractarianism."

2
A Feminist Defence of Kant

In this chapter I defend the Kantian moral framework from two related criticisms, both of which claim that this framework is unsuitable for feminist purposes. One of these criticisms focuses on Kant's privileging the rational over the animal; the other focuses on his privileging the rational over the emotional. I argue that if feminists are willing to look to Kant we can find ways of understanding certain psychological harms of oppression, and find ways of addressing these harms, that we otherwise risk losing sight of. In particular, I argue that without a Kantian account of duties to the self, feminists cannot properly explain what is wrong with the gendered norms of self-sacrifice that have historically exploited women.

A good number of feminists make no secret of their dislike of Kant.[1] For this reason, I think it is worth starting off by explaining why I, as a feminist, find it appropriate to use a Kantian framework to analyse the experiences of women's oppression. This is admittedly a somewhat controversial philosophical move. Kant has served as a whipping boy for feminists of all stripes who assert, among other things, that his conception of personhood is committed to an overly narrow conception of rationality that cannot account for the embodied and emotional character of human life. I recognize the obstacles to employing Kant in a feminist critique of women's oppression, but I maintain that Kant's account of what our rational nature is, why it is valuable, how it can be compromised and deformed, and why it must be fostered and protected, provides conceptual resources that feminists cannot afford to ignore. Before advancing this argument, however, a word of caution needs to be expressed.

After all, Kant himself says some horrifically misogynistic things about women, particularly in some of his more peripheral works. Some of his more egregious examples include the following gems:

> [Scholarly women] use their books somewhat like a watch, that is, they wear the watch so it can be noticed that they have one, although it is usually broken or does not show the correct time.[2]
>
> [A] woman makes no secret in wishing that she might rather be a man, so that she could give larger and freer latitude to her inclinations; no man, however, would want to be a woman (A 222).
>
> Nature was concerned about the preservation of the embryo and implanted fear into the woman's character, a fear of physical injury and a timidity towards similar dangers. On the basis of this weakness, the woman legitimately asks for masculine protection (A 219).
>
> A woman who has a head full of Greek, like Mme. Dacier, or carries on fundamental controversies about mechanics, like the Marquise du Châtelet, might as well even have a beard, for perhaps that would express more obviously the mien of profundity for which she strives.[3]
>
> [Women's philosophy is] not to reason, but to sense.... I hardly believe that the fairer sex is capable of principles (O 132–133).[4]

It is clear enough that Kant himself was no friend to women. I am not going to pretend otherwise. But I count myself among the feminist philosophers who think there is no reason to insist that these anthropological views must fully infect Kant's central philosophical views.[5] It comes as a surprise to no one that the society in which Kant lived was deeply sexist; that this sexism is sometimes apparent in the works of someone writing against such background social conditions should be just as unsurprising. Kant was writing in a social milieu that took women's subordination to men completely for granted. But some feminists have insisted that while we might be able to excuse the sexist claims Kant makes about women, and while it is not self-evident that the Kantian corpus is irredeemably misogynist, we cannot simply ignore Kant's sexism and neatly translate his claims into gender-neutral language.[6] In what follows, I will propose that this is, in fact, precisely what we can do. I argue that much of what is most important in Kant's work can be read in a gender-neutral manner and thus we can use his moral framework for explicitly feminist purposes.

Both the *Anthropology* and the *Observations on the Feeling of the Beautiful and Sublime* are widely regarded as peripheral pieces in the Kantian canon. It turns out that there are only two places where explicit misogyny creeps into the *central* works of Kant's practical philosophy. In a passage from the *Doctrine of Right* in the *Metaphysics of Morals*, Kant refers in passing to the "natural superiority of the husband to the wife."[7] Later in the *Doctrine of Right*, Kant claims that women (along with anyone who is "an apprentice in the service of a merchant or artisan; a domestic servant (as distinguished from a civil servant); [or] a minor") lack "civil personality," that is, they lack both the ability and the right to participate in civil society, and are thus "passive citizens" who are "mere underlings of the commonwealth because they have to be under the direction or protection of other individuals, and so do not possess civil independence" (*MM* 6:314–315).

These passages are problematic for a number of reasons, but they can be made sense of as reflections of the social mores of Kant's time. While it is clear that Kant did believe in men's "natural" superiority over women, he never felt the need to explicitly defend or justify this belief.[8] Furthermore, it is worth noting that Kant's mention of husbands' "natural superiority" in the first passage takes place in the larger context of his discussion of what he took to be the "natural *equality* of a couple" in marriage (*MM* 6:279).[9] And it is worth noting that Kant goes on to insist, in the second passage, that laws must never be passed that are "contrary to the natural laws of freedom and of the equality of everyone in the people corresponding to this freedom, namely that *anyone can work his way up from this passive condition to an active one*" (*MM* 6:315).[10] Even while he endorsed some of the most despicable social norms and institutions of his time, Kant recognized that the tenets of his theory committed him to the view that *all* people are fundamentally equal and deserve to be treated as such.

Thus, while Kant himself was no feminist, I contend that the resources exist within Kant's work to support a robustly feminist moral theory. But, before showing how Kant's work on rationality gives us the conceptual tools to make sense of what is wrong with some of the worst harms of sexist oppression, let us first address what I take to be the two most pressing feminist objections to Kant.

The embodiment objection

Many feminist philosophers have argued that Kantianism is fundamentally ill-suited for feminist theorizing. A theme that is common to many of these feminist criticisms has to do with Kant's views about human nature. According to the Kantian picture of human nature, we are fundamentally split beings, simultaneously *rational* and *animal*. This splitting of the person into animal and rational is seriously problematic for a number of reasons. Martha Nussbaum puts the criticism this way:

> [f]irst, [this Kantian split] ignores the fact that our dignity is just the dignity of a certain sort of animal. It is the animal sort of dignity, and

> that very sort of dignity could not be possessed by a being who was not mortal and vulnerable.... Second, the split wrongly denies that animality can itself have a dignity; thus it leads us to slight aspects of our own lives that have worth, and to distort our relation to the other animals. Third, it makes us think of the core of ourselves as self-sufficient, not in need of the gifts of fortune; in so thinking we greatly distort the nature of our own morality and rationality, which are thoroughly material and animal themselves; we learn to ignore the fact that disease, old age, and accident can impede the moral and rational functions, just as much as other animal functions. Fourth, it makes us think of ourselves as a-temporal. We forget that the usual human lifecycle brings with it periods of extreme dependency, in which our functioning is very similar to that enjoyed by the mentally or physically handicapped throughout their lives.[11]

Nussbaum contends that this split "goes wrong in both directions: it suggests...that our rationality is independent of our vulnerable animality; and it also suggests that animality, and non-human animals, lack intelligence, are just brutish and 'dumb'."[12] Both wrong directions are morally problematic. It is the first wrong direction, however, that she thinks makes Kantianism particularly inadequate for feminist purposes. I will call this – the criticism that Kantianism is committed to a split between the rational and the animal that undermines its suitability for feminist theorizing – the *embodiment objection*. According to this embodiment objection, the problem with the Kantian view of human nature is that it profoundly misrepresents the sorts of creatures we are. For Kant our animality is important only insofar as it supports our rationality. But there is a dignity, the thought goes, even in those parts of us that have nothing to do with our rationality, and the Kantian picture that locates every bit of our value in our rationality captures none of this. This misrepresentation of human nature encourages contemptuousness toward the inevitable stages of our lives in which we are dependent on others (including infancy, childhood, and elderly disability). And this contemptuousness, aside from being bad for its own sake, has implications for women in the following way.

Because Kantianism characterizes our rational nature and our animal nature as conceptually independent, proponents of the embodiment objection argue that it ignores the fundamentally embodied and social character of our rational nature.[13] Kant's emphasis on rationality has made it easy for some Kantian theorists to be led to think only about fully or ideally rational persons. Thus proponents of the embodiment objection accuse Kant, like most other theorists in the social contract tradition, of subscribing to what has been called the "fiction of competent adulthood."[14] According to this fiction, people are fundamentally free, equal, and independent. As Seyla Benhabib has put the point, this fiction of competent adulthood postulates that we live in "a strange world: it is one in which individuals are grown up before they have been born; in which boys are men before they have been children; a world where neither mother, nor sister, nor wife exist."[15]

Most proponents of the embodiment objection, of course, agree that people who actually *are* competent adults should generally be treated as if they are free, equal, and independent. But they remind us that no one is born free, equal, or independent, and that no one remains this way forever. Each of us is asymmetrically dependent on other people for large parts of our lives. When these facts of human dependency are ignored, or relegated to the periphery of one's conception of the human condition, these critics claim that it is *inevitable* that the work of caring for dependent people will be taken for granted and that those responsible for this work will be at risk of exploitation.[16] Kantianism's failure to respond appropriately to these facts of asymmetrical dependency is thus of concern to feminism because the lion's share of the work involved in caring for asymmetrically dependent people falls to women. Being held disproportionately responsible for this work, usually without pay or even the recognition that it *is* work, disadvantages women.[17] Kant's central focus on rationality as that which is of fundamental moral importance is therefore problematic for feminism, according to proponents of the embodiment objection, because, among other things, this way of thinking about human beings leads to women's exploitation.

In defence of Kant

Proponents of the embodiment objection are clearly right about Kant's split between the animal and the rational in at least the following sense: it is true that Kant thinks we are, in an important sense, fundamentally distinct from the rest of nature. Other animals are capable of acting only from instinct, Kant thinks; this makes these animals, bound by the mechanical laws of nature, always act in predictable ways. Rational animals like us, however, are not bound like this. We are free. We are fundamentally separate from nature in this respect then, because we have the capacity to make free choices about what we do.[18] Regardless of what our more animalistic inclinations might tempt us to do, we are always capable of denying these inclinations and choosing to act out of duty. It is this capacity to act freely, in accordance with the moral law, that Kant thinks makes us candidates for having the ultimate moral value.[19] The embodiment objection has it right, then, when it says that in a Kantian picture our animality is valuable primarily insofar as it makes our rationality possible. But, as we will see, these critics are wrong to insist that this prioritizing of the rational over the animal is *necessarily* inimical to feminist goals.

Kant's attempt to ground rationality in the noumenal rather than the phenomenal realm has also led proponents of the embodiment objection to interpret him as conceiving of rationality as *fundamentally immune* from the sorts of harms that our animal bodies are vulnerable to. Their accusations are, remember, that Kantianism "makes us think of the core of ourselves as a-temporal," that it distorts "the nature of our...morality and rationality, which are thoroughly material and animal," that it encourages us "to ignore the fact that disease, old age, and accident can impede the moral and rational functions, just as much as other animal functions," and that it makes us "forget that the usual human lifecycle brings with it periods of extreme dependency."[20] But such critics are simply mistaken in their claim that Kant characterizes rational capacities as being, in every way, utterly unlike our other animal capacities. Kant himself actually recognizes much of what these proponents of the embodiment objection accuse him of ignoring or denying.

Kant appreciates, for example, that our rational capacities do not spring into existence fully developed. While our capacity to act rationally is innate, this capacity develops gradually as we learn and mature. It is something that we *acquire*.[21] This capacity requires a great deal of training and experience to develop properly.[22] Kant recognizes that we need to be taught how to achieve the ends we have set for ourselves, that the rational capacities necessary for this free choice are capacities that need to be developed. One implication of this is that he thinks that before our rational capacity has developed fully we cannot be held completely responsible for what we do.[23] Kant also discusses various pedagogical issues throughout his practical philosophy; what he says about the importance of education in these works clearly indicates that he is aware that our rational capacities are similar to our other animal capacities, at least in the respect that they require a great deal of cultivation.

Kant also appreciates that our rational capacities are similar to our more ordinary animal capacities in the sense that they are subject to damage and degradation. It is a presupposition of many of his most central moral prohibitions that rational capacities can be damaged or degraded; the claim that one ought not damage oneself or others in certain ways presupposes that it is *possible* for one to do so. So, for example, Kant recognizes that rational capacities can be destroyed – this follows from his claim that suicide and murder are immoral.[24,25] He also recognizes that rational capacities can be temporarily incapacitated – this follows from his claim that drunkenness and gluttony are immoral.[26] It is true that Kant's examples tend not to focus on the sorts of damage and degradation many proponents of the embodiment objection have in mind – those resulting from "disease, old age, and accident," which are the sorts of things that are an inevitable part of the human condition and result in those asymmetrically dependent people whom women are largely responsible for caring for. But, following a version of the principle of "ought implies can," we can see that Kant recognizes perfectly well that rational capacities are subject to damage and degradation. He would not bother telling us why these harms are bad if he did not think they were possible.

Still, a proponent of the embodiment objection would probably be right to accuse Kant of underemphasizing the *inevitability* of this damage and degradation. This oversight leads him to misrepresent the human condition in an important way. This misrepresentation makes him fail to incorporate the need for asymmetrically dependent people's care into the core of his practical philosophy, and, uncorrected, this failure might well lead a Kantian to overlook or even condone the exploitation of women who are responsible for most of this care. But there is nothing preventing a Kantian feminist from inserting a more robust account of our moral lives – one that addresses these asymmetrical dependencies and the relationships in which they occur – into Kant's framework. There is nothing inherent in the Kantian framework that prevents us from recognizing that we are embodied and social creatures. And there is nothing that prevents us from doing the work that Kant did not, nothing that prevents us from applying his framework to a more comprehensive, inclusive, and diverse account of the human condition – one that reflects the experiences of *all* human beings, not merely those in relatively privileged social positions, such as the one Kant himself occupied.

The emotions objection

The second criticism I want to take up has to do not with Kant's privileging of the rational over the animal, but with his privileging of the rational over the emotional. Many philosophers – not just feminists – have claimed that the problem with Kantian morality is that its focus on rationality denigrates the importance of the emotional aspects of our lives. Because Kant sometimes speaks as if inclinations are nothing more than a hindrance to the possibility of morality,[27] he is criticized for mischaracterizing our moral lives by making morality a cold, unfeeling, and impersonal matter of acting from duty at the expense of our feelings and our personal commitments.[28] Friedrich Schiller was one of the first such critics of Kant, arguing in 1794 that, "[m]an can be self-opposed in a twofold manner; either as savage, if his feelings rule his principles, or as barbarian, if his *principles destroy his feelings.*"[29] Bernard Williams renewed this debate in the 1970s and 1980s when he argued that Kantian morality both devalues and estranges us from our emotions insofar as it rejects the possibility that emotions could serve as morally acceptable motivations for action.[30] Carol McMillan characterizes Kant in this way: "Kant goes so far as to say that no action springing from natural inclination can have moral worth. For him, an action has genuine moral worth only when it is done solely out of duty, without any liking or preference for it."[31] These and other critics contend that morality has as much to do with the emotions as it does with reason, and they criticize Kant for pretending otherwise. Many of the most trenchant contemporary versions of this criticism come from feminists. I will call this – the criticism that Kantianism prioritizes the rational over the emotional in a manner that undermines its suitability for feminist theorizing – the *emotions objection*. This objection, at its roots, boils down to an insistence that Kant is wrong to think that morality must be grounded in something non-contingent.

One reason this criticism of Kant is of special interest to feminists is because of the historical, and continuing, association of men with reason and women with the emotions.[32] Women have been, and often still are, seen as less rational and more emotional than men. They have been seen as better suited to the mundane and trivial work of managing relationships, less apt to be able to transcend the particular in favour of the universal, and less capable of the abstract reasoning abilities that make us distinctively human and more tied to the emotional and affective responses that we share with animals. As we saw above, Kant himself explicitly held this view. When Kant denigrates the emotions, then, many feminists worry that he is simultaneously denigrating women. A common feminist response to this worry, put forward especially by those feminists who endorse the ethics of care, argues that we must revalue both women *and* the emotions.[33] This revaluing of the emotions often brings with it a simultaneous denigration of a certain conception of reason. As Annette Baier writes, "[w]here Kant concludes 'so much the worse for women', we can conclude 'so much the worse for the male fixation on the special skill of drafting legislation, for the bureaucratic mentality of rule worship, and for the male exaggeration of the importance of independence over mutual interdependence'."[34]

Different care ethicists unpack this argument in very different ways. Some embrace the claim that women are naturally more emotional and intuitive than men and argue that the solution to a whole host of moral, social, and political problems lies in attending to the knowledge and perspectives that women have always had. Others endorse this conclusion without affirming the gender essentialism implied by it; they argue that we have much to gain by attending to the emotions, but they deny that women are necessarily any better at this type of moral reasoning than men are. In any case, what these approaches share in common is an insistence that the emotional and affective parts of our lives must play a fundamental and central role in moral theorizing. These proponents of the emotions objection argue that the lived experience of morality often has less to do with respecting abstract rules of reciprocal non-interference with strangers than it does with attending to the emotional nuances of the relationships we have with those people we love and care about. Pretending otherwise – pretending that morality is fundamentally a matter of "a controlling reason dictating to possibly unruly passions"[35] – is, even as a necessary minimum, an impoverished picture of our moral lives. Their insistence on attending to the emotional experiences of mutual interdependence involved in our relationships with others leads proponents of the emotions objection to reject those moral theories, such as Kant's, that focus exclusively or primarily on rationality.

In defence of Kant

However, contemporary Kantians have given a number of convincing defences of the Kantian moral framework against various versions of the emotions objection.[36] Some argue that instead of thinking of the role of duty in Kant as at odds with our emotion-derived motivations, we should think of duty as requiring from us a general commitment to conform our behaviour to morality's demands. This general commitment amounts to having a particular attitude of respect toward the moral law. Given the broad scope of this commitment – it is one that regulates all our actions, and is life-long – it would be virtually impossible to fulfil successfully if one's emotions were consistently drastically out of step with it.[37] Nothing in Kant's view implies that acting in the absence of emotions, or in opposition to them, is required or even desirable from a moral point of view. When our emotions are in line with duty, after all, we face fewer psychological obstacles to acting from duty – this makes the cultivation of the right emotions something to be encouraged from Kant's point of view. And Kant explicitly counsels us to cultivate sympathetic feelings so that we are well-prepared to recognize when others need our help.[38]

Kant is clear that duty is always a limiting condition on what we do (it must always place limits on what we may do), but it need not be our primary motive (it need not provide the motivation to perform the act in question) for every act we perform. When it comes to acts that are merely morally permissible (as opposed to acts that are morally required), certain emotions are actually necessary, because they must be present to provide motivation for the act that can then be vetted by the moral law. When it comes to acts that are morally required, however, our commitment to morality must be necessary and sufficient for acting.[39] This is not to say that emotional motives cannot also be present for these acts, however. There is nothing wrong with acting out of an emotional attachment to those we love, for example. Our actions are usually overdetermined anyway; as long as the motive of duty, by itself, would be sufficient to make us do what is right, then if we happen to perform an action also because we possess another emotional motive, there is nothing amiss. All Kant is saying is that if what we do is going to count as moral, then the motive of duty must be, by itself, capable of making us do what is right.

Kant does hold that reason must take precedence over emotion when the two are in conflict. But, despite what proponents of the emotions objections might hold, this is not actually a shortcoming of the Kantian moral framework. This is because conflicts between the demands of reason and the emotions will arise only when our emotions are telling us to do something *immoral*. The rest of the time, there is no reason to think that that the demands of reason and the emotions will not be in line. A common example of this sort of conflict is when our emotions tell us to prefer the interests of our intimates at the expense of the interests of everyone else while reason tells in favour of impartiality and equal consideration of everyone's ends. Proponents of the emotions objection sometimes suggest that Kantian morality would have us abandon the preferential treatment of our intimates in the name of universalizable impartiality,[40] but this is a misleading caricature of Kant's views. Most of the time, preferential treatment of intimates falls into the category of what is morally permissible; often it is actually morally required (e.g., given that we live in a society where the raising of children is usually undertaken in small nuclear family units, raising these children successfully often requires prioritizing their interests over the interests of others). The demands of reason are thus not usually at odds with the demands of the emotions when it comes to how we may, or must, treat those we love most. And the small number of cases where reason demands one course of action and the emotions demand another will be those where our emotions are demanding something *immoral* of us (e.g., ignoring our obligations to society at large).

It is true that the emotions cannot serve as the ground of morality for Kant, but this is ultimately a good thing because emotions are, in themselves, morally indifferent. It is, after all, ultimately a contingent matter whether someone happens to possess kind or sympathetic emotions toward others. If morality were to be grounded in a contingent matter such as this, then were these sympathetic emotions absent a person would have neither motivation nor reason to do what morality requires.[41] Kant's insistence that morality must not be grounded in anything contingent thus leads him to disqualify the emotions from being able to ground morality and to insist that reason (and the sense of duty that is informed by it) must play this role. This rejection of the contingency of the emotions in favour of the necessity of reason amounts to an insistence that we need a moral backstop against a certain kind of self-centred thinking to which Kant thinks we are especially prone.[42] Even if we do not like people we may not behave immorally toward them; even if we hate ourselves we must respect ourselves; even if we love someone there is only so much preferential treatment we can give to them at the expense of those we do not love.

Making reason, rather than emotion, the ground of morality does not saddle Kantians with a cold and unfeeling moral theory, at least not in any bad sense. And the sense in which this move saddles us with an impersonal moral theory is not something that is to be apologized for. It is true that when our personal projects and desires conflict with the demands of morality it is morality that must take precedence. But this is just to recognize that we have obligations to other members of our moral community, obligations that trump our personal interests and projects when there is a conflict. The impartial moral standpoint Kant advocates is not inhuman; it is unselfish.[43] By requiring that morality be grounded in reason rather than emotion, Kant is, in effect, warning us that if we let what we do be determined solely by our personal interests and projects, we risk losing sight of ourselves as members of a moral community with obligations to others, and we risk forgetting that our actions have consequences for the lives of other members of this moral community. This is a warning that proponents of the emotions objection should find welcome; being able to provide a robust explanation of the moral importance of attending to the needs of others is, after all, a central concern of the ethics of care.

This is why Kant's refusal to grant the emotions a central place in morality does not disqualify his theoretical framework from proving useful for feminists. While Kant did accept the historical association of women with the emotions, and accepted the denigration of women that was taken for granted in his day, both of these mistakes can and should be conceptually disentangled from his views on the role of the emotions in morality. Because Kant himself accepted commonly-held beliefs that simultaneously associated and derogated women and the emotions, this admittedly lends itself to the possibility of his authority being used to perpetuate sexist beliefs about women's inferiority. But this possibility is not an inevitability. Because the sexism of Kant himself does not infect the whole of Kant's moral theory, this theory remains one that feminists should not ignore.

Therefore, while proponents of the emotion objection are certainly right to criticize Kant's own derogatory association of women with the emotions, and probably right to revalue the importance of the emotions in certain moral contexts – particularly in explaining the richness of the lived experience of our moral lives – they are wrong to denigrate the moral importance of reason, wrong to defend a moral framework that attempts to explain all moral obligations by appealing to emotional responses that will always be contingent, and wrong to argue that Kant's focus on reason makes the Kantian moral framework unsuitable for feminist purposes. Contemporary commentators have convincingly dispelled most of the worries that might stem from Kant's privileging of the rational over the emotional.

I do not mean to suggest here that all is completely well between Kant and feminism. There is much to be learned from both the embodiment and emotions objections, I think. We should grant that Kant, like so many other philosophers in the liberal tradition, is often guilty of taking for granted much of the work that goes into turning asymmetrically dependent, needy individuals into free, equal, and independent adults. And we should grant that this oversight means that in a Kantian framework it is possible to overlook or condone the exploitation of the women who are largely responsible for this work. Finally, we should grant that Kant's central focus on reason instead of the emotions risks overlooking much of the richness and nuance that we experience in our moral lives. For these reasons I think we should be open to the possibility that there might be aspects of our moral lives that the Kantian framework cannot properly accommodate. A fully comprehensive moral theory might need to be supplemented with other, non-Kantian, theoretical perspectives. But, I will argue, a Kantian framework is indispensable for certain things.

I hope to have established that the oversights and inadequacies highlighted by the embodiment and emotions objections are insufficient grounds for a necessary dismissal of Kantianism. I will argue next that Kantianism has the resources within it both to show us the extent of the psychological harms that people can experience when they live under oppressive social conditions, and to suggest novel ways to ameliorate these harms, that we might otherwise not see. If we reject the Kantian framework because of the sorts of considerations emphasized by the embodiment and emotions objections we risk, in effect, throwing the baby out with the bathwater.

Kant's contribution: rational nature and self-respect

What sets Kant apart from almost every other thinker in the Western philosophical canon is his ability to make sense of *duties to the self*, particularly the *duty of self-respect*. Kant has been so influential on this point that most contemporary philosophers who write about duties to the self do so within the Kantian tradition.[44] What these philosophers see in Kantianism is an account that tells us who we are, why we are valuable, how we must be treated in virtue of this value, and why these constraints on permissible treatment apply not only to how we may treat others but also to how we may treat ourselves. Kant's duty of self-respect is a duty each of us has to recognize the value of the rational nature within us and to respond accordingly. It is worth looking at Kant's arguments for all this in closer detail.

The value of rational nature

The central concept here is what Kant calls our *humanity*. Humanity, for Kant, is not the whole of human nature, but is, rather, a particular subset of characteristics that are often associated with human nature, specifically those having to do with *rational* nature. In the most general terms, humanity is the capacity to act on principles or maxims: that is, to act for reasons.[45,46] More specifically, humanity includes the capacity to follow certain hypothetical imperatives or to act from rational principles of prudence and efficiency;[47] it also includes the capacity to follow categorical imperatives or to act from certain unconditional principles of conduct independently of the fear of punishment or the promise of reward.[48] Humanity also includes the capacity, which is lacking in lower animals, to anticipate future consequences, to adopt long-term goals, to resist short-term temptations, and to adopt ends for which one has no sensuous inclinations.[49,50] Finally, humanity includes the capacity to understand the world and reason abstractly. In short, humanity is our *rational nature*, our capacity to set and pursue ends through reason.[51]

For Kant, humanity does not belong only to human beings. Rather, humanity is attributable to "the human being and every rational being in general" (G 4:428). Kant must allow that humanity could exist in something other than human beings because of the particular role humanity plays in his practical philosophy. As we have seen, Kant is famously committed to the idea that moral principles must not be dependent on anything contingent.[52,53] Yet, if humanity were simply human nature then it, like human nature, could have been otherwise. Because humanity is what grounds the moral law, it must not be dependent on what human nature happens to be. Humanity is therefore distinct from human nature. Humanity must instead be attributable to *any* being with the capacity for rationality.

It is a matter of some controversy precisely how to interpret Kant's argument for the value of humanity. However, a fairly well-accepted interpretation of the Formula of Humanity, that section of the *Groundwork* where Kant establishes the value of rational nature, takes the following form.[54] Kant begins by pointing out that ordinary things have value only insofar as someone actually values them.[55] Because the relation between value and reason is such that we can have a reason to perform an action only if the goal of that action is valuable to us, ordinary things can give us reasons for action only if we happen to value them.[56] If anything is to give us reasons for action that are independent of what we contingently value – that is, if we can have reason to do something other than if we just happen to want to do it – it must be something with intrinsic and absolute value to provide these reasons.[57,58] Whatever this is, it must be objectively good according to standards that hold for every rational being. In other words, it must be an *end in itself*.[59] Kant asserts that there *is* something that has this sort of value: our rational capacity to make decisions about what is valuable.[60] And so, in virtue of our rational capacity to make value judgements, *we* have this sort of value. Our objective value means we have value independently of whether anyone happens to value us. Unlike the things we value contingently, our value is intrinsic and absolute.[61]

Rational nature is objectively valuable, then, because its objective value is *presupposed* by every value judgement. It is objectively valuable because it is a presupposition of our value judgements (and of any other act of practical rationality) that whatever is making these judgements – whatever is setting these ends according to reason – is a respectable authority on such matters. Unless we respect our rational nature as objectively good, none of the value judgements we make with our rational nature – none of the ends we set – can be objectively good. So, if there is to be any objective goodness in the world – if any of the ends we set are to be objectively good – this goodness must be grounded in our rational nature (which we must view as objectively valuable, as an end in itself). And *each* rational individual, insofar as she is rational, must necessarily[62] recognize this about herself, that because *her* rational nature grounds the objective value of all other things, *her* rational nature is an end in itself.[63] But each rational individual, insofar as she is rational, also must necessarily recognize that, just as this holds true for her rational nature, it holds true for *anyone else* with the same (i.e., rational) nature.[64] The judgement that one's own rational nature is an end in itself thus generalizes to the judgement that rational nature in general is an end in itself. This, then, is how we reach the Formula of Humanity's derivation of the Categorical Imperative: "*So act that you use humanity, whether in your own person or in the person of any other, always at the same time as an end, never merely as a means*" (G 4:429).

It is worth noting here the way in which this interpretation of Kant's argument is *conditional*: Kant is arguing that *if* there is anything that is objectively prescriptive (i.e., capable of telling us what to do categorically, not hypothetically), it must be explained by appealing to the objective value of our rational nature. In other words, the objective value of our rational nature is a precondition of the possibility of objectively prescriptive morality. The conditional nature of this argument means that it is no answer to the amoralist; it is not meant to convince anyone who is sceptical about the very existence of morality (i.e., of objectively prescriptive judgements). The argument is meant to address an audience who already acknowledges that morality exists and is inquiring merely after an explanation of its nature.

The necessity of respecting rational nature follows straightforwardly from the sort of value it has. Anything with this sort of value must be respected accordingly, Kant argues. Something that is an end in itself may neither be regarded nor treated as a mere means to some other end; this would be to regard or treat it as if its value were instrumental rather than intrinsic. We thus may neither regard nor treat ourselves or others as only instrumentally valuable; unlike mere things, we must, in virtue of our rational nature, be respected as ends in ourselves.[65] This means rational beings must never be treated merely as things. Because we are rational, we are worthy of a certain kind of respect.

What does the Kantian duty to respect humanity require?

What, precisely, is required by the obligation to respect people in virtue of their rational nature? Remember, Kant's Formula of Humanity famously commands you to act so *"that you use humanity, whether in your own person or in the person of any other, always at the same time as an end, never merely as a means"* (G 4:429). What does it mean to treat people's humanity – that is, their rational nature – as an end, rather than merely as a means?

Respecting people's rational nature clearly rules out the permissibility of other people casually killing or injuring us in ways that would prevent the future exercise of our rational nature. This obligation also requires people to appeal to our reason and never to coerce or manipulate us; forcing or tricking us would be using our rational nature as a means to someone else's ends. The only way for others to obtain our cooperation, and still treat us as ends in ourselves, is for them to let us decide matters for ourselves by appealing to our reason. We should therefore be free to set and pursue our own ends and not have ends imposed upon us against our will.

The injunction to treat people as ends in themselves is generally taken to mean that respecting people's rational natures forbids *using* people in certain ways. We may not use another person to achieve our purposes, no matter how good those purposes might be, because this would be to treat this person as a mere means to our ends rather than as an end in herself. Anyone who has rational nature may not be used merely as an instrument, the way ordinary objects are used.

Kant also says of rational nature that it is not an *end to be effected*, but is instead an *independently-existing end*.[66] What he means by this is that rational nature is not something that we have an obligation to try to produce when it does not yet exist, but when it does exist it is valuable and thus must be respected. So, in the Kantian picture, the appropriate response to the recognition that people have intrinsic value in virtue of their rational nature is not that we must try to *maximize* instances of that value (by, say, creating as many new people with rational nature as possible). Rather, the appropriate response to the recognition that people have intrinsic value in virtue of their rational nature is that we must have a certain attitude of *respect* toward people who already have this nature. This attitude of respect requires not only that we protect this nature from being harmed; we must also foster its development. We are obligated not just to refrain from damaging other people's rational nature, but also to enable the exercise of this rational nature in various ways.

The obligation to respect rational nature is fundamental in the Kantian picture; the obligation to respect individual people in virtue of their rational nature derives from this more basic obligation. This means that the obligation to respect people in virtue of their rational nature applies equally to anyone with rational nature; this obligation applies to one's own rational nature in precisely the same way that it applies to the rational nature of others. Just as we must recognize the intrinsic value that other people have and respect them accordingly, we must recognize this about our own value and respect ourselves accordingly. This, then, is how Kant ultimately derives the duty of self-respect.

Are obligations to the self possible?

However, despite its importance in Kant's moral framework, the thought that one could have an obligation to oneself is far from uncontroversial. The question of whether there can be obligations to the self is usually pursued in the context of the more specific question of whether a particular kind of obligation – that which arises from making promises to oneself – is intelligible. The canonical argument against the possibility of such obligations comes from M.G. Singer, who argues against the possibility of promises to the self for two reasons.[67] Interestingly, versions of the criticisms put forth by Singer are actually anticipated by Kant, who admits that the "Concept of a Duty to Oneself Contains (at First Glance) a Contradiction" (*MM* 6:417). The first problem with obligations to the self that Singer points out is that, when it comes to standard cases of obligation, the party to whom the obligation is owed can *release* the party who owes the obligation. And, since no one can release oneself from an obligation, Singer thinks, it is therefore impossible that one could have an obligation to oneself in the first place. Kant echoes this concern in the *Doctrine of Virtue*:

> One can...bring this contradiction to light by pointing out that the one imposing obligation (*auctor obligationis*) could always release the one put under obligation (*subiectum obligationis*) from the obligation (*terminus obligationis*), so that (if both are one and the same subject) he would not be bound at all to a duty he lays upon himself. This involves a contradiction (*MM* 6:417).

Singer's second argument for the impossibility of obligations to the self takes a similar form to his first. He argues that, in standard cases of obligation, if one party has an obligation to another, then the party to whom the obligation is owed has a *right* against the party who owes the obligation. And, since it is absurd to think that one could have a right against oneself, Singer thinks, it is therefore impossible that one could have an obligation to oneself in the first place. Kant echoes something very much like this concern in the *Doctrine of Virtue* as well:

> If the I *that imposes obligation* is taken in the same sense as the I *that is put under obligation*, a duty to oneself is a contradictory concept. For the concept of duty contains the concept of being passively constrained (I am *bound*). But if the duty is a duty to myself, I think of myself as *binding* and so as actively constraining (I, the same subject, am imposing obligation). And the proposition that asserts a duty to myself (I *ought* to bind myself) would involve being bound to bind myself (a passive obligation that was still, in the same sense of the relation, also an active obligation), and hence a contradiction (*MM* 6:417).

But Kant thinks this contradiction is merely apparent; he takes himself to have a "Solution of This Apparent Antimony" (*MM* 6:417). Kant's defence of the possibility of obligations to the self relies on his metaphysical conception of the self. He solves the apparent contradiction that results when the person who is doing the obligating is the same person who is obligated by arguing that, in such cases, the *noumenal* self obligates the *phenomenal* self.[68] Obligations to the self are possible because the noumenal self (the aspect of the self that we know must exist, despite having no direct sensible access to it, because without it we would not be capable of freedom) obligates the phenomenal self (the aspect of the self to which we have direct sensible access), Kant argues.

Now, I admit it is not at all clear that this argument actually works.[69] And even if it did, Kant's metaphysical conception of the self is admittedly controversial. I have no intention of launching into a defence of this metaphysical picture here; nothing in my account hangs on such a defence. Luckily for those not inclined to buy into the more contentious aspects of Kant's metaphysical framework, Thomas Hill has a defence of the possibility of obligations to the self that is less contentious (and ultimately more successful, probably) than Kant's.[70] Hill argues, contra Singer's first argument, that there *are* things one can do to release oneself from an obligation.[71] If one reconsiders a promise to oneself in light of unanticipated new information, if one is not doing so because of anticipated temptations, and if one explicitly declares the promise cancelled, Hill argues that this constitutes a legitimate release from an obligation to oneself. Thus Singer's argument that obligations to the self are impossible because the obligator must be able to release the obligatee from the obligation does not go through. Hill responds to Singer's second argument as well. Hill argues that much of the force of this second argument (that one cannot have a right against oneself) comes from the first argument (that one cannot release oneself from an obligation). As we have just seen, Hill takes himself to have a response to the first argument, so he is understandably not terribly moved by the second. Furthermore, while he admits that it might be a bit strange to talk of violating one's own rights or pressing one's rights against oneself, Hill thinks this strangeness is not enough to undermine the conceptual possibility of promises to the self. And so, despite the apparent dissimilarities between obligations to the self and obligations to others, and despite the apparent peculiarities that attach to obligations to the self, obligations to the self are nevertheless possible. With Hill, I believe that the most fruitful way to think about these obligations is as being grounded ultimately in self-respect.

What does the Kantian duty of self-respect require?

What is required by the Kantian duty of self-respect? Most obviously, it requires that we do what we can to prevent others from damaging our rational nature. But it also requires that we try to cultivate and exercise our rational nature. Someone who fails to cultivate her rational nature, or who allows her rational nature to deteriorate, or who simply does not bother to exercise her rational nature when it is appropriate for her to do so, cannot be said to be respecting this nature in herself. Similarly, we fail to treat our rational nature as an end in itself when we trade or sacrifice it for something else we happen to want. This would be to treat this nature as a mere means to some other end.

Kant's discussion of the demands placed on us by the obligation of self-respect takes place mostly in the context of his articulation of the various attitudes we should not have, and the various actions we should not perform, if we are to have proper self-respect. Kant says much more about how we should *not* regard or treat ourselves than he does about how we *should*. He does, however, give some concrete examples of what it would be to fail to fulfill the obligation of self-respect:

> Be no man's lackey. – Do not let others tread with impunity on your rights. – Contract no debt for which you cannot give full security. – Do not accept favours you could do without, and do not be a parasite or a flatterer or (what really differs from these only in degree) a beggar.

Be thrifty, then, so that you will not become destitute. – Complaining and whining, even crying out in bodily pain, is unworthy of you, especially if you are aware of having deserved it; .... – Kneeling down or prostrating oneself on the ground, even to show your veneration for heavenly objects, is contrary to the dignity of humanity, as is invoking them in actual images; for you then humble yourself, not before an *ideal* represented to you by your own reason, but before an *idol* of your own making (*MM* 6:436–437).

Though these examples are obviously a bit dated – they clearly reflect the social mores of Kant's time – they are nevertheless telling. What the examples have in common is that they are all cases where one is subordinating oneself to another or where one is expressing the belief that one is not the moral equal of others. One of the ways that someone might lack self-respect, then, is by failing to recognize that her moral status is equal to that of all rational beings or by failing to act as if she recognizes this about herself.[72] That is, someone could fail to have self-respect by failing to respect the fact that her basic status as a human being entitles her to certain kinds of equal treatment with others.

While clearly central for Kant, a failure to recognize one's equal moral status with others is not the only way one could fail to fulfill the obligation of self-respect. There are other ways one might fail to have self-respect, suggested by the Kantian framework, that Kant does not explicitly consider. Someone might fail to have self-respect, for example, by underestimating or undervaluing, or by acting as if she undervalues or underestimates, something that she has legitimately earned. If someone does not properly appreciate and respect her merits, achievements, acquired talents, or earned social position – or if she acts as if she does not appreciate these things – she has failed to respect herself in a certain way.[73] As we will explore in more detail next, failing to respect one's own rights or one's own merits can be particularly likely to occur when an individual lives in conditions of oppression.

Self-respect under oppression

What is by far the most prominent Kantian account of the importance of self-respect is put forward by Thomas Hill in his "Servility and Self-Respect."[74] Hill argues that an individual fails to respect herself insofar as she fails to acknowledge that she has certain basic moral rights, or insofar as she fails to value these rights properly; he calls such a person "servile." What is morally objectionable about servility is that it involves a public and systematic willingness to disavow one's moral status and this, Hill argues, is incompatible with a proper regard for morality. While the most obvious instances of a lack of respect for morality tend to involve violating the rights of others, the servile person's lack of respect for morality lies in her acting in ways that demonstrate that she either does not know or does not care about her own status as a moral equal. Servile people do not violate their own rights, Hill thinks, so much as they fail to properly respect the system of morality that gives them those rights: "A person who fully respected a system of moral rights would be disposed to learn his proper place in it, to affirm it proudly, and not to tolerate abuses of it lightly. This is just the sort of disposition the servile person lacks."[75] The moral failing of servility, then, is that it is a failure to fulfill the duty of self-respect by failing to properly respect one's equal status under the moral law.

Hill gives several archetypal examples of servile people; the one most relevant to the issues at hand is what he calls the *Deferential Wife*. Hill's Deferential Wife is completely devoted to serving her husband. She does not tend to form her own interests, values, or ideals, and, in the cases where she does, she does not consider them to be as important as her husband's. The Deferential Wife believes that her proper role as a woman is to serve her family, and, as such, she puts their interests before her own. Hill argues that the Deferential Wife is not blameworthy for her servility if it results from a lack of viable options, from socially fostered ignorance, or from the mistaken belief that she has a moral obligation to be servile. But, if the Deferential Wife knows what she is doing and is servile because she is too lazy or timid to change, or because she stands to gain some minor advantage by not changing, then she is blameworthy.

It would be hard to overstate the influence Hill's work has had on how philosophers think about duties of self-respect. Hill's analysis has proven particularly useful for articulating precisely why self-respect is important for people who are oppressed. A number of contemporary feminist philosophers, for example, have seized upon his archetype of the Deferential Wife to explore both the moral failings of servility and the sexist social norms that encourage women to adopt servile behaviours in the first place.[76]

Robin Dillon has expanded fruitfully on Hill's work on self-respect in oppressive contexts.[77] In her analysis of how oppressive social conditions can undermine self-respect, Dillon argues that self-respect requires that we understand that we are persons who are fundamentally equal to all others, that we live lives that express who we are as individuals in accordance with our ideals and commitments, and that we properly appreciate ourselves as agents. Properly appreciating our agency means taking our responsibilities seriously, she thinks, because it is only in virtue of our agency that we have responsibilities at all. Having respect for ourselves thus requires that we take to heart the importance of our responsibilities, including our responsibility to protect those features of us in virtue of which we are owed respect.

Self-respect is important, Dillon thinks, not merely because it happens to be the case that without it we tend not to take care of ourselves, nor stand up for ourselves, nor pursue our commitments with determination. While it is true that self-respect does play this instrumental psychological role, Dillon argues that its primary importance goes far beyond this; self-respect is a constituent element of many of our most morally important features, one that is "tightly bound up with such morally important things as personhood, rights, agency, autonomy, integrity, responsibility, identity, character."[78] That is, self-respect matters morally.

> Self-respect is inextricably connected with what is constitutive of human worth.... [S]elf-respect is respect of things with great moral significance – our personhood and standing in the moral community; our agency and capacity to be critically self-appraising, self-defining, and self-directing; our strivings to become persons it is worth being.[79]

One thing Dillon is careful to establish is that people who lose their self-respect are not necessarily responsible nor blameworthy for this loss. This is a consideration that we will return to repeatedly in the chapters that follow. Dillon emphasizes this because she believes there is a distinct political dimension to self-respect; there are social factors outside an individual's control that lie behind both self-respect and its loss.

> [A] person's lacking self-respect is not simply a fact about her psychology but is an integral part of both her personal relationships and the social structures to which certain classes of persons are relegated and in which they are generally denied respect, thus coming to view themselves as not worthy of even their own respect.[80]

Whether or not one has self-respect is not something that is entirely within one's control. It depends, at least in part, on the background social conditions one finds oneself in. And, Dillon argues, oppressive social conditions clearly undermine, rather than bolster, the self-respect of those who are oppressed.

Dillon also argues that damaged self-respect is a gendered phenomenon – one connected directly to oppression. Women are more likely than men to have damaged self-respect, she argues; this damage is both a straightforward result of women's subordination in a sexist society and also one of the principal means of carrying out this subordination. Damaged self-respect is a result of having our views about ourselves, our worth, and our place in the world formed in social, cultural, and political contexts that are oppressive. When these contexts are pervaded by the message that the category of persons to which we belong is inferior, this inferiority is internalized and can decimate self-respect. This lack of self-respect then functions as a means of entrenching the oppressive status quo; people will be much less likely to stand up for themselves, to assert their moral equality, or to decry infringements on their rights, when they have internalized the message that their membership in an oppressed group of people means they are not entitled to anything better. Dillon thereby shows how an account of the importance of self-respect is crucial for solving the problem of adaptive preferences. I take my account here to be a contribution to the discussion started by Hill and picked up by philosophers such as Dillon.[81] Properly responding to the realities of oppression thus requires a robust appreciation of the importance of self-respect. And, I will argue, Kant's moral framework provides the most promising theoretical foundation for this task.

Rationality, oppression, and self-respect: what is the baby?

Kant's defence of the ultimate moral importance of our rational nature is something that feminists cannot afford to ignore. This is because, as we will see in detail in Chapter 4, harms to one's rational nature are among the worst harms an oppressed person can face. It is critically important for feminists to have something to say about why harms to women's rational capacities are seriously morally problematic because these harms are among the most egregious problems that arise from women's oppression.

Feminists have been discussing the devastating psychological effects of sexist oppression for quite some time. Mary Wollstonecraft and J.S. Mill argued, in the eighteenth and nineteenth centuries respectively, that prevailing sexist social norms of polite society and motherhood, and prevailing sexist legal institutions such as marriage and property, could damage women's rational capacities by depriving them of equal opportunities with men to develop their talents.[82,83] Simone de Beauvoir argued that women's traditional gender roles offer them very few, if any, opportunities to make existentially authentic choices; when women take on the role of a wife or the role of a mother, their lives can become completely defined by their relationships to their husbands or their children and they can, in effect, lose their sense of self and become an "Other."[84] Sandra Bartky has argued that women can internalize sexist oppression, come to believe that they are actually inferior to men, and thus experience a kind of "psychic alienation" that damages their rational capacities by making them less capable of autonomous action.[85] Ann Cudd has discussed how oppression can cause both material and psychological harms to its victims when oppressed people come to believe in, are weakened by, and are even motivated to fulfill, the stereotypes that represent them as inferior.[86] Sally Haslanger has drawn on the resources of psychology to explain how the phenomenon of stereotype threat can negatively affect the cognitive performance of people who identify as members of marginalized groups; when someone is aware of a stereotype that portrays people like her as less capable in a given domain, this awareness can manifest itself in anxiety, intrusive thoughts, extreme cautiousness, decreased performance expectancy, and disengagement, all of which negatively affect her ability to learn and perform.[87] And then, as we have seen, there is the feminist literature on adaptive preferences, which shows us how oppressive social circumstances that condition women to believe that they are inferior to men can result in failures of rationality whereby these women believe they do not deserve their fair share of even basic social and material goods.

Kantianism gives us a way to explain what is wrong with these harms. Despite what Kant himself might have thought, we know that women's rational capacities are no different from men's. Thus, we know that women are just as deserving of respect as men. And we know that the respect that women are owed in virtue of their rational capacities is incompatible with the harms to women's rationality that can result from oppression. Feminists therefore have good reason to take Kantianism seriously since Kant's work on rationality gives us the conceptual tools to make sense of what is wrong with some of the worst harms of sexist oppression. But Kantianism is hardly the only moral framework that has the resources to explain what is wrong with harming women's rational capacities. What then, precisely, is the baby feminists risk throwing out with the Kantian bathwater?[88]

The baby, I hope it is clear by now, is the Kantian duty of self-respect. Because Kant provides such a robust account of duties to the self, his account is unparalleled in its ability to fully explain the moral importance of self-respect. We will see next that his account is also unparalleled in its ability to condemn certain gendered norms of self-sacrifice.

Condemning the exploitation of women that results from gendered norms of self-sacrifice requires ruling out the possibility that one could be obligated to sacrifice one's own interests to foster or protect the interests of others. It is only if the duty to foster and protect one's own interests is at least as important as the duty to do so for others that feminists can rule out the permissibility of this exploitation in all cases. Thus feminists must defend the existence of duties to the self, must appreciate the importance of duties of self-respect, and, because Kant is the most central figure in the western canon to articulate an account of these duties, feminists must not dismiss the Kantian moral framework out of hand. I am not the first to have defended a version of this claim. Jean Hampton also uses the Kantian moral framework, particularly its emphasis on the intrinsic and equal value of each individual person, to explore the moral failings of gendered self-sacrifice.[89]

Gendered self-sacrifice

Failures of self-respect are of special interest to feminism because sacrificing one's own interests in favour of the interests of those for whom one is responsible for caring is, unfortunately, a distinctively feminine virtue. Soren Kierkegaard, someone not generally admired for his feminist credentials, put the lie to this false virtue in his description of a uniquely feminine form of self-abnegating sin that disguises itself as virtuous devotion, wherein "the woman in proper womanly fashion throws herself, throws her self, into whatever she abandons herself to. If you take that away, then her self vanishes too, and her despair is: not wanting to be herself."[90] De Beauvoir, more sympathetic to women's plight but no less critical of the social roles they participate in, also described this distinctively feminine desire to serve, and thus lose oneself in, one's beloved:

> for in responding to her lover's demands, a woman will feel that she is *necessary*; she will be integrated with his *existence*, she will share his *worth*, she will be *justified*. ... Thus she gives up her transcendence, subordinating it to that of the essential other, to whom she makes herself vassal and slave. It was to find herself, to save herself, that she lost herself in him in the first place; and the fact is that little by little she does lose herself in him wholly; for her the whole of reality is in the other.[91]

Elizabeth Cady Stanton, an early advocate of women's rights, is famously said to have declared that "self-development is a higher obligation than self-sacrifice," and "the thing which most retards and militates against women's self-development is self-sacrifice."[92]

Each of these thinkers was responding to what were then the predominant cultural ideals of feminine virtue, ideals that valourized devotion and self-abnegation as ideal traits of character for women. It has long been women's traditional role to foster and protect the interests of others, even at the expense of their own interests. Convincing women to sacrifice their own interests to further the interests of others is a hallmark of sexist oppression. This convincing does not only take place when those women who are willing to cooperate with these ideals of self-sacrifice are valourized; it also takes place when the social status of all women is denigrated, causing individual women not to value their own interests enough to prioritize them over others'. It is, in other words, another instance of the problem of adaptive preferences. As Mary Daly puts it, "since those kept in a state of being unacceptable to themselves feel worthless, self-sacrifice is a logical conclusion of their condition."[93] All of this, many feminists have argued, continues to occur today, and it amounts to nothing less than systematic exploitation.[94]

Without an account that defends the existence of duties to the self, feminists ultimately do not have the resources to fully explain what is wrong with this kind of exploitation. The difficulty arises here because self-sacrifice is not inherently morally problematic. In fact, it is usually considered to be a virtue. Being willing to sacrifice one's interests for the sake of others can be one of the noblest forms of altruism. It is thus not clear that accounts that deny the existence of duties to the self can provide feminists with an explanation of what is wrong with *gendered* self-sacrifice, nor explain why it is so often exploitative.

One might attempt to reply, on behalf of those who would deny the existence of duties to the self, that although self-sacrifice is not wrong *per se*, the specific sort of self-sacrifice that gendered norms require of women is still morally problematic. One route that could be taken here would be to argue that what is wrong with gendered self-sacrifice is not that it harms the individual woman who chooses to engage in it, but that it harms *other* women.[95] Participating in these norms is what ultimately entrenches and perpetuates them; thus, when one woman goes along with these expectations of self-sacrifice, she makes it more likely that other women will be expected to make similar sacrifices. But then what, according to this explanation, is wrong with these other women's participating in gendered norms of self-sacrifice? Nothing, in itself. The only thing that is wrong with these further self-sacrifices is that they make it more likely that still other women will have to make these sorts of sacrifices. This regress is vicious. This other-oriented explanation of what is wrong with gendered norms of self-sacrifice fails to explain the moral harm that a woman *herself* has experienced when she chooses to go along with her exploitation, and fails to capture the general intuition that there is something seriously morally problematic about permitting oneself to be exploited.

Another other-oriented explanation of what is wrong with gendered self-sacrifice might take a different route, arguing that the moral problem here is that, on balance, these norms harm women more than they benefit the people for whom women make sacrifices. In other words, what is wrong with these norms is that ultimately they *do more harm than good*. But this, too, will not do. Norms like these remain in place for a reason, after all. Gendered norms of self-sacrifice, and the sexist status quo they help perpetuate, benefit some people enormously. Injustice can be terribly efficient. Sexist social institutions, and the norms that sustain them, remain in place, in part, because they are good at serving the interests of a great number of people. There is no reason to think that the benefits of these norms that accrue to others do not outweigh the harms of these norms that accrue to women. Feminists should be extremely wary of trying to make the immorality of gendered norms of self-sacrifice hinge on the all-things-considered balance of benefits and harms, because there is a real chance that this calculation might show that, so much the worse for the women who are pressured to sacrifice their interests in accordance with these norms, everyone is better off for them doing so.

Furthermore, even if the calculation did not go this way and it turned out that the balance of harms to women caused by gendered norms of self-sacrifice *did* outweigh the benefits to others, there would still be something wrong with a social norm that systematically required certain members of society, but not others, to sacrifice their interests disproportionately. This is because there is something wrong, in itself, with a social system that is set up in such a way that it consistently demands self-sacrifice from some, but not all, of its members. Unequal expectations of self-sacrifice transform what should be an individual virtue into a demand that is incompatible with the equal respect for individuals that morality requires. A norm like this – one that is systematically disproportionate and asymmetrical in the demands that it makes on individuals – is incompatible with justice because such a norm, in effect, prioritizes the interests of the group over the interests of the individuals that make up that group. If individual people freely choose to sacrifice their interests for the sake of others in their group, this need not be morally problematic. (It could, in fact, be virtuous.) We can even concede that if everyone in a group is *equally* required to make certain sacrifices for the survival or flourishing of the group, this might not be strictly compatible with the principle just articulated, but the egalitarianism behind such an arrangement makes it, at least conceivably, morally justifiable. Moral considerations of fairness also probably justify disproportionate or asymmetrical sacrifices made by those who are better off for the sake of those who are less well off (adults sacrificing for children, say, or the wealthy sacrificing for the poor).[96] But absent this kind of countervailing moral justification, if only some people are required to sacrifice their interests for the sake of the group or if some people are required systematically to sacrifice their interests disproportionately, this will be incompatible with the equal respect for individuals that morality requires.

Accounts that explain the wrongness of acquiescing in gendered norms of self-sacrifice solely in terms of the harms that accrue to other women cannot adequately accommodate this because they cannot categorically rule out the permissibility of such norms. Only if we have an account that permits duties to the self can we make complete sense of what is wrong with this kind of exploitation. Given the ubiquity of this exploitation, this is of critical importance to feminism. But what is perhaps the most predominant strain of feminist moral thinking – the ethics of care – has a surprisingly difficult time accounting for this. This is because care ethics characterizes the central issues of morality as having to do with caring for those with whom we are in intimate relationships. Just as care ethics can have difficulty explaining the moral importance of attending to the needs of nonintimate others, it can have difficulty explaining the moral importance of attending to the needs of the self. Insofar as care ethics denigrates the individualism that it sees as fundamental to the justice perspective, it risks losing the ability to explain why individuals must not allow the interests of others always to take precedence over their own interests. Because care ethics prioritizes the moral importance of caring for intimate others, it risks losing the ability to explain why individuals must first care for themselves; if caring for oneself is justified only when it enables one to care for others, then care ethics has the potential to condone or even encourage women's exploitation.[97] Insofar as care ethics denigrates the justice perspective's emphasis on individuals asserting their own rights while respecting others', it risks losing the ability to guard against these very infringements. In contrast, the justice perspective's conception of people as free, independent, and equal individuals might have its problems, but failing to explain why it might be morally problematic for an individual to sacrifice her interests for the sake of others is not one of them. Likewise, the justice perspective's conception of morality as fundamentally a matter of reciprocal non-interference might also have its problems, but failing to explain why individuals must not permit themselves to be exploited is not one of them.

Kantianism is perhaps the most derided theory within the justice perspective. As we have seen, it is caricatured as a cold, impersonal, and unfeeling moral theory, incapable of accounting for the richest and most personal parts of our moral lives and incapable of accommodating either our emotions or our embodiment. But Kantians can and do respond to these charges, giving us a moral framework that makes sense of the possibility of duties to the self and that recognizes the importance of the duty of self-respect, both of which are necessary in order to categorically rule out the permissibility of gendered norms of self-sacrifice. As we will see in the chapters that follow, Kant's accounts of rationality, autonomy, self-respect, and self-sacrifice bear directly on the lives of oppressed individuals and their communities, often in ways that Kant himself could not have anticipated.

Notes

1. See, for example, Jaggar, *Feminist Politics and Human Nature;* Nancy Hartsock, *Money, Sex, and Power* (Boston: Northeastern University Press, 1988); MacKinnon, *Toward a Feminist Theory of the State,* and *Feminism Unmodified;* Carole Pateman, *The Problem of Political Obligation: A Critique of Liberal Theory* (Berkeley: University of California Press, 1979), and *The Sexual Contract;* and Sally Sedgwick, "Can Kant's Ethics Survive the Feminist Critique?," *Pacific Philosophical Quarterly* 71 (1990): 60–79.
2. Immanuel Kant, *Anthropology from a Pragmatic Point of View,* Louden (trans.) (Cambridge: Cambridge University Press, 2006 [1798]), 221. 'A' in parenthetical documentation hereafter refers to this work.
3. Immanuel Kant, *Observations on the Feeling of the Beautiful and Sublime,* Frierson and Guyer (eds) (Cambridge: Cambridge University Press, 2011 [1764]), 78. 'O' in parenthetical documentation hereafter refers to this work.
4. Tempering this somewhat, Marcia Baron points out that Kant adds to this claim that "these are also extremely rare in the male" (*O* 231). Marcia Baron, "Kantian Ethics and Claims of Detachment" *Feminist Interpretations of Kant,* Schott (ed.) (University Park: Pennsylvania State University Press, 1997), 166, note 1.
5. Other philosophers who use Kant for feminist purposes include, for example, Baron, "Kantian Ethics and Claims of Detachment"; Lara Denis, "Kant's Ethical Duties and their Feminist Implications," *Feminist Moral Philosophy: Canadian Journal of Philosophy Supplementary* 28 (2002): 157–187; Robin Dillon, "Toward a Feminist Conception of Self-Respect," *Hypatia* 7 (1992): 52–69, "Respect and Care: Toward Moral Integration," *Canadian Journal of*

Philosophy 22 (1992): 105–132, and "'What's a Woman Worth? What's Life Worth? Without Self-Respect!': On the Value of Evaluative Self-Respect," *Moral Psychology: Feminist Ethics and Social Theory*, DesAutels and Walker (eds) (Lanham: Rowman and Littlefield, 2004), 47–66; Jean Hampton, "Selflessness and the Loss of Self," *Social Philosophy and Policy* 10 (1993): 135–165, and "Feminist Contractarianism"; Barbara Herman, "Could it be Worth Thinking about Kant on Sex and Marriage?," *A Mind of One's Own: Feminist Essays on Reason and Objectivity*, Antony and Witt (eds) (Boulder: Westview, 2002), 53–72; Sarah Clark Miller, "A Kantian Ethic of Care?," *Feminist Interventions in Ethics and Politics: Feminist Ethics and Social Theory*, Andrew, Keller, & Schwartzman (eds) (Lanham: Rowman and Littlefield, 2005), 111–127. Kurt Mosser, "Kant and Feminism," *Kant-Studien* 90 (1999): 322–353; Herta Nagl-Docekal, "Feminist Ethics: How It Could Benefit from Kant's Moral Philosophy," Morgenstern (trans.), *Feminist Interpretations of Kant*, Schott (ed.) (University Park: Pennsylvania State University Press, 1997), 101–124; Lina Papadaki, "What is Objectification?" *Journal of Moral Philosophy* 7 (2010): 16–36; Janice Richardson, "On Not Making Ourselves the Prey of Others: Jean Hampton's Feminist Contractarianism," *Feminist Legal Studies* 15 (2007): 33–55; and Anita Superson, "Privilege, Immorality, and Responsibility for Attending to the 'Facts about Humanity'," *Journal of Social Philosophy* 35 (2004): 34–55, "Deformed Desires and Informed Desire Tests," and "The Deferential Wife Revisited: Agency and Moral Responsibility," *Hypatia* 25 (2010): 253–275.
6. See, for example, Pauline Kleingold, "The Problematic Status of Gender-Neutral Language in the History of Philosophy: The Case of Kant," *Philosophical Forum* 24 (1992–1993): 134–150.
7. Immanuel Kant, *The Metaphysics of Morals*, Gregor (ed. and trans.) (Cambridge: Cambridge University Press, 1996 [1797]), 6:279. 'MM' in parenthetical documentation hereafter refers to this work.
8. As Susan Mendus puts it, Kant "gestures at reasons, sometimes he merely states baldly that this is so, but nowhere does he spell out explicitly and consistently exactly why women cannot be active citizens." Susan Mendus, "'An Honest but Narrow-Minded Bourgeois'?" *Essays on Kant's Political Philosophy*, Williams (ed.) (Chicago: University of Chicago Press, 1992), 179.
9. Italics mine.
10. Italics mine.
11. Martha Nussbaum, "The Future of Feminist Liberalism," *Varieties of Feminist Liberalism*, Baehr (ed.) (Lanham: Rowman and Littlefield, 2004), 106.
12. Nussbaum, "The Future of Feminist Liberalism," 106.
13. Those who have defended versions of this claim include, for example, Linda Alcoff, "Phenomenology, Post-structuralism, and Feminist Theory on the Concept of Experience," *Feminist Phenomenology*, Fisher and Embree (eds) (Norwell: Kluwer Academic Publishers, 2000), 39–56; Eva Feder Kittay, "Human Dependency and Rawlsian Equality," *Feminists Rethink the Self*, Meyers (ed.) (Boulder: Westview, 1997), 219–266, *Love's Labor*, and "When Caring is Just and Justice is Caring," *The Subject of Care: Feminist Perspectives on Dependency*, Kittay and Feder (eds) (Lanham: Rowman and Littlefield, 2002), 257–276; Mark Johnson, *The Body in the Mind: The Bodily Basis of Meaning, Imagination, and Reason* (Chicago: University of Chicago Press, 1987); George Lakoff and Mark Johnson, *Philosophy in the Flesh: The Embodied Mind and Its*

Challenge to Western Thought (New York: Basic Books, 1999); Bonnie Mann, "Dependence on Place, Dependence in Place," *The Subject of Care: Feminist Perspectives on Dependency*, 348–368, and *Women's Liberation and the Sublime* (New York: Oxford University Press, 2006); and Carole Pateman, "Self-Ownership and Property in the Person: A Tale of Two Concepts," *The Journal of Political Philosophy* 10 (2002): 20–53.

14. Nussbaum, "The Future of Feminist Liberalism," 105.
15. Benhabib, "The Generalized and the Concrete Other," 162.
16. See especially, for example, Kittay, *Love's Labor*; and Okin, *Justice, Gender, and the Family*.
17. See, for example, Scott Coltrane, "Research on Household Labor: Modeling and Measuring the Social Embeddedness of Routine Family Work," *Journal of Marriage and the Family* 62 (2000): 1208–1233; Arlie Hochschild, *The Second Shift* (New York: Avon, 1989); and Okin, *Justice, Gender, and the Family*.
18. "That choice which can be determined by *pure reason* is called free choice. That which can be determined only by *inclination* (sensible impulse, *stimulus*) would be animal choice (*arbitrum brutum*). Human choice, however, is a choice that can indeed by *affected* but not *determined* by impulses, and is therefore of itself (apart from an acquired proficiency of reason) not pure but can still be determined to actions by pure will. *Freedom* of choice is this independence from being *determined* by sensible impulses; this is the negative concept of freedom. The positive concept of freedom is that of the ability of pure reason to be of itself practical. But this is not possible except by the subjection of the maxim of every action to the condition of its qualifying as a universal law" (*MM* 6:213–214).
19. "*Autonomy* is therefore the ground of the dignity of human nature and of every rational nature." Immanuel Kant, *Groundwork of the Metaphysics of Morals*, Gregor (ed. and trans.) (Cambridge: Cambridge University Press, 1998 [1785]), 4:436. '*G*' in parenthetical documentation hereafter refers to this work.
20. Nussbaum, "The Future of Feminist Liberalism," 106.
21. "The very concept of virtue already implies that virtue must be acquired ... for a human being's moral capacity would not be virtue were it not produced by the strength of his resolution in conflict with powerful opposing inclinations. Virtue is the product of pure practical reason as it gains ascendancy over such inclinations with consciousness of its supremacy (based on freedom)" (*MM* 6:477).
22. "[M]an is an animal, who requires discipline, without which he grows up to be not unlike a wild animal, and this is where Rousseau makes a mistake, when he believes that discipline flows from the nature of man" (*A* 25:447).
23. "Degrees of imputation depend on the degree of freedom. The subjective conditions of freedom are the ability to act, and further, that we know what pertains thereto, that we are aware of the motivating ground and the object of the action. In the absence of these subjective grounds there is no imputation. Thus when children destroy something useful, it cannot be imputed to them, because they know not what they do." Immanuel Kant, *Lectures on Ethics*, Heath (ed. and trans.) (Cambridge: Cambridge University Press, 2001), 27:291. '*LE*' in parenthetical documentation hereafter refers to this work.

24. "A human being, however, is not a thing and hence not something that can be used *merely* as a means, but must in all his actions always be regarded as an end in itself. I cannot, therefore, dispose of a human being in my own person by maiming, damaging, or killing him" (G 4:429).
25. "The first, though not the principal, duty of a human being to himself as an animal being is *to preserve himself* in his animal nature. The contrary of this is willful *physical death* or killing oneself (*autochiria*), which can be thought of as either total, suicide (*suicidium*), or only partial, mutilating oneself. Mutilating oneself can in turn be either *material, depriving* oneself of certain integral, organic *parts*, that is, maiming oneself, or *formal, depriving* oneself (permanently or temporarily) of one's *capacity* for the natural (and so indirectly for the moral) *use* of one's powers" (MM 6:421).
26. "Brutish excess in the use of food or drink is misuse of the means of nourishment that restricts or exhausts our capacity to use them intelligently. *Drunkenness* and *gluttony* are the vices that come under this heading. A human being who is drunk is like a mere animal, not to be treated as a human being. When stuffed with food he is in a condition in which he is incapacitated, for a time, for actions that would require him to use his powers with skill and deliberation. It is obvious that putting oneself in such a state violates a duty to oneself. The first of these debasements, below even the nature of an animal, is usually brought about by fermented drinks, but it can also result from other narcotics, such as opium and other vegetable products. They are seductive because, under their influence, people dream for a while that they are happy and free from care, and even imagine that they are strong; but dejection and weakness follow and, worst of all, they create a need to use the narcotics again and even to increase the amount. Gluttony is even lower than that animal enjoyment of the senses, since it only lulls the senses into a passive condition and, unlike drunkenness, does not even arouse imagination to an *active* play of representations; so it approaches even more closely the enjoyment of cattle" (MM 6:427).
27. "To be subject to emotion and passions is probably always an illness of mind because both emotion and passion, exclude the sovereignty of reason" (A 155).
28. This point has been made, both directly and indirectly, by such diverse thinkers as, for example, Mark Johnson, *The Body in the Mind*; George Lakoff and Mark Johnson, *Philosophy in the Flesh*; John Kekes, "Morality and Impartiality," *American Philosophical Quarterly* 18 (1981): 295–303; Michael Stocker, "The Schizophrenia of Modern Ethical Theories," *Journal of Philosophy* 73 (1976): 453–466; Peter Winch, "Moral Integrity," in *Ethics and Action* (London: Routledge, 1972); and Susan Wolf, "Moral Saints," *Journal of Philosophy* 79 (1982): 419–439.
29. Friedrich Schiller, *The aesthetic letters, essays, and philosophical letters of Schiller*, Weiss (trans.) (Boston: Little and Brown, 1854 [1794]), 14. *Italics mine*. Schiller attempted to overcome the dualism established by Kant between form and sense, suggesting that between the "sensuous drive" (*Sinnestrieb*) and the "formal drive" (*Formtrieb*) there is a third mediating "play drive" (*Spieltrieb*). He was one of the first to criticize Kant for overemphasizing the rational nature of ethical conduct. Human conduct, according to Schiller, always operated in the middle ground between sensation and rationality.

30. Bernard Williams, "A Critique of Utilitarianism," in Smart and Williams, *Utilitarianism: For and Against* (Cambridge: Cambridge University Press, 1972), "Morality and the Emotions," in *Problems of the Self* (Cambridge: Cambridge University Press, 1972), "Persons, Character and Morality," "Moral Luck," and "Utilitarianism and Moral Self-Indulgence," in *Moral Luck* (Cambridge: Cambridge University Press, 1981).
31. Carol McMillan, *Women, Reason and Nature* (Princeton: Princeton University Press, 1982), 20.
32. See especially Genevieve Lloyd, *The Man of Reason* (Minneapolis: University of Minnesota Press, 1981).
33. See, for example, Baier, *Moral Prejudices*; Gilligan, *In a Different Voice*; Virginia Held, *The Ethics of Care: Personal, Political, and Global* (New York: Oxford University Press, 2006); Noddings, *Caring*; Walker, *Moral Understandings*.
34. Baier, *Moral Prejudices*, 26.
35. Baier, *Moral Prejudices*, 30.
36. See, for example, Marcia Baron, "The Alleged Moral Repugnance of Acting from Duty," *Journal of Philosophy* 81 (1984): 197–220, and *Kantian Ethics Almost Without Apology* (Ithaca: Cornell University Press, 1995); Barbara Herman, "On the Value of Acting from the Motive of Duty," *Philosophical Review* 90 (1981): 359–382, and "Integrity and Impartiality," *Monist* 66 (1983): 233–250; and Thomas Hill, "The Importance of Autonomy," *Women and Moral Theory*, Kittay and Meyers (eds) (Totowa: Rowman and Littlefield, 1987), 129–138.
37. This argument is made by Marcia Baron in "The Alleged Moral Repugnance of Acting from Duty" and *Kantian Ethics Almost Without Apology*.
38. "Sympathetic Feeling is Generally a Duty...Sympathetic joy and sadness (*sympathia moralis*) are sensible feelings of pleasure or displeasure (which are therefore to be called 'aesthetic') at another's state of joy or pain (shared feeling, sympathetic feeling). Nature has already implanted in human beings receptivity to these feelings. But to use this as a means to promoting active and rational benevolence is still a particular, though only a conditional, duty. It is called the duty of *humanity* (*humanitas*) because a human being is regarded here not merely as a rational being but also as an animal endowed with reason. ... But while it is not in itself a duty to share the sufferings (as well as the joys) of others, it is a duty to sympathize actively in their fate; and to this end it is therefore an indirect duty to cultivate the compassionate natural (aesthetic) feelings in us, and to make use of them as so many means to sympathy based on moral principles and the feeling appropriate to them" (*MM* 6:356–357).
39. This argument is made by Barbara Herman in "On the Value of Acting from the Motive of Duty" and "Integrity and Impartiality."
40. See, for example, Gilligan, *In a Different Voice;* and Wolf, "Moral Saints."
41. "To be beneficent where one can is a duty, and besides there are many souls so sympathetically attuned that, without any other motive of vanity or self-interest they find an inner satisfaction in spreading joy around them and can take delight in the satisfaction of others so far as it is their own work. But I assert that in such a case an action of this kind, however it may conform with duty and however amiable it may be, has nevertheless no true moral worth but is on the

same footing with other inclinations, for example, the inclination to honour, which, if it fortunately lights upon what is in fact in the common interest and in conformity with duty and hence honourable, deserves praise and encouragement but not esteem; for the maxim lacks moral content, namely that of doing such actions not from inclination but *from duty*. Suppose, then, that the mind of this philanthropist were overclouded by his own grief, which extinguished all sympathy with the fate of others, and that while he still had the means to benefit others in distress their own troubles did not move him because he had enough to do with his own; and suppose that now, when no longer incited to it by any inclination, he nevertheless tears himself out of this deadly insensibility and does the action without any inclination, simply from duty; then the action first has its genuine moral worth. Still further: if nature had put little sympathy in the heart of this or that man; if (in other respects an honest man) he is by temperament cold and indifferent to the sufferings of others, perhaps because he himself is provided with the special gift of patience and endurance toward his own sufferings and presupposes the same in every other man or requires it; if nature had not properly fashioned such a man (who would in truth not be its worst product) for a philanthropist, would he not still find within himself a source from which to give himself a far higher worth than what a mere good-natured temperament might have? By all means! It is just then that the worth of character comes out, which is moral and incomparably highest, namely that he is beneficent not from inclination but from duty" (*G* 4:398–399).
42. "[W]e like to flatter ourselves by falsely attributing to ourselves a nobler motive, whereas in fact we can never, even by the most strenuous self-examination, get entirely behind our covert incentives, since, when moral worth is at issue, what counts is not actions, which one sees, but those inner principles of actions that one does not see" (*G* 4:407).
43. "Pure practical reason merely *infringes upon* self-love, inasmuch as it only restricts it, as natural and active in us even prior to the moral law, to the condition of agreement with this law, and then it is called *rational self-love*. But it *strikes down* self-conceit altogether, since all claims to esteem for oneself that precede accord with the moral law are null and quite unwarranted because certainty of a disposition in accord with this law is the first condition of any worth of a person..., and any presumption prior to this is false and opposed to the law." Immanuel Kant, *The Critique of Practical Reason*, Gregor (ed. and trans.) (Cambridge: Cambridge University Press, 1997 [1788]), 5:73. '*CPR*' in parenthetical documentation hereafter refers to this work.
44. See, for example, Stephen Darwall, "Two Kinds of Respect," *Ethics* 88 (1977): 36–49; Lara Denis, "Kant's Ethical Duties and their Feminist Implications," and "Kant's Ethics and Duties to Oneself," *Pacific Philosophical Quarterly* 78 (1997): 321–348; Robin Dillon, "Self-Respect: Moral, Emotional, Political," *Ethics* 107 (1997): 226–239, "How to Lose your Self-Respect," *American Philosophical Quarterly* 29 (1992): 125–139, and "Toward a Feminist Conception of Self-Respect"; Thomas Hill, "Self-Respect Reconsidered," *Tulane Studies in Philosophy* 31 (1982): 129–137, and "Servility and Self-Respect," *The Monist* 57 (1973): 87–104; Rawls, *A Theory of Justice*, 178–183, 251–257, 440–446; Elizabeth Telfer, "Self-Respect," *Philosophical Quarterly* 18 (1968): 114–21; Larry Thomas, "Rawlsian Self-Respect and the Black Consciousness

Movement," *Philosophical Forum* 9 (1977–78): 303–314, and "Morality and Our Self-Concept," *Journal of Value Inquiry* 12 (1978): 258–268.

For an argument that attempts to problematize the Kantian grounds of these accounts of self-respect, see Cynthia Stark, "The Rationality of Valuing Oneself: A Critique of Kant on Self-Respect," *Journal of the History of Philosophy* 35 (1997): 65–82.

45. "Only a rational being has the capacity to act *in accordance with the representation* of laws, that is, in accordance with principles, or has a *will*. Since *reason* is required for the derivation of actions from laws, the will is nothing other than practical reason.... If reason infallibly determines the will, the actions of such a being that are cognized as objectively necessary are also subjectively necessary, that is, the will is a capacity to choose *only that* which reason independently of inclination cognizes as practically necessary, that is, as good" (*G* 4:412).

46. "The capacity to set oneself an end – any end whatsoever – is what characterizes humanity" (*MM* 6:392).

47. "[Hypothetical imperatives] represent the practical necessity of a possible action as a means to achieving something else that one wills (or that it is at least possible for one to will).... Since every practical law represents a possible action as good and therefore as necessary for a subject practically determinable by reason, all imperatives are formulae for the determination of action that is necessary in accordance with the principle of a will which is good in some way. Now, if the action would be good merely as a means *to something else* the imperative is *hypothetical*;... One can think of what is possible only through the powers of some rational being as also a possible purpose of some will" (*G* 4:414–415).

48. "[T]here is one imperative that, without being based upon and having as its condition any other purpose to be attained by certain conduct, commands this conduct immediately. This imperative is **categorical**. It has not to do with the matter of the action and what is to result from it, but with the form and the principle from which the action itself follows; and the essentially good in the action consists in the disposition, let the result be what it may. This imperative may be called the imperative **of morality**.... [O]nly law brings with it the concept of an *unconditional* and objective and hence universally valid *necessity*, and commands are laws that must be obeyed, that is, must be followed even against inclination" (*G* 4:416).

49. "*Will* is a kind of causality of living beings insofar as they are rational, and *freedom* would be that property of such causality that it can be efficient independently of alien causes *determining* it, just as *natural necessity* is the property of the causality of all nonrational beings to be determined to activity by the influence of alien causes" (*G* 4:446).

50. "[Imperatives] say that to do or to omit something would be good, but they say it to a will that does not always do something just because it is represented to it that it would be good to do that thing. Practical good, however, is that which determines the will by means of representations of reason, hence not by subjective causes but objectively, that is, from grounds that are valid for every rational being as such. [The practical good] is distinguished from the *agreeable*, as that which influences the will only by means of feeling from merely subjective causes, which hold only for the senses of this or that one, and not as a principle of reason, which holds for everyone" (*G* 4:413).

51. For more detailed accounts, and slightly differing interpretations, of the Kantian conception of humanity, see, for example, Guyer, *Kant on Freedom, Law and Happiness*, Hill, "Humanity as an End in Itself," Korsgaard, "Kant's Formula of Humanity," and Wood, "The Formula of Humanity as an End in Itself."
52. "Everyone must grant that a law, if it is to hold morally, that is, as a ground of obligation, must carry with it absolute necessity; that, for example, the command 'thou shalt not lie' does not hold only for human beings, as if other rational beings did not have to heed it, and so with all other moral laws properly so called; that, therefore, the ground of obligation here must not be sought in the nature of the human being or in the circumstances of the world in which he is placed, but a priori simply in concepts of pure reason" (*G* 4:389–390).
53. "[I]t is of the utmost importance to take warning that we must not let ourselves think of wanting to derive the reality of this principle from the *special property of human nature*. For, duty is to be practical unconditional necessity of action and it must therefore hold for all rational beings (to which alone an imperative can apply at all) and *only because of this* be also a law for all human wills" (*G* 4:425).
54. Wood and Korsgaard advance different versions of this interpretation, in "The Formula of Humanity as an End in Itself," and "Kant's Formula of Humanity," respectively.
55. "All objects of the inclinations have only a conditional worth; for, if there were not inclinations and the needs based on them, their object would be without worth. ... Thus the worth of any object *to be acquired* by our action is always conditional" (*G* 4:428).
56. "The ends that a rational being proposes at his discretion as *effects* of his actions (material ends) are all only relative; for only their mere relation to a specially constituted faculty of desire on the part of the subject gives them their worth. ... Hence all these relative ends are only the ground of hypothetical imperatives" (*G*4:428).
57. "But suppose there were something the *existence of which in itself* has an absolute worth, something which as *an end in itself* could be a ground of determinate laws; then in it, and in it alone, would lie the ground of a possible categorical imperative, that is, of a practical law" (*G* 4:428).
58. "[S]ince without it nothing of *absolute worth* would be found anywhere; but if all worth were conditional and therefore contingent, then no supreme practical principle for reason could be found anywhere" (*G* 4:428).
59. "If, then, there is to be a supreme practical principle and, with respect to the human will, a categorical imperative, it must be one such that, from the representation of what is necessarily an end for everyone because it is an *end in itself*, it constitutes an *objective* principle of the will and can thus serve as a universal practical law" (*G* 4:428–429).
60. "Now I say that the human being and in general every rational being *exists* as an end in itself, *not merely as a means* to be used by this or that will at its discretion" (*G* 4:428).
61. "Beings the existence of which rests not on our will but on nature, if they are beings without reason, still have only a relative worth, as means, and are therefore called *things*, whereas rational beings are called *persons* because their nature already marks them out as an end in itself, that is, as something

that may not be used merely as a means, and hence so far limits all choice (and is an object of respect). These, therefore, are not merely subjective ends, the existence of which as an effect of our actions has a worth *for us*, but rather *objective ends*, that is, beings the existence of which is in itself an end, and indeed one such that no other end, to which they would serve *merely* as a means, can be put in its place" (G 4:429).

62. The force of this necessity, to be clear, is *rational* rather than psychological or metaphysical.
63. "The human being necessarily represents his own existence in this way; so far it is thus a *subjective* principle of human actions" (G 4:429).
64. "But every other rational being also represents his existence in this way consequent on just the same rational ground that also holds for me; thus it is at the same time an *objective* principle from which, as a supreme practical ground, it must be possible to derive all laws of the will" (G 4:429).
65. "[I]n the order of ends the human being (and with him every rational being) is an *end in itself*, that is, can never be used merely as a means by anyone (not even by God) without being at the same time himself an end, and that humanity in our person must, accordingly, be *holy* to ourselves: for he is the *subject of the moral law* and so of that which is holy in itself, on account of which and in agreement with which alone can anything be called holy" (*CPR* 5:131–132).
66. "Rational nature is distinguished from the rest of nature by this, that it sets itself an end. This end would be the matter of every good will. But since, in the idea of a will absolutely good without any limiting condition (attainment of this or that end) abstraction must be made altogether from every end to be *effected* (this would make every will only relatively good), the end must here be thought not as an end to be effected but as an *independently-existing* end, and hence thought only negatively, that is, as that which must never be acted against and which must therefore in every volition be estimated never merely as a means but always at the same time as an end" (G 4:437).
67. Marcus G. Singer, "Duties and Duties to Oneself," *Ethics* 73 (1963): 133–142.
68. "When a human being is conscious of a duty to himself, he views himself, as the subject of duty, under two attributes: first as a *sensible being*, that is, as a human being (a member of one of the animal species), and second as an *intelligible being* (not merely as a being that has reason, since reason as a theoretical faculty could well be an attribute of a living corporeal being). The senses cannot attain this latter aspect of a human being; it can be cognized only in morally practical relations, where the incomprehensible property of *freedom* is revealed by the influence of reason on the inner lawgiving will.... Now the human being as a *natural being* that has reason (*homo phaenomenon*) can be determined by his reason, as a *cause*, to actions in the sensible world, and so far as the concept of obligation does not come into consideration. But the same human being thought in terms of his *personality*, that is, as being endowed with inner *freedom* (*homo noumenon*), is regarded as a being that can be put under obligation and, indeed, under obligation to himself (to the humanity in his own person). So the human being (taken in these two different senses) can acknowledge a duty to himself without falling into contradiction (because the concept of a human being is not thought in one and the same sense)" (*MM* 6:417–418).

69. For a discussion of why Kant's argument in defence of imperfect duties probably does not work see, for example, Andrews Reath, "Self-Legislation and Duties to Oneself," *Southern Journal of Philosophy* 36 (1997): 103–124. Reath argues that Kant's distinction between the noumenal and phenomenal self will not solve the problem here because Kant himself admits that it is our noumenal self that is both "endowed with inner freedom" and "can be put under obligation." According to Kant's own view, then, our noumenal self both recognizes a duty and chooses whether to obey it. So, even with Kant's distinction between noumenal and phenomenal, the same sense of self – the noumenal self – is what does the obliging and is what is obliged.
70. For other defences of the possibility of duties to the self that are more explicitly wedded to Kantianism, see, for example, Denis, "Kant's Ethics and Duties to Oneself"; Margaret Paton, "A Reconsideration of Kant's Treatment of Duties to Oneself," *The Philosophical Quarterly* 40 (1990): 222–233; and Jens Timmerman, "Kantian Duties to the Self, Explained and Defended," *Philosophy* 81 (2006): 505–530. These commentators all agree that there *is* a sense in which there are two selves involved when it comes to duties to the self; these two senses of the self are the self understood as the *legislator* of the moral law and the self understood as the *subject* of the moral law.
71. Thomas Hill, "Promises to Oneself," *Autonomy and Self-Respect* (New York: Cambridge University Press, 1991), 138–154.
72. Cynthia Stark defends a similar account of what Kant thinks it means to lack self-respect in "The Rationality of Valuing Oneself: A Critique of Kant on Self-Respect."
73. Thomas Hill considers both these kinds of lack of self-respect, as well as a third kind. He argues that one can fail to have self-respect in a way that is independent of either one's rights or one's merits. To fail to have self-respect in this third way is to fail to live up to certain *personal* standards. The sorts of standards Hill has in mind are those according to which someone judges her own conduct, but which she does not extend to others. This sort of self-respect requires of people that they develop and live by certain (morally permissible) standards – be they ideals one strives for, or simply lines one cannot cross without disgracing oneself in one's own eyes. I think Hill has put his finger on a legitimate way that one can fail to have self-respect here, but because it bears less directly on my project than the other sorts of failures of self-respect just considered – failures to respect rights or merits – I set it aside. (See Thomas Hill, "Self-Respect Reconsidered.")
74. Hill, "Servility and Self-Respect."
75. Hill, "Servility and Self-Respect," 99.
76. See, for example, Susan Babbitt, "Feminism and Objective Interests: The Role of Transformation Experiences in Rational Deliberation," *Feminist Epistemologies* Alcoff and Potter (eds) (New York: Routledge, 1993), 245–265; Marcia Baron, "Servility, Critical Deference and the Deferential Wife," *Philosophical Studies* 48 (1985): 393–400; Samantha Brennan, "Reconciling Feminist Politics and Feminist Ethics on the Issue of Rights," *Journal of Social Philosophy* 30 (1999): 260–275; Marilyn Friedman, "Moral Integrity and the Deferential Wife," *Philosophical Studies* 47 (1985): 141–150; John Tomasi, "Individual Rights and Community Virtues," *Ethics* 101 (1991): 521–536; Superson, "Deformed Desires and Informed Desire Tests," and "The Deferential Wife Revisited";

and Andrea Westlund, "Selflessness and Responsibility for Self: Is Deference Compatible with Autonomy?" *The Philosophical Review* 112 (2003): 483–523.
77. See, for example, Dillon, "Self-Respect: Moral, Emotional, Political," "How to Lose your Self-Respect," and "Toward a Feminist Conception of Self-Respect."
78. Dillon, "How to Lose your Self-Respect," 134–135.
79. Dillon, "How to Lose your Self-Respect," 135.
80. Dillon, "How to Lose your Self-Respect," 125.
81. Others who have used Kant's account of self-respect for explicitly feminist purposes include Lara Denis, "Kant's Ethical Duties and their Feminist Implications;" Jean Hampton, "Selflessness and the Loss of Self," and "Feminist Contractarianism;" Janice Richardson, "On Not Making Ourselves the Prey of Others;" and Anita Superson, "The Deferential Wife Revisited."
82. Mill, "The Subjection of Women."
83. Mary Wollstonecraft, "Of the Pernicious Effects which Arise from the Unnatural Distinctions Established in Society," *A Vindication of the Rights of Woman* (Cambridge: Cambridge University Press, 1995 [1792]).
84. Simone de Beauvoir, *The Second Sex*, Parshely (trans.) (Harmondsworth: Penguin, 1984 [1949]).
85. Sandra Bartky, "On Psychological Oppression," *Femininity and Domination: Studies in the Phenomenology of Oppression* (New York: Routledge, 1990).
86. Ann Cudd, "Psychological Explanations of Oppression," *Theorizing Multiculturalism: A Guide to the Current Debate*, Willett (ed.) (Malden, MA: Blackwell, 1998), 187–215.
87. Haslanger, "Changing the Ideology and Culture of Philosophy."
88. Thanks to Ann Garry for putting the question to me in this particularly evocative way.
89. See Jean Hampton, "Selflessness and Loss of Self" and "Feminist Contractarianism."
90. Soren Kiergaard, *The Sickness unto Death*, Hannay (trans.) (Harmondsworth: Penguin, 1989 [1849]), 80–81. As cited in Hampton, "Selflessness and Loss of Self," 61.
91. de Beauvoir, *The Second Sex*, 650–561. Italics in original.
92. Cited in Judith Nies, *Nine Women: Portraits from the American Radical Tradition* (Los Angeles: University of California Press, 2002), 67.
93. Mary Daly, *Gyn/Ecology: The Metaethics of Radical Feminism* (Boston: Beacon Press, 1978), 378.
94. The potential exploitation of women, for whom caring and self-sacrifice are seen as distinctive virtues, is described by a number of feminists, including, for example, Larry Blum, Marcia Homiak, Judy Housman, and Naomi Scheman, "Altruism and Women's Oppression," *Philosophical Forum* 5 (1974): 222–247; Gilligan, *In a Different Voice*; Hampton, "Feminist Contractarianism"; Held, *Feminist Morality*; Kittay, *Love's Labor*; Ruddick, *Maternal Thinking*; and Judith Tormey, "Exploitation, Oppression and Self-Sacrifice," *Philosophical Forum* 5 (1974): 206–221.
95. As we will consider in more detail in Chapter 4, Ann Cudd advances a version of this argument. See Cudd, *Analyzing Oppression*.
96. Thanks to an anonymous referee for pressing this point.
97. This argument has been made, for example, by Dillon, "Toward a Feminist Conception of Self-Respect"; Sarah Hoagland, "Some Concerns About Nel Noddings' *Caring*," *Hypatia* 5 (1990): 109–114; and Barbara Houston, "Caring and Exploitation," *Hypatia* 5 (1990): 115–119.

3
The Obligation to Resist Sexual Harassment

Sexual harassment has received a great deal of attention from both feminist activists and feminist scholars, who have explained at great length why it is morally problematic, how it harms women, and what should be done to eradicate it. But what has not received much attention is the issue of what moral expectations, if any, we should have of women who find themselves subjected to sexual harassment. This is hardly surprising. As I discuss below, a number of different considerations might make us think that women never have an obligation to confront those who sexually harass them. Perhaps the most important among these considerations is feminists' perfectly appropriate reticence to be guilty of victim-blaming. A woman who has been sexually harassed has been subjected to a moral harm, and it seems strange to suggest that being subjected to a moral harm might actually impose moral obligations on the victim, instead of the perpetrator. Strange as it might initially seem, I want to consider just this possibility. In the end, I make a case for the claim that a woman who has been sexually harassed has a moral obligation to confront her harasser. It will turn out that this obligation arises as a special case of a woman's obligation to preserve and protect her own autonomy or moral agency.

A concrete example might lend plausibility to this admittedly rather unintuitive claim. In an essay for *Harper's* magazine, "Getting Away from Already Being Pretty Much Away from It All," David Foster Wallace describes his visit to the Illinois State Fair. The friend who goes with him, whom he calls Native Companion because she is a local, gets on one of the rides. While she is hanging upside down, the men operating the ride stop it so that her dress falls over her head and they can ogle her. What follows is the exchange that takes place between Wallace and Native Companion immediately after she gets off the ride.

[Wallace asks,] "Did you sense something kind of sexual-harassmentish going on through that whole little sick exercise?"

"Oh for fuck's sake...it was *fun*."...

"They were looking up your *dress*. You couldn't see them, maybe. They hung you upside down at a great height and made your dress fall up and *ogled* you. They shaded their eyes and made comments to each other. I saw the whole thing."

"Oh for fuck's sake."...

"So this doesn't bother you? As a Midwesterner, you're unbothered? Or did you just not have an accurate sense of what was going on back there?"

"So if I noticed or I didn't, why does it have to be *my* deal? What, because there's assholes in the world I don't get to ride on The Zipper? I don't get to ever spin? Maybe I shouldn't ever go to the pool or ever get all girled up, just out of fear of assholes?"...

"So I'm curious, then, about what it would have taken back there, say, to have gotten you to lodge some sort of complaint with the Fair's management."

"You're so fucking *innocent*...," she says. "Assholes are just assholes. What's getting hot and bothered going to do about it except keep me from getting to have fun?"...

"This is potentially key....This may be just the sort of regional politico-sexual contrast the swanky East-Coast magazine is keen for. The core value informing a kind of willed politico-sexual stoicism on your part is your prototypically Midwestern appreciation of fun...whereas on the East Coast, politico-sexual indignation *is* the fun. In New York, a woman who'd been hung upside down and ogled would go get a whole lot of other women together and there'd be this frenzy of politico-sexual indignation. They'd confront the ogler. File an injunction. Management'd find itself litigating expensively – violation of a woman's right to nonharassed fun. I'm telling you. Personal and political fun merge somewhere just east of Cleveland, for women."...

"They might ought to try just climbing on and spinning and ignoring assholes and saying Fuck 'em. That's pretty much all you can do with assholes."[1]

Right, then. I think this exchange raises some very interesting questions. Is a decision to ignore behaviour that stems from oppressive norms a legitimate way to react to oppressive social conditions? Or is ignoring one's oppression tantamount to acquiescence? What sort of obligation do women have to resist patriarchal oppression? What sort of obligation do women have to stand up to perpetrators of sexual harassment? If, as Native Companion suggests, all you can do with harassers is ignore them, what are the prospects for real social change?

What follows is an attempt to answer these questions. My goal here is to establish that women often do have a moral obligation to confront the men who harass them. Furthermore, I will argue that this obligation is not overridden by many of the considerations that can override other moral obligations. But first, some preliminary issues must be dealt with. We must be clear on exactly what sort of harm someone like Native Companion has undergone. After analysing the particular harms of sexual harassment, I will argue that Native Companion's experience with sexual harassment has the potential to affect her autonomy in a number of morally problematic ways. I argue that her obligation to resist these harms means that she has an obligation to resist her harassment, but then move on to consider whether the fact that sexual harassment occurs under oppression might give rise to either practical and normative considerations that could override a woman's obligation to confront her harassers. I conclude that these considerations are generally insufficient to override the obligation. Then I respond to an objection to an earlier version of my argument – that the harms of oppression are almost never sufficiently restrictive to affect one's autonomy – by analyzing the relationship between autonomy and responsibility in general. I close with a preliminary analysis of the possibility that resisting oppression might permit multiple courses of action, a consideration taken up more fully in the following chapter.

The harm of sexual harassment

Exactly what sort of harm has Native Companion undergone? Wallace calls the situation "sexual-harassmentish," but Native Companion does not seem willing to acknowledge that she has been harmed at all. Has she been sexually harassed? Most feminist analyses of sexual harassment restrict their focus to harassment in the workplace – probably because much of this work has been done by legal scholars, who have succeeded in having sexual harassment made illegal in this context – and relatively few focus on what is known as 'street harassment'. This restricted focus might make sense for practical legal purposes, but Margaret Crouch argues that the artificial separation of the workplace from other public places:

> tends to obscure the function and effect of all harassment – to keep women in their place. Sexual harassment is a means of maintaining

women's status as subordinate in society; it is also a means of keeping women in certain physical spaces and out of others, or, at least, of controlling women's behavior in those spaces. In this way, sexual harassment constrains women's freedom of movement both in terms of status and place.[2]

Drawing on a number of feminists' accounts, I will argue that this is precisely the harm that Native Companion has experienced. I will argue that sexual harassment has three interrelated elements. First, sexual harassment occurs against a cultural backdrop of gender-specific *stereotypes* and assumptions about the sexual roles, desires, behaviours that are appropriate for men and women. The upshot of these stereotypes is that sexual harassment both derives from, and is a manifestation of, the greater social power that men have over women in an oppressive society. Second, sexual harassment stems from sexual *objectification*. The upshot of this objectification is that sexual harassment both derives from, and is a manifestation of, women's unequal moral status in an oppressive society. Finally, the *systematicity* of oppression means that sexual harassment ultimately functions, either directly or indirectly, to undermine women's *autonomy*. Let us look more closely at these three elements of sexual harassment.

Stereotypes

In a sexist society such as ours, certain stereotypes about the sexual natures of men and women are held ubiquitously. There is both a descriptive and a prescriptive element to these sexual stereotypes. That is, they both purport to describe what sexual character traits men and women do in fact possess, and also to prescribe what sexual character traits are appropriate for men and women to possess. Because stereotypes are simultaneously descriptive and prescriptive, they are self-perpetuating, encouraging gendered behaviours which then reinforce and perpetuate the stereotypes. Sexist stereotypes thus simultaneously draw on and reinforce oppressive sexist social norms.

The sexual stereotypes and norms behind Native Companion's sexual harassment include beliefs about women's inferiority to men and about the appropriateness and permissibility of men's sexual aggressiveness and women's sexual passivity. Sandra Bartky says the content of sexist sexual stereotypes portray men as sexually aggressive, dominant, and promiscuous, and women as sexually passive, frigid, submissive, cautious, and monogamous. There are racist elements to these sexual stereotypes as well, Bartky points out: white and Asian women are usually placed on the more passive end of this spectrum, while black and Latina women are more likely to be seen as "hot-blooded" or "spitfires" (although still not as lustful as the men of their respective races); men of colour are more likely to be seen as predatorily sexual, particularly when a white woman is the object of their interest. These stereotypes play into sexual harassment in a particular way. Regardless of race, when a man behaves in sexually aggressive ways, actively pursuing a woman who responds by behaving in sexually passive ways, both are merely displaying gender-appropriate behaviour. But these behaviours will tend to systematically place women at a social disadvantage. Bartky argues that the content of women's stereotypes threatens their autonomy because femininity is neither:

> too self-regarding [nor] independent.... [W]hite women, at least, are psychologically conditioned not to pursue the kind of autonomous development that is held by the culture to be a constitutive feature of masculinity.... [This means they] cannot be autonomous ... without in some sense ceasing to be women.[3]

Women's disadvantages are exacerbated when they internalize the stereotypes about them. Bartky argues that internalized stereotypes threaten women's autonomy by leaving them with inferior, truncated, or depreciated senses of self. She argues that internalized stereotypes are problematic on existentialist grounds (because they prevent an authentic choice of self), on psychological grounds (because they prevent self-actualization), and on moral grounds (because they prevent the development of autonomy and moral agency).

As we saw in Chapter 2, internalized stereotypes can disadvantage those who identify as members of oppressed groups via the phenomenon of stereotype threat, which undermines people's abilities by encouraging decreased performance when they are aware of a stereotype that portrays people like them as less capable in a given domain. As we saw in Chapter 1, the problem of adaptive preferences illustrates what happens when oppressed people internalize negative stereotypes and come to believe that they are inferior, either treating themselves as such or accepting such treatment from others. The problem of adaptive preferences also illustrates how internalized sexist stereotypes can disadvantage women by encouraging them to rule out adopting certain worthwhile ends because they are preoccupied with more trivial ones. For example, a woman might devote more time and energy to presenting herself as sexually attractive than she devotes to her studies or career because she has accepted the sexist message that it is more important that she be attractive to men than that she be intelligent or independent.[4] Similarly, internalized stereotypes can limit oppressed people's exposure to possible forms of life that, were they exposed to them, they might decide were valuable. When someone's experiences are constrained, this can constrain her sense of what is possible for people like her. For example, Native Companion's sense of what is possible for her is limited by oppression, insofar as she cannot imagine what it would be like to not have to deal with men's predatory sexuality.

Men's stereotypically gender-appropriate behaviours give them a competitive advantage over women, whose stereotypically gender-appropriate behaviours disadvantage them. This competitive advantage translates into social power. As we saw in Chapter 1, one characteristic of oppression is that the members of non-oppressed groups benefit from the oppressive harms experienced by the members of oppressed groups. This benefit often takes the form of relative advantage, where members of a group that does not face systematic hardships are better situated to compete for limited resources than members of a group that does. And these stereotypes can disadvantage women even when everyone involved considers themselves to be egalitarian. As we saw in Chapter 1, there is reason to think we are all subject to the phenomenon of implicit bias, which occurs when people consciously reject negative stereotypes and support anti-oppressive policies but simultaneously retain unconscious negative associations. This means that a commitment to equality is no guarantee that sexist stereotypes are not at play. The upshot of these stereotypes is that sexual harassment both derives from, and is a manifestation of, the greater social power that men have over women in an oppressive society.

Objectification

The second element of sexual harassment is that it stems from sexual objectification. In a sexist society such as ours, sexual objectification involves dehumanizing women so that they may be regarded or treated as sexual objects. Sexually objectifying a woman involves the (at least implicit) assumption that she is the sort of being who exists fundamentally not for her own purposes but for the purposes of her objectifier. Linda LeMoncheck argues that this dehumanization demeans or degrades women's equal moral status, resulting in their being treated as if they have fewer rights to well-being and freedom than the men who objectify them.[5] When women are viewed as if their primary function is men's sexual gratification, women's own goals, interests, and preferences are inevitably granted less importance than those of their objectifiers. When women are viewed as existing primarily for men's sexual purposes, they are granted a second-class moral status. The way women are viewed affects the way they are treated, and the way they are treated affects the way they are viewed; in this way, women's sexual objectification both derives from and contributes to sexist oppression.

Of course, as both LeMoncheck and Martha Nussbaum point out, it is important not to confuse treating women as sex objects, which is morally problematic, with treating them as sexually attractive or as the objects of sexual desire, which need not be morally problematic.[6] There are many contexts in which it is perfectly appropriate to treat a woman as sexually attractive or as the object of sexual desire; what is common to all these contexts is that the woman's sexuality is actually relevant to the situation and that she is treated as a moral equal. The morally problematic kind of sexual objectification occurs only when a woman is treated as sexually attractive in a context where her sexuality is, or ought to be, irrelevant, or when she is not treated as a moral equal because of her sex. This happens when women are treated as if their subjectivity and autonomy – their feelings and experiences, and their decisions about what they would like to do or how they would like to be treated – do not matter.

I argued above that one of the most pernicious ways that the culture of sexual objectification underlying Native Companion's harassment might harm her occurs when sexist stereotypes are internalized. Given the ubiquity of sexual objectification, this internalization is far from unlikely. Catharine MacKinnon famously claims that "all women live in sexual objectification the way fish live in water;"[7] Nussbaum interprets this metaphor to mean, "not only that objectification surrounds women, but also that they have become such that they derive their very nourishment and sustenance from it."[8] There is good reason to suspect that Native Companion has, at least in this respect, internalized her oppression. This is evident in her taking the attitudes of her harassers – men who "look at [her] like she's food, which she ignores"[9] – for granted. She minimizes the egregiousness of her harassers' behaviour and insists that the only thing to do is ignore them. She believes that men are just naturally sexually aggressive and that the only appropriate response to this aggressiveness that is open to women is to do nothing. She has, it seems, accepted the inevitability of being treated like she is a piece of meat. This indicates that, despite her feistiness, Native Companion has internalized the gendered sexual roles of dominance and submission that many feminists criticize.

One can sexually objectify a woman simply by thinking about her in a certain way; the woman need not be aware that she has been objectified for it to be the case that she has been. If this were all objectification amounted to, it would not be nearly as morally problematic. But Bartky points out that this is not usually the way things go. She describes an experience of sexual harassment not unlike Native Companion's, that of enduring the catcalls and whistles of strange men:

> While it is true that for these men I am nothing but, let us say, a "nice piece of ass," there is more involved in this encounter than their mere fragmented perception of me. They could, after all, have enjoyed me in silence. Blissfully unaware, breasts bouncing, eyes on the birds in the trees, I could have passed by without having been turned to stone. But I must be *made* to know that I am a "nice piece of ass": I must be made to see myself as they see me. ... It is unclear what role is played by sexual arousal or even spontaneous connoisseurship in encounters like these. What I describe seems less the spontaneous expression of a healthy eroticism than a ritual of subjugation.[10]

Bartky argues that sexual objectification is usually not just a "way of perceiving"; instead, it almost always also serves as a "way of maintaining dominance."[11] And sexual harassment is the outward behaviour that thereby usually arises from this sort of sexual objectification.

Crouch characterizes this aspect of sexual harassment as a breach of the "civil inattention" that is the norm that usually holds in public spaces.[12] Erving Goffman gives this label to the way we respectfully engage with people we do not know – for example, by briefly making eye contact with a stranger and then averting our eyes as we walk by them, thereby acknowledging that we see the other person but signaling that we do not intend to invade their personal space – and argues that its effect is a sort of privacy in public that is necessary for anonymous life in urban settings.[13] Civil inattention holds among men, and among women, but in a sexist society it does not always hold between men and women. Instead, men may treat women as "open persons," people who are worthy of so little respect that they may be ogled, commented on, and approached at will. These breaches of civil inattention constitute sexual harassment.

However, just because a woman must be aware of the offending behaviour in order to be sexually harassed, she need not take herself to have been harassed in order for her to have actually been harassed. If the behaviour occurs because a woman has been sexually objectified, the behaviour is sexual harassment, regardless of how it is perceived. Native Companion's treatment at the hands of the carnival workers is a clear case of sexual harassment since they treat her as worthy of so little respect that they act as if they are perfectly justified in "ogling her nethers."[14] One does not ogle the nethers of a moral equal without her permission. And riding The Zipper hardly constitutes permission to be ogled. These men have treated Native Companion as a sexual object in a situation where her sexuality ought to be irrelevant. So, whether she feels affronted or not, Native Companion has been sexually harassed.

Experiences of sexual harassment take place in cultural contexts where the sexual objectification of women is rampant and where the gendered sexual roles of dominance and submission that derive from this objectification result in disproportionately high rates of sexual violence against women.[15] How women are perceived in a sexist society clearly has some bearing on how women are treated in such a society. Feeling entitled to sexually objectify women, feeling entitled to sexually harass women, and feeling entitled to sexually assault women are not unconnected phenomena. This is, of course, not to suggest that every individual man who feels entitled to do the former will inevitably progress to doing the latter; it is merely to insist that all of these behaviours exist on a spectrum whose common element is the view that the fundamental purpose of women's sexuality is to serve men's sexual needs. Less extreme manifestations of this view, such as sexual objectification and harassment, function to both legitimize and minimize the perceived egregiousness of more extreme manifestations of this view, such as sexual assault. Native Companion is at a greater risk of being subjected to sexual violence simply in virtue of being a woman; living one's life in the shadow of this risk counts as an indirect sort of harm, regardless of whether one is fortunate enough to escape more extreme forms of sexual violence.

The systematicity of oppression and its effects on autonomy

A full appreciation of the harms of sexual harassment requires attending to the *systematicity* of oppression. Remember, as Marilyn Frye's birdcage metaphor suggests, the systematicity of oppression means that the detrimental effects of oppression are usually only fully evident from a perspective that takes into account, all at once, their effects on a person's life prospects. So, while the carnies' harassment might not directly harm (or perhaps even threaten to harm) Native Companion, it is important to notice that this harassment does not occur in a social vacuum. This means that, at the very least, this harassment harms (or at least threatens to harm) Native Companion indirectly.

The systematicity of oppression also means that there is a sense in which the harm a woman experiences when she is sexually harassed is not aimed at her as an individual. Instead, harassers are able to harass her because she is a member of an oppressed group whose members they do not accord the appropriate moral respect. Anita Superson argues that this is a constitutive element of sexual harassment.[16] The harm of sexual harassment thus differs from other kinds of harms because it both draws on and reinforces certain oppressive social norms. This means that when a particular woman is sexually harassed, all women are, at least indirectly, harmed.

As we have seen, when a woman is sexually harassed, or sexually objectified more generally, she has not been treated as a moral equal. Failing to treat someone as a moral equal amounts to failing to accord her the respect of an autonomous agent. But sexual harassment is not merely *evidence* of a lack of respect for women's autonomy; it can also *undermine* their autonomy. It can, in a sense, make them less autonomous. This is because sexual harassment does not just occur within the context of women's oppression under patriarchy. It also simultaneously entrenches this oppression by participating in, and thereby reinforcing and legitimating, certain sexist attitudes about women's inferiority to men and about the sex roles it is appropriate for women to occupy. That is, sexual harassment is not just a manifestation of the sexist attitudes of patriarchal society; it also contributes to and legitimates these attitudes. These attitudes, in turn, reinforce patriarchal oppression.

In her groundbreaking analysis of oppression, Frye emphasizes the double binds that oppressed people very often experience, describing situations where their "options are reduced to a very few and all of them expose [them] to penalty, censure or deprivation."[17] Such double binds are a clear manifestation of how oppression can restrict the autonomy of those who are oppressed. Crouch argues, we saw, that sexual harassment functions to "keep women in their place," restricting women's freedom by maintaining their subordinate social status and controlling their behaviour in public spaces. These restrictions amount to restrictions on women's autonomy. Oppression undermines women's autonomy by restricting the quantity and quality of choices available to them. Because oppression undermines the autonomy of those who are oppressed, insofar as sexual harassment both draws on and contributes to patriarchal oppression, it undermines women's autonomy. Thus, the moral harm of sexual harassment goes beyond any individual instance of a woman not having her autonomy respected. Rather, the moral harm of sexual harassment is that it can actually *make women less autonomous*. And because sexual harassment both draws on and reinforces the oppressive social norms of patriarchy, when a particular woman is sexually harassed, all women are, in fact, harmed.

The obligation to protect autonomy and the obligation to resist sexual harassment

The distinctive moral harm of sexual harassment, I have just argued, is that it undermines women's autonomy. It does this by reinforcing and legitimating the sexist attitudes that underlie patriarchal oppression. Now, if autonomy is a necessary condition for the possibility of moral obligation, then it seems reasonable to think there is a fundamental moral obligation to protect one's own autonomy. After all, it is a woman's autonomy that makes her capable of being subject to obligations in the first place. Since the possibility of being subject to moral obligations is at least partially constitutive of moral agency, a woman's autonomy is necessary for her to be a moral agent.

This means that the obligation to protect one's own autonomy translates into an obligation to resist sexual harassment. It looks like Native Companion is wrong to say there is nothing she is obligated to do in her situation. Because she is obligated to protect her autonomy, she is obligated to resist her sexual harassment. This obligation to resist sexual harassment is, in essence, an obligation to resist that which undermines her capacity for obligation, to resist that which undermines her moral agency. Seen in this way, women's obligation to confront the men who sexually harass them is not just a general obligation to confront some random moral harm. It is primarily a moral obligation to confront and resist behaviour that undermines one's ability to be morally obligated at all. It is a special case of an obligation to preserve and protect one's moral agency.

This means that a woman's obligation to confront the men who sexually harass her is primarily an obligation she has *to herself*. As we saw in the previous chapter, obligations to the self, particularly in the context of oppression, are most fruitfully thought of in terms of the Kantian duty of self-respect. This duty is one each of us has to recognize the value of the rational nature within us and to respond accordingly, respecting both our rights and our merits. Failures of self-respect involve a public and systematic willingness to disavow one's equal moral status, and this is incompatible with a proper regard for the moral law. These failures can be particularly likely to occur under oppression, both resulting from people's subordination in an oppressive society and functioning as one of the principal means of carrying this subordination out. I argued in Chapter 2 that the Kantian duty of self-respect is one that feminists cannot afford to ignore. In the remainder of this book, I will argue that this duty translates into an obligation to resist one's own oppression.

However, I will restrict my focus in this chapter, for the most part, to the narrower claim that the obligation to protect one's autonomy means there is an obligation to resist sexual harassment. But, as we will consider next, there are good reasons to think that the fact that sexual harassment takes place under patriarchal oppression might give rise to either practical or normative considerations that can override women's obligation to confront the men who sexually harass them.

Autonomy and obligation under oppression

Obviously, women can have an obligation to confront their harassers only if they are actually autonomous. If sexist oppression completely prevents the possibility of autonomous action for women, then the question of what moral obligations women have will obviously not arise. It is clear that women's range of options and choices are restricted in ways they would not be in the absence of this oppression. Many of the ostensibly free choices that women make take place under circumstances where the range of meaningful options is so limited that one begins to wonder whether such choices are meaningfully autonomous at all. Furthermore, the problem of adaptive preferences shows us that women can actually internalize their oppression; because patriarchal social factors function illicitly to influence their preferences, women can end up with preferences that are inimical to their own interests. Because women's preferences can end up distorted under patriarchy, even those choices that appear to be unproblematic cases of simple preference-satisfaction are suspect. For if oppressive forces have perverted the content of a preference, it is hard to see how that preference can really be called an autonomous one.

But to claim that women are usually, or even often, incapable of any meaningful degree of autonomy under patriarchy would be to go too far. As soon as we think of autonomy as a concept that admits of degrees, we have the conceptual resources to argue that, while women would clearly be more autonomous without patriarchy, they are (almost always) not entirely without a significant degree of autonomy even under patriarchy. Despite their oppression, most women usually still have a morally significant amount of control over their lives. This is true not only of women in Western liberal democracies, who enjoy historically unprecedented social and political freedoms, but probably also of most women in the developing world. Uma Narayan has criticized the tendency to portray the agency of Third World women as if it were completely "pulverized" by patriarchy; she thinks this effaces the value and significance of the choices these women make "from the point of view of the women who make them."[18] These women are neither "dupes" nor "prisoners" of patriarchy, Narayan argues. While the choices made by many Third World women are undeniably distorted by oppression, she argues that there is still active agency involved in their compliance with oppressive social structures. She advocates thinking of these women as "bargaining with patriarchy," and counsels us to attend to not just how an oppressive practice imposes constraints on women's choices, but also how women are capable of making choices within these constraints.

Still, oppression obviously undermines women's autonomy in a very real way. There is good reason to think this should affect decisions about which moral obligations it is fair to say women have. The question of whether women like Native Companion are responsible for confronting their harassers must be considered within an overall picture that recognizes that women are already subject to conditions of oppression when they are harassed. The thought that we need to take women's oppression into account when deciding which moral obligations they have is not a new one. For example, Superson argues that it is morally inappropriate for feminists to require women who conform to traditional gender roles to change their behaviour. She thinks this is the case even though she admits that this behaviour contributes not only to the oppression of those who conform, but also to the oppression of *all* women. She argues that it is unfair to say that these women have an obligation to change their behaviours because "their choice of lifestyle, and the values and beliefs accompanying it,...takes place in the context of severe restrictions of their freedom caused mainly by patriarchy. Their lifestyle, in turn, significantly limits their choices further."[19] To say that they have an obligation to change is to "expect them to act in ways that restrict their choices even further," and would be tantamount to blaming the victim. Superson's argument lines up nicely with my claim that the decision about what obligations an agent has is a normative one. And, whether or not we agree with her conclusion that oppressed women do not have obligations to resist the factors of their oppression (as will become even more apparent, I do not), an analysis like hers gives us good reason to take seriously the ways in which the fact that someone is oppressed can influence what degree of obligation she has.

There are several reasons why the fact that sexual harassment takes place under the oppressive conditions of patriarchy is relevant to the decision of whether women have an obligation to confront their harassers. First, there are some purely practical considerations. On the one hand, demanding responsibility might give an agent an incentive to act in ways that would end up increasing her autonomy; holding someone responsible for something can influence what she actually does, when she knows that she is being held responsible.[20] But given how prevalent situations of sexual harassment are in a patriarchal society, confronting every single perpetrator is probably not logistically possible. Furthermore, confronting every harasser could be potentially exhausting and could lead to a sense of victimization that could leave women unable to appreciate their own potential for responsible opposition.

Another practical consideration worth considering is that it just might not be worth confronting harassers because it will not do any good. This seems to be the thrust of Native Companion's claim that the only thing you can do with harassers is ignore them. It is true that for any individual case of confrontation the effect on overarching social oppressions will probably be negligible. But, on a larger scale, such pessimism is unwarranted. For if all, or even most, cases of harassment were confronted, harassers would soon get the message that such behaviour was inappropriate. To those who would object that harassers already know this behaviour is inappropriate, but simply do not care, the response can be that perpetual confrontation might give them reason to care. If harassers found that when they harassed women they were subject to acerbic retorts, belittlement, embarrassment, or other undesired consequences, such as negative implications for their career, they would quickly begin to think twice about whether their behaviour was worth it. I suspect that when most men harass women, they do so because they think they can get away with it. Ignoring harassment only confirms this.

A good general strategy for confronting sexual harassers, particularly in cases like Native Companion's, is to attempt to force the harasser to see you as a person worthy of being treated with respect. Perhaps the most effective way to do this is to remind them of other women they already respect (or would, at the very least, probably purport to respect). Ask them, "Would you say that to your mother? Your sister? What about your daughter? No? Then what makes you think you can say it to me?" Of course, the problem with this strategy is that while it generally does force an empathetic response from a harasser, there is no guarantee that he will have the right kind of empathetic response. When confronting a harasser the goal is to get him to see that you, and *all other women*, are worthy of respect, not merely the women to whom he has familial or affectional ties. The problem with asking a harasser, "What if I was your sister?" is that it is open for him to respond, "But you aren't."

Not only is there a concern that this strategy does not really require a harasser to respect you, but there is also a very real possibility that he does not have the right kind of respect for the women he does purport to respect. Patriarchy has long demanded a certain kind of respect for the particular women in a man's family, but this respect has been the sort of respect one has for one's property; traditionally (and currently, in some places), women have had the status of chattel. This is hardly the kind of respect Kant had in mind, and there is nothing in this strategy that requires a harasser to treat you as an end in yourself in the Kantian sense.

Furthermore, Bonnie Mann has pointed out that there is a "long patriarchal tradition of protectionism" that goes hand in hand with harassment and abuse.[21] Cultural narratives of masculinity require women to be victims so that there is someone to be saved. Sexual harassment and masculine protectionism are thus two sides of the same coin. The reason a harasser (at least purportedly) respects the particular women to whom he is related draws on an archetype Mann calls "the hero," who is "a narcissistic subject, whose hero story, nourished by broader misogynist social arrangements, requires victims to rescue [and whose] obsessive displays of agency pre-empt and undermine the world-making capacities of the ones he sets out to save."[22] Trying to get a harasser to respect you by appealing to his purported respect for certain other women only feeds into the cultural narratives of protectionist masculinity that are ultimately responsible for the harassment in the first place.

Crouch echoes this concern, reporting that, when surveyed, some men express their disapproval of street harassment in the language of chivalry.[23] The problem with this is that, despite its pretences, the institution of chivalry fails to protect many women; its protections are reserved for those women who are not seen as a threat to the patriarchal status quo. Crouch describes accounts from women who report that when they fail to respond to a street harasser in the manner he desires, particularly if they respond with anger instead, the situation often escalates to one of overt hostility and abuse. This, she argues, should be interpreted as the harasser's attempt to regain the dominance that he initially displayed by harassing, and that is threatened by a woman's angry assertion of her equality.

These various considerations show that even if there is an obligation to confront harassers, the background social conditions of oppression can make effective practical strategies for confrontation exceedingly hard to come by. In addition to these practical considerations, a number of normative considerations are relevant here, all of which emphasize how *unfair* it is to hold women responsible for resisting sexual harassment. We need to recognize that a woman who has been harassed suffers real harm – psychological, social, and emotional harm – and by saying that she has an obligation to confront her harasser, we impose a further burden on her. Because she has not done anything wrong, it seems unfair to demand that she take on the burden of trying to rectify the situation. We might think that oppressive social factors have left her with enough on her plate and that the last thing she needs is to be answerable to further moral demands. As Frye puts the point:

> Can we hold ourselves, and is it proper to hold each other, responsible for resistance? Or is it necessarily both stupid cruelty and a case of 'blaming the victim' to add yet one more pressure in our lives, in each others' lives, by expecting, demanding, requiring, encouraging, inviting acts and patterns of resistance and reconstruction which are not spontaneously forthcoming?[24]

Considerations of safety can also come into play when determining whether to require a woman to confront her harasser. In many cases of harassment, a woman should have every reason to think that confronting her harasser will put her in danger. One of the many harms caused by sexual harassment is that women can end up feeling afraid, not only of their harasser but also of their vulnerability in a society that permits such behaviour. This fear is not entirely unjustified. As noted above, one of the things that makes sexual harassment particularly problematic is that it treats women as morally inferior to their harassers. If a woman knows that her harasser does not consider her to be a moral equal, she has every reason to be concerned that he will not accord her the sort of respect that would prevent him from harming her in other ways as well. Because the conditions of women's oppression add an element of danger that is not present in non-oppressive situations, our concern for women's safety might completely override any moral obligations we would otherwise require of them. If we have good reason to think women would be at risk of further harm if they have an obligation to confront their harassers, then we cannot morally require this of them. But if we have some assurance that a woman would not face too much further risk by confronting her harasser, we should think seriously about saying that she has an obligation to do so. We cannot afford to be too vague about what counts as potential danger. If we err on the side of caution in every case and never require women to confront their harassers, then the prospects for social change will be very dim. Patriarchy is not likely ever to be eradicated if it is never resisted.

There is also a concern that obliging women to resist sexual harassment risks shifting the moral burden away from harassers and onto their victims. The men who sexually harass women do not just fail to fight patriarchy; they actively perpetuate it. If saying that women have an obligation to confront men who sexually harass them even *appears* to diminish the moral culpability of men who are guilty of contributing to patriarchy, there is a serious reason to think that we shouldn't be doing this. There is a real concern that thinking about women's obligations to resist their oppression in the way I am advocating might be blaming the victims and unfairly shifts the burden of rectifying the wrongs of patriarchy onto those who suffer under it, instead of onto those who benefit from it.

In the same vein, there also seems to be something deeply unfair about saying that being harassed gives women a special obligation to fight oppression that is somehow different from everyone's general obligation to fight oppression. Sexist oppression is clearly unjust; is it not the case that everyone is *equally* obligated to fight it? Is society in general not remiss if it does not reform itself so that it neither allows nor tolerates sexual harassment? If the obligation that women have to fight their own oppression is somehow different from the obligations that everyone else has, then there is a concern that women who neglect this obligation will be seen as morally derelict, in a way that others are not. Further, remember that even men who do not actively contribute to patriarchy still benefit from it. Social institutions, such as the family, the academy, and the workplace in general, favour sexist and nonsexist men alike. Feminist men can refuse to benefit from some of the advantages patriarchy offers them, such as their assumed exemptions from the lion's share of household duties and childcare responsibilities. But other advantages, such as men's increased earning power, social mobility, and relative sense of security that comes from not having to fear being raped, cannot easily be given up, if they can be given up at all. Because men benefit from patriarchy, they are almost certainly better situated to fight it than women; why not think this gives *men* a special obligation to fight women's oppression? Similarly, why not think that women who are otherwise relatively privileged in virtue of intersectional considerations such as race, class, and sexual orientation have a special obligation to fight oppression on behalf of women who do not enjoy such privileges and are thus likelier to be harmed by sexist oppression as well? In other words, why not focus on the obligations that *bystanders* have to resist oppression, instead of the obligations of those who are oppressed?[25]

To be clear, I certainly do not mean to imply that men, relatively privileged women, or bystanders in general are excused from their obligations to fight sexist oppression. Make no mistake, those who do not resist patriarchy are neglecting a moral obligation to fight injustice. Society in general has an obligation to divest itself of unjust institutions. Women are certainly not the only ones who have an obligation to oppose patriarchy. But I am also no apologist for patriarchy. I do not want to excuse or justify the ways in which it harms women. If it turns out that one of the ways that patriarchy harms women is that it burdens them with unfair obligations, then this is just one more reason to eliminate it. I think there is good reason to believe that women's obligations to resist their oppression – and thus to confront their harassers – *are* unfair. But unfair obligations are obligations nonetheless.

An objection: autonomy and responsibility

James Stacey Taylor has pointed out that there is a potential ambiguity in my claim that sexual harassment can undermine women's autonomy.[26] I might be making the rather strong claim that this loss of autonomy renders women less able to *make their own decisions* than they would have been before this loss. In the Frankfurtian terms that are popular in the literature on personal autonomy, this loss of autonomy would make women "wantons" – agents who are less able to make their own decisions because they are less able reflect on their desires and consider whether they wish to act to satisfy them.[27] Or, Taylor argues, I might instead be making a weaker claim, that sexual harassment renders women less autonomous insofar as they are less able to *exercise* their autonomy. In this interpretation, sexual harassment would not actually affect women's internal ability to reflect on their desires and decide what they would like to do, but it would affect their external ability to successfully achieve the satisfaction of these desires. Taylor argues that, properly speaking, this loss of autonomy would not really make women less autonomous, because it would not affect their ability to decide what they would like to do. Instead, it would merely restrict the available avenues open to women to actually express their autonomy.

Taylor goes on to argue that the first way of interpreting my claim that sexual harassment can make women less autonomous is implausible, because these harms are not usually severe enough to completely destroy women's ability to make their own decisions. And he argues that the second way of interpreting my claim that sexual harassment makes women less autonomous, while plausible, does not support my claim that women are morally obligated to resist sexual harassment in virtue of their moral obligation to protect their autonomy because it does not establish that sexual harassment actually makes women less autonomous. After all, he points out, not being able to successfully fulfil all of one's autonomously chosen desires is a very different (and, presumably, much less severe) harm than not being able to autonomously form one's desires in the first place.

> [Women's] autonomy is compromised only in that they are less able to exercise it insofar as the patriarchal society in which they find themselves restricts the options for the expression of their autonomy that are open to them. But such restriction does not render them any less morally responsible for their decisions and actions, even if it might mitigate their culpability for some of them.[28]

This less severe harm is not sufficiently restrictive to affect one's moral responsibility for one's actions, he argues, and I need to establish that women's responsibility is affected by sexual harassment in order to establish my conclusion that they have an obligation to resist it.

Further extrapolating on this connection between autonomy and responsibility, Taylor goes on to appeal to a distinction that Marina Oshana makes between local and global autonomy. According to Oshana, the scope of local autonomy consists of individual acts, while the scope of global autonomy consists of the general "direction of one's life." Taylor affirms Oshana's view that only local autonomy is necessary for moral responsibility. To support this view, Oshana argues that we intuitively would think that even a slave – an agent with virtually no global autonomy – is locally autonomous, and thus morally responsible with respect to behaviour such as loving and nurturing his children, as long as "his capacities for love and nurturance have not been obliterated or misshapen by his situation."[29] Taylor argues that, because the only plausible interpretation of my view is that the sexist oppression that sexual harassment contributes to affects women's global autonomy and not their local autonomy, my argument that women have an obligation to resist sexual harassment because they have a responsibility to protect their very capacity to be morally responsible fails.

Responses to Taylor

I have a number of responses to Taylor's criticisms. First, I want to express doubt about whether the distinction between global and local autonomy can be made as cleanly as he and Oshana suggest. What is the freedom to make decisions about the direction of one's life, really, except the cumulative freedom to make decisions about individual acts? I think it is clear enough what the latter freedom consists of, but I am wary of their claim that there is a difference in kind between this kind of freedom and the freedom to make decisions about one's life. Because of our own temperaments, we philosophers probably tend to mistakenly assume that people have the temperament to engage in far more reflective decision-making about the direction of their lives than the vast majority of people actually do. Because of our own privileges, we also probably tend to mistakenly assume that people have a great deal more control over the direction of their lives than the vast majority of people actually do. I think a great deal more needs to be said about exactly how much control over the direction of one's life is required, or how much reflection needs to take place, for an individual to possess global autonomy. If, for example, global autonomy requires a perfect lack of unwanted outside restrictions, or perfect existential responsibility, virtually no one will count as globally autonomous.

Now, given that Taylor and Oshana do not think that moral responsibility requires global autonomy, perhaps they would be comfortable with this conclusion. But I think there are significant problems with their pretending that there is a sharp line to be drawn between global and local autonomy, and with their pretending that attributions of moral responsibility pertain only to the latter. Instead, it is more helpful to think of attributions of both autonomy and obligations as existing in degrees, mitigated by the concrete social circumstances in which the agent finds herself. This means that I reject Taylor's characterization of my argument as asserting that oppression affects only global autonomy. I am arguing that sexual harassment and other manifestations of oppression are capable of undermining both the local and the global autonomy of the agents they affect. We looked at some of the ways this can happen above, and will look at a great many more in the following chapters.

Given this, I want to deny that Taylor's central distinction – between the autonomous ability to internally reflect on one's desires in order to make decisions and the autonomous ability to externally achieve the satisfaction of these desires – plays out under actual oppressive circumstances in the way he suggests. As we have seen, the problem of adaptive preferences shows that oppression is capable of affecting not only one's ability to successfully enact one's decisions, but also what one actually decides to do in the first place. A proper appreciation of this problem makes clear that we cannot leave the content of people's desires unanalyzed; it shows that oppressive social factors can affect what desires people choose, not just their ability to successfully fulfil these desires. Thus, while Taylor argues that it is implausible to suggest that sexual harassment can make women less autonomous by interfering with their ability to reflect on their own desires, I want to insist that this is precisely what it, in conjunction with other oppressive factors, can sometimes do. Sexual harassment never occurs in a social vacuum; as one of the wires in Frye's birdcage it functions in concert with other manifestations of sexist oppression that can and do undermine women's autonomy.

Sexual harassment's effects on women's autonomy can affect their moral obligations in both of Taylor's cases, whether the harm is that of interfering with women's ability to reflect on their desires or merely their ability to fulfil them. Taylor would be correct to insist that the effect is *greater* in cases where the effect on autonomy is stronger (that is, in those cases where sexual harassment affects women's ability to reflect on their desires), but he is wrong to argue that one's obligations are not affected *at all* in those cases where the effect on autonomy is weaker (that is, in those cases where sexual harassment merely affects women's ability to successfully fulfil their desires). The plausibility of this will be made much clearer, I think, by picking upon a distinction that Taylor introduces but does not explore – the distinction between responsibility and culpability. To unpack this distinction, I turn now to an examination of exactly what the relationship is between autonomy and moral obligation in general.

Autonomy and obligation

In general, we hold people morally responsible only for actions that are undertaken to some degree autonomously. If one has no autonomy, one has no moral obligations; if one is fully autonomous, one is fully subject to all possible moral obligations that might exist in a situation. And if we think that someone is partially autonomous, we might think that she is partially subject to some or all of the potential moral obligations that exist for someone in a situation like hers. Perhaps the appropriate amount of moral obligation to demand of someone is always directly proportional to the degree of autonomy she has. Is this the best way to view the relationship between autonomy and moral responsibility? We might think the two concepts are interdefined, where moral responsibility *just is* what is demanded of autonomous moral agents, and autonomous moral agents *just are* those agents who have certain moral responsibilities. If this is the relationship between the two concepts, it is easy to see why nonautonomous agents are not subject to moral responsibilities, and why fully autonomous agents are fully subject to moral responsibilities. We can even explain those cases of partial autonomy where the amount of moral responsibility is directly proportional to the degree of autonomy. But perhaps the story is not as straightforward as this. In order to see why this could be the case, let us consider more closely what we might mean when we say that an autonomous agent is responsible for her actions.

Sometimes responsibility attributions are intended to indicate that other people are entitled to evaluate the reasons that an agent is capable of providing for her actions. An attribution of this kind of responsibility amounts to an affirmation that an agent is the appropriate subject of praise or blame. Let us call this kind of responsibility *moral responsibility*.[30] Determinations of whether an agent has this kind of responsibility are not matters of degree. This is not to deny that it might be a matter of controversy to explain when and why others are entitled to evaluate an agent's reasons and actions, or to quantify precisely how much reflective ability an agent must have in order to have this kind of responsibility. But, ultimately, these potentially controversial questions have determinate answers, and an agent either is or is not the appropriate subject of praise or blame, and thus either does or does not have this kind of responsibility. Once an agent possesses sufficient rational capacities to pass a particular threshold, she is objectively responsible in this sense. An agent can be held morally responsible for her actions if others are entitled to praise or blame her morally after evaluating the reasons she is capable of providing for her actions.

A different kind of responsibility attribution tracks judgements of the degree to which an agent is morally responsible for her reasons and actions. Let us call this kind of responsibility *culpability*. After affirming that an agent is the appropriate subject of praise or blame, we can go on to judge whether she faces extenuating circumstances that affect how praise- or blameworthy she is. To be perfectly clear, this is not the same as judging how much praise or blame an agent has actually earned; this would be a judgement that morally evaluates an agent's reasons and actions, which is not a matter of attributing moral responsibility to an agent, but of analyzing the moral worth of her reasons and actions after it has been determined that she is in fact a subject who can be held morally responsible. Instead, attributions of this kind of responsibility hinge on judgements that consider whether an agent who is morally responsible has a legitimate excuse that affects how morally culpable she is for her actions. Determinations of whether an agent has this kind of responsibility are matters of degree; different extenuating circumstances will have differing effects on this kind of responsibility.[31] What sorts of extenuating circumstances do I have in mind here? If, for example, we discover that an agent was unaware of what she was doing, we think she is less culpable than if she was operating in full knowledge. If we discover that she was unaware, but could reasonably have been expected to be aware, we think she is more culpable than if she could not have been reasonably expected to have been aware. If we discover that she intended the consequences of her actions we think she is more culpable than if these consequences were accidental. If we discover the existence of certain unjust incentive structures that give her reason to act in ways that she would not have in the absence of such structures, we think she is less culpable. These, and other, extenuating circumstances are all instances of cases where the concrete details of an agent's situation affect determinations of how morally responsible we think it reasonable to hold her, without leading us to judge that she has no moral responsibility whatsoever (that is, without judging that she is no longer the appropriate subject of praise or blame). In other words, these are all cases where we think a morally responsible agent has an excuse that makes her less culpable than she would be in the absence of such an excuse. An agent can be held more or less culpable for the actions for which she is morally responsible, depending on whether she faces extenuating or exculpatory circumstances.

To recap quickly: moral responsibility requires that an agent have sufficient rational abilities such that others are entitled to evaluate the reasons for her actions and praise or blame her accordingly, while culpability requires that the concrete details of a morally responsible agent's situation do not provide her with an excuse that makes her less responsible than she otherwise would be. The relationship between autonomy and these two kinds of responsibility is as follows. Moral responsibility is both necessary and sufficient for autonomy. In other words, we need to determine whether an agent has the rational capacities required to reflect on her reasons for acting, and thus whether she is the appropriate subject of praise or blame, in order to determine whether she is a fully autonomous agent. Autonomy, however, like culpability, admits of degrees. How autonomous an agent is can affect how culpable she is, such as in cases where unjust incentive structures influence an agent's reasons for her actions so strongly that they qualify as coercive. An agent is made less autonomous by such coercions, and this diminished autonomy translates into diminished culpability.

Why exactly do attributions of autonomy track attributions of moral responsibility and culpability in this way? The reason we do not impose moral responsibility on those who completely lack autonomy is that it would be profoundly unfair to require moral obligations of someone who was incapable of actually fulfilling them. And the reason we do impose moral responsibility on those who are fully autonomous is that it is fair to require morally responsible behaviour from someone who is capable of living up to what morality requires of them. This is to say that the judgement of whether an autonomous agent is morally responsible – the judgement of whether an agent is the appropriate subject of praise or blame – is itself a normative judgement. The judgement of how culpable an autonomous agent is for her actions is also a normative judgement, one that looks to considerations of fairness to determine whether extenuating circumstances affect the degree of moral culpability it is fair to impose on an agent. Because culpability and autonomy both admit of degrees, it is possible that they are not always directly proportional to one another. There will be cases in which the appropriate amount of culpability to impose on an agent is directly proportional to the degree of autonomy she has. But there will also be cases in which the appropriate amount of moral culpability to impose on an agent does not appear to be in direct proportion to the amount of autonomy she has.

How does all of this bear on the question of whether women are obligated to resist oppression? In very extreme cases – those where oppression has damaged a woman's rational abilities severely enough that others are no longer entitled to evaluate the reasons for her actions – a woman might not be the appropriate subject of praise or blame. In such cases a woman's autonomy has been damaged to the point where she is no longer morally responsible; thus she cannot have an obligation to resist her oppression because she cannot have obligations at all. Much more commonly, however, oppression will damage a woman's autonomy only to the point where she remains a morally responsible agent, thus has an obligation to resist, but the factors of her oppression lessen her culpability for failing to do so. As we just saw, there can be both practical and normative reasons to vary the amount of moral culpability imposed on a person who is oppressed.

What are we to make of the case of Native Companion in particular? The very fact that we are asking what she is obligated to do here means we are assuming Native Companion is the appropriate subject of praise or blame; she therefore definitely has moral responsibility. If the preceding analysis of responsibility is correct, the question of whether Native Companion has an obligation to resist her sexual harassment really boils down to the question of whether her experience of oppression has undermined her autonomy in such a way as to translate into diminished culpability, or whether other normative considerations affect how culpable she is for resisting or failing to resist these harms. Properly speaking, it is her culpability, not moral responsibility, that is affected by her oppression. Taylor is right that we should not pretend that Native

Companion is rendered completely un-autonomous by her oppression. But it is important to note that, even though Native Companion's oppression is not severe enough to undermine her autonomy to the point where she is no longer the appropriate subject of praise and blame, it does not follow that her autonomy has not been undermined at all. I will further develop my argument for *why* she is obligated to resist this harm in the next chapter. But first I want to begin to address the question of *what* she is obligated to do.

Self-respect, confronting, and resisting

As far as Native Companion and Wallace are concerned, there seem to be just two available options here: confront the carnies or ignore them. Wallace does bring up the possibility of complaining to the fair's management, or filing an injunction and "litigating expensively," but it is fairly clear that he does not really take these more extreme measures to be live options. Thus far, I have been happy to grant this characterization of the situation. I have argued that the relevant duty here is a duty of self-respect, and I have argued that this duty means Native Companion has an obligation to resist her oppression. But I have been assuming throughout that resisting oppression requires confronting sexual harassers, conflating resistance with confrontation.

This assumption fits well with an argument made by Bernard Boxill, who argues that self-respecting people must protest their mistreatment at the hands of oppressors.[32] The point of protesting, Boxill claims, is to express "a righteous and self-respecting concern" for oneself.[33] Elsewhere, he argues that oppressed people have a responsibility "to repudiate the insult and falsehood of oppression" that holds that they are the "tools and dependents" of those who oppress them.[34] Self-respect requires protest not because a protester has a reasonable hope of her protest convincing others that she has rights; Boxill recognizes that this, unfortunately, is far from guaranteed by most acts of protest. He also recognizes that resisting oppression does not necessarily require changing the status quo: "One may resist and fail to stop what one is resisting. The idea of successful resistance is not redundant, and the idea of unsuccessful resistance is not self-contradictory. And there is a profound difference between unsuccessful resistance and no resistance at all."[35] Because protesting is, in many cases, an ineffective means of changing the status quo, or of persuading others to acknowledge that one has value or rights, the point of protest must have something to do with the effect it has on oneself.

Just what this effect is supposed to be is not entirely straightforward, however. Boxill points out that someone can believe perfectly consistently that she has value or rights, even if she does not protest when she is treated in ways that deny this value or violate these rights; she simply has to believe that those who are mistreating her are mistaken in their beliefs about her value or rights. And, as we will consider in detail in the chapters to come, there can be good reasons to refrain from protesting; the incentives or rewards offered to those who acquiesce in their mistreatment, and the punishments attached to protesting, can tempt even self-respecting people into at least to pretending to be servile. But pretending at servility is dangerous, Boxill thinks, because it shakes one's confidence in her self-respect. This, then, is the point of protest: *to assure oneself that one has self-respect.* While protest is an "indifferent way of getting others to acknowledge and thus to confirm that one has worth," it can be "an excellent way of confirming that one has faith in one's worth."[36] Even pretending to be servile can undermine one's confidence in one's value. Eventually this threatens to destroy one's self-respect. Protest is what rights all this, Boxill thinks. A self-respecting person is

> driven to make his claim to self-respect unmistakable. Therefore, since nothing as unequivocally expresses what a person thinks he believes as his own emphatic statement, the ... self-respecting person will declare his self-respect. He will protest. His protest affirms that he has rights. More important, it tells everyone that he believes he has rights and that he therefore claims self-respect.[37]

Because Boxill thinks the duty of self-respect requires protesting one's treatment at the hands of oppressors, he would argue that Native Companion does have an obligation to confront the men who harassed her. He would seem to agree with her characterization of the situation as one in which the two available options are resisting oppression by confronting the carnies or doing nothing and ignoring them.

However, in what follows, I will consider the possibility that while the duty of self-respect does require Native Companion to resist her oppression, this duty might not always require direct confrontation or protest. Protest, as Boxill seems to conceive of it, is an inherently public act: it involves a public declaration that one respects oneself. But, as I will discuss in more depth in the next chapter, protesting is merely one of many different ways to resist oppression. Boxill is correct to argue that protest is the morally appropriate course of action to take in resisting certain cases of oppression. But in other cases, as we will see, resisting one's oppression by protesting publicly can have disastrous consequences. There must be ways to resist one's oppression, I will argue, that do not require one to protest publicly. Resisting oppression thus belongs to a broader category of action than merely protesting it. And, it will turn out, there are often many different ways to resist one's oppression.

Notes

1. David Foster Wallace, "Getting Away from Already Pretty Much Being Away From it All," *A Supposedly Fun Thing I'll Never Do Again* (Boston: Little, Brown, 1997), 101.
2. Margaret A. Crouch, "Sexual Harassment in Public Places," *Social Philosophy Today* (2010): 137. (Emphasis removed.)
3. Bartky, "On Psychological Oppression," 24.
4. Bartky bemoans how women can "become infatuated with [their] female personae and waste [their] powers" trying to attain physical perfection. She describes how the "essentially infantile narcissism" of this internalized sexual objectification is then shattered by unrealistic standards of female beauty; a woman can, quite literally, never be beautiful enough. And she argues that "[a]nyone who believes that such concerns are too trivial to weigh very heavily with most women has failed to grasp the realities of the feminine condition." See Bartky, "On Psychological Oppression," 28.
5. Linda LeMoncheck, "What's Wrong with Being a Sex Object?" *Living with Contradictions: Controversies in Feminist Social Ethics*, Jaggar (ed.) (Boulder: Westview Press, 1994), 199–206, and "The Power of Sexual Stereotypes and the Sexiness of Power," *Sexual Harassment: Issues and Answers*, LeMoncheck and Sterba (eds) (New York: Oxford University Press, 2001), 264–269.
6. See LeMoncheck, "What's Wrong with Being a Sex Object?," 202, 205; and Martha Nussbaum, "Objectification," *Philosophy and Public Affairs* 24 (1995): 249–291.
7. MacKinnon, *Toward a Feminist Theory of the State*, 124.
8. Nussbaum, "Objectification," 250.
9. Wallace, "Getting Away from Already Pretty Much Being Away From it All," 97.
10. Bartky, "On Psychological Oppression," 27.
11. Bartky, "On Psychological Oppression," 27.
12. Crouch, "Sexual Harassment in Public Places."
13. Erving Goffman, *Behavior in Public Places* (New York: Free Press, 1963), and *Interaction Rituals* (New York: Pantheon, 1967).
14. Wallace, "Getting Away from Already Pretty Much Being Away From it All," 101.
15. The most influential defenders of this claim have been Catharine MacKinnon and Andrea Dworkin. See, for example, Catharine MacKinnon, *Sexual Harassment of Working Women: A Case of Sex Discrimination* (New Haven: Yale University Press, 1979); and Catharine MacKinnon and Andrea Dworkin, *In Harm's Way: The Pornography Civil Rights Hearings* (Cambridge: Harvard University Press, 1987); and MacKinnon, *Toward a Feminist Theory of the State*.

16. See Anita Superson, "A Feminist Definition of Sexual Harassment," *Journal of Social Philosophy* 24 (1993): 46–64, and "Right-Wing Women: Causes, Choices, and Blaming the Victim," *Journal of Social Philosophy* 24 (1993): 40–61.
17. Frye, *The Politics of Reality*, 2.
18. Narayan, "Minds of Their Own," 422.
19. Superson, "Right-Wing Women," 40.
20. Susan Wendell has argued for a similar point. See Susan Wendell, "Oppression and Victimization: Choice and Responsibility," *Hypatia* 5 (1990): 15–46.
21. Bonnie Mann, "Creepers, Flirts, Heroes, and Allies: Four Theses on Sexual Harassment," *APA Newsletter on Feminism and Philosophy* 11 (2012): 24–31.
22. Mann, "Creepers, Flirts, Heroes, and Allies," 29.
23. Crouch, "Sexual Harassment in Public Places."
24. Marilyn Frye, "History and Responsibility," *Hypatia* 8 (1985): 215–216.
25. For a fruitful discussion about the obligations that bystanders have to resist oppression, see the symposium discussion between Bernard Boxill, Jean Harvey, Thomas Hill, and Sarah Buss in the *Journal of Social Philosophy* 41 (2010): 1–49.
26. Taylor discusses this ambiguity in his rebuttal of the version of my argument that appeared in Carol Hay, "Whether to Ignore Them and Spin: Moral Obligations to Resist Sexual Harassment," *Hypatia* 20 (2005): 94–108. See James Stacey Taylor, "Autonomy, Responsibility, and Women's Obligation to Resist Sexual Harassment," *International Journal of Applied Philosophy* 21 (2007): 55–63. As will become apparent, I believe that he correctly identifies a problematic vagueness in my earlier argument, but ultimately I do not accept his terms of the debate nor his utilitarian alternative to my Kantian account.
27. See Harry G. Frankfurt, "Freedom of the Will and the Concept of a Person," *Journal of Philosophy* 68 (1971): 5–20.
28. Taylor, "Autonomy, Responsibility, and Women's Obligation to Resist Sexual Harrassment," 6.
29. Marina Oshana, "Autonomy and Free Agency," *Personal Autonomy: New Essays on Personal Autonomy and Its Role in Contemporary Moral Philosophy*, Taylor (ed.) (Cambridge: Cambridge University Press, 2005), 202, n. 18.
30. This conception of moral responsibility owes much to P.F. Strawson's account of reactive attitudes. See P.F. Strawson, "Freedom and Resentment," *Proceedings of the British Academy* 48 (1962): 1–25.
31. For discussions of this phenomenon, see Sarah Buss, "Justified Wrongdoing," *Noûs* 31 (1997): 337–369; Anita Superson, "The Deferential Wife Revisted: Agency and Moral Responsibility," *Hypatia* 25 (2010): 253–275; and Susan Wolf, "Asymmetrical Freedom," *The Journal of Philosophy* 77 (1980): 151–166.
32. Bernard R. Boxill, "Self-Respect and Protest," *Philosophy and Public Affairs* 6 (1976): 58–96.
33. Boxill, "Self-Respect and Protest," 61.
34. Bernard R. Boxill, "The Responsibility of the Oppressed to Resist Their Own Oppression," *Journal of Social Philosophy* 41 (2010): 10.
35. Boxill, "The Responsibility of the Oppressed to Resist Their Own Oppression," 7.
36. Boxill, "Self-Respect and Protest," 66.
37. Boxill, "Self-Respect and Protest," 67.

4
The Obligation to Resist Oppression

In 1944, the year after the Great Bengal Famine, 45.6 per cent of widowers surveyed ranked their health as either "ill" or "indifferent." Only 2.5 per cent of widows made the same judgement. This subjective ranking belied their actual situations since, as a group, the widows' basic health and nutrition tended to be particularly abysmal. These women were starving and yet most of them claimed not to be sick. One explanation for this unwarranted stoicism is that, unlike men who were similarly situated, these women reacted to the scarcity of food by coming to believe that what little food there was should not be wasted on them.[1] This is (literally) a textbook case of the problem of adaptive preferences; the reason the Bengali women formed these desires while the men did not is that they had already internalized prevalent sexist social mores that granted women's interests less importance than men's.[2] Because these women did not believe their interests mattered as much as others', they did not experience their starvation as worth complaining about.

It is a terrible thing that, to satisfy the less dire needs of the men around them, these women were willing to give up the food that they needed to live. And it is a terrible thing that this happened because these women came to believe that their own needs were unimportant when compared to those of men. But I also think that the women had something to answer for. Rather than standing up for themselves, they accepted starvation. And, when they were being conditioned by sexist social norms to think that this was right, they did not (or did not effectively) reject this idea. In short, while these women were terribly wronged by an oppressive society, they also wronged themselves by failing to resist this oppression.

That it is wrong to oppress others, to take the food they need or deny them the social conditions necessary for the self-respect they deserve, is hardly controversial. But that those who are oppressed can also do wrong in not resisting their oppression is rather more so.³ In this chapter I defend this claim; I argue that people have an obligation to resist their own oppression and that this obligation is rooted in an obligation to protect their rational nature. This defence will rely on the Kantian moral framework that was defended in Chapter 2. Rather than focusing on how oppression can affect autonomy and responsibility, as I did in Chapter 3, I focus here on how oppression can affect rational nature. First, I present a Kantian account of the obligation to resist one's oppression as an obligation oppressed people have to protect their rational nature; next, I defend this Kantian account by demonstrating some of the ways oppression can harm people's rational nature; and finally, I show how the obligation to resist one's oppression need not be as overly onerous as it might initially appear.

The obligation to resist one's oppression

The usual reason to think that someone's acquiescence in her or his oppression is morally problematic is other-oriented. By acquiescing in oppression, one might argue, someone is at least failing to help, and quite possibly actually *harming*, other people.⁴ This idea has merit. After all, no one is oppressed in a social vacuum. The extent to which an individual goes along with her own oppression typically affects the oppression of others who share her social category. Accepting one's oppression can make oppression appear acceptable, or, even worse, it can make oppression appear not to be oppression at all.⁵ And doing this is no better than endorsing oppression: sending the message that it is permissible to treat me in these ways in virtue of my being a woman sends the message that it is permissible to treat others in these ways in virtue of their being women as well.

But there is also a self-directed account of the obligation to resist one's oppression. Someone who is oppressed should stick up for herself, you might think, because, by acquiescing in her oppression, she is behaving in a way that is wrong regardless of how others are affected. The claim that women have special obligations to themselves under oppression that are in some way obligations to the self is not unprecedented in the feminist canon. Mary Wollstonecraft, one of feminism's earliest writers, argued that women ought not to abide by conventional social mores that valued them solely for their beauty and charm. Following on the heels of the Enlightenment, Wollstonecraft extended the ideals of rationality and individualism to women. She argued that women's primary obligation is to themselves as rational beings and that fulfilling this obligation requires resisting many of the conventional gender roles prescribed by genteel society:

> The being who discharges the duties of its station is independent; and, speaking of women at large, their first duty is to themselves as rational creatures, and the next, in point of importance, as citizens.... The rank in life which dispenses with their fulfilling this duty, necessarily degrades them by making them mere dolls.[6]

Elizabeth Cady Stanton, another early advocate of women's rights, is famously said to have declared that "self-development is a higher obligation than self-sacrifice."[7] As we saw in Chapter 2, Cady Stanton's dedication to the cause of American women's suffrage led her to speak out against prevailing social expectations that pressured women to sacrifice their interests for the interests of their family. Women have an obligation to themselves, she argued, to put their interests first, to develop their talents and abilities in order to be able to participate as the full members of democratic society she knew they were capable of being.

Simone de Beauvoir ushered in the Second Wave of feminism by arguing that women who consent to their oppression fail in their obligation to themselves to live existentially authentic lives. In explaining why, unlike members of other oppressed groups, women have not resisted their oppression, de Beauvoir argued that women acquiesce in their oppression because to do otherwise would be to renounce the few advantages they *do* get from their oppressive relationships with men. Acquiescing in their oppression not only affords many women some degree of material protection, it also allows women to avoid taking existential responsibility for their lives. De Beauvoir believed, along with many other existentialists, that living an existentially authentic life can be difficult, even terrifying. Most people, existentialists believe, are cowardly and prefer to avoid taking on the responsibility of defining for themselves what their lives will be about. But the act of making self-defining choices is what existentialists take to be distinctive of an authentic human existence. Social roles in general are existentially problematic; in effect, they make these self-defining choices for people inauthentically. But women's social roles are particularly problematic, de Beauvoir argues, since women's socially prescribed gender roles offer them very few, if any, opportunities to make existentially authentic choices. When women take on the role of a wife or a mother, their lives become completely defined by their relationships to their husbands or their children. In effect, women lose their sense of self; they become an "Other," in de Beauvoir's terms. But adopting the role of the Other is easier, and less frightening, than carving out for oneself a life that has value and meaning. This is why it can seem like an advantage for women to acquiesce in their oppression by taking on these roles. De Beauvoir condemns this failure to take existential responsibility for oneself as a form of cowardice and argues that, essentially, women have an obligation to reject the conventional gender roles that lead them down this path.

> To decline to be the Other, to refuse to be party to the deal – this would be for women to renounce all the advantages conferred upon them by their alliance with the superior caste. Man-the-sovereign will provide woman-the-liege with material protection and will undertake the moral justification of her existence; thus she can evade at once both economic risk and the metaphysical risk of a liberty in which ends and aims must be contrived without assistance. Indeed, along with the ethical urge of each individual to affirm his subjective existence, there is also the temptation to forgo liberty and become a thing. This is an inauspicious road, for he who takes it – passive, lost, ruined – becomes henceforth the creature of another's will, frustrated in his transcendence and deprived of every value. But it is an easy road; on it one avoids the strain involved in undertaking an authentic existence.[8]

This is, of course, far too quick a sketch of these feminists' accounts. I mean only to show here that they are historical examples of feminists who have advocated different versions of the claim that people have an obligation to themselves to resist elements of their own oppression. The distinctiveness of my account here will thus not be the claim that women have an obligation to themselves to resist their oppression – this much has been argued by others – but rather that this obligation to the self is of a particular sort. That is, I argue that this obligation is best thought of as akin to a Kantian obligation of respect for one's own rational nature.

Remember, Kant's case for our obligations to ourselves, like his case for our obligations to others, begins with the value of our rational nature. Kant's argument for why rational nature in general is valuable relies on his second formulation of the Categorical Imperative, also known as the *Formula of Humanity*. This formulation of the Categorical Imperative famously commands you to "Act so that you use humanity in your own person, as well as in the person of every other, always at the same time as an end, never merely as a means" (G 4:429). The ground, or explanatory justification, of this moral principle, according to Kant, is that "[r]ational nature exists as an end in itself" (G 4:429). Kant says that insofar as we are rational we must conceive of ourselves as having a rational nature, and we must recognize that our rational nature confers upon us a value that requires that we always be treated as an end and never merely as a means. That is, insofar as we are rational we must view our rational nature as conferring on us a value that restricts the ways we may be treated. The obligation of self-respect, then, is an obligation to recognize the value of the rational nature within us and to respond accordingly. This obligation is an instance of the more general obligation to respect rational nature, wherever one finds it.

As we saw in Chapter 2, there are other Kantian accounts of why people have an obligation to recognize the value of their rational nature and to respond appropriately to that value, the most influential of which is found in Thomas Hill's "Servility and Self-Respect." The moral failing of servility, remember, is that a servile person fails to fulfil the obligation of self-respect by failing to properly respect her equal status under the moral law. Regardless of whether any particular case of servility is blameworthy, Hill thinks it is morally objectionable, "at least in the sense that it ought to be discouraged, that social conditions which nourish it should be reformed, and the like."[9] And, insofar as servile behaviour represents a failure of the obligation of self-respect, Hill seems to imply that servile people have an obligation to change their behaviour. But, while Hill recognizes that servility is a moral failing, he does not come out and say explicitly that people have an obligation to resist this moral failing.

Although I am deeply sympathetic to Hill's account, the account that I defend here differs from his in several respects. One difference has to do with their relative scopes: because Hill's focus is on servility rather than oppression, his account will apply to a different class of cases than mine. This is because it is possible for there to be both cases of acquiescing in one's oppression that do not involve servility, and cases of servility that do not involve acquiescing in one's oppression. The problems of servility and acquiescing in one's oppression are closely related, to be sure, but the two are conceptually distinct. Another difference between our accounts is that mine attempts to flesh out what respecting rational nature actually requires of us in a way that Hill's does not. If you focus exclusively, as Hill does, on how acquiescing in one's oppression is a failure to respect the value of one's rational nature, then you might overlook some of the concrete ways one's rational nature can actually be *harmed* by this acquiescence. These are moral harms that deserve to be taken very seriously. For this reason, I argue that once we recognize that rational nature can be harmed by oppression we will see there is an obligation not merely to *respect* rational nature but also to *protect* it. Hill's focus is on the *attitudes* one must have toward rational nature; my focus is on the particular *actions* one must take to actually protect this nature.

A clear virtue of Robin Dillon's analysis of these issues, on the other hand, is that it details exactly how oppression can undermine the self-respect of those who are oppressed. Her account also gestures toward an explanation of why having self-respect is incompatible with acquiescing in one's own oppression. Like mine, her arguments owe much to Hill's, and are rooted firmly in the Kantian tradition. But, ultimately, Dillon's focus has more to do with articulating the practical effects that oppression can have on self-respect than it does with articulating a theoretical justification for the importance of self-respect under oppression; on this latter count she is content to rest with the assertion that self-respect is "bound up with," or "inextricably connected with," morally important features of people who are oppressed. Furthermore, while she defends the importance of self-respect, and while she shows how oppression can function to damage self-respect, like Hill, Dillon does not argue explicitly for an obligation to resist this damage. My account differs from Dillon's, then, because this is precisely the obligation I mean to establish.

So I want to tell a somewhat different story, but one that also draws heavily from Kant. I argue that if Kant is right and our rational nature has ultimate value, then we ought to protect this nature by protecting all of it, including our capacity to act rationally. Oppression can harm rational capacities in a number of ways, we will see. Because one has an obligation to prevent harm to one's rational nature, and because oppression can harm one's capacity to act rationally, one has an obligation to resist one's oppression. What I am doing here is applying the Kantian obligation to respect rational nature in ways that have not been recognized before. In identifying the possibility that oppression can harm people's rational capacities, I have uncovered a new class of instances that the general Kantian obligation to respect rational nature can be applied to. This application should be of special interest to feminist theorists, and to any others interested in oppression more generally.

Of the various things that might be controversial about this line of thought, one that might stand out at this point is the claim that oppression harms one's capacity to act rationally (or at least often does so in familiar contexts of oppression). The goal of what comes next, then, is to show how oppression harms oppressed people's capacity to act rationally.

How oppression harms rational nature

Departing somewhat from many interpretations of Kant, I contend that we should think of our capacity for practical rationality as an ordinary human capacity, as susceptible to harm as many other human capacities.[10] Our capacity for practical rationality can be harmed when damage is done to either our capacities to form reasonable practically relevant beliefs, or to our capacities to form reasonable – that is, consistent – intentions on the basis of these beliefs, or to our capacities to practically deliberate from beliefs to intentions. Our capacity for practical rationality can also be harmed when we face illegitimate restrictions on the full and proper exercise of these capacities. For clarity's sake, I will refer to the former sort of harm – when one's rational capacities are prevented from functioning in a way that also threatens their future functioning – as *damage* to one's rational nature, and the latter sort of harm – when one encounters an unfair temporary interference with the full exercise of one's rational capacities – as a *restriction* on one's rational nature. The line between these two sorts of harm will not always be completely clear, but this vagueness is unimportant given our purposes here because both sorts of harm are seriously morally problematic.

Now, if development through childhood builds our rational capacities, and trauma or neglect tears them down, then why not think that other forces are capable of affecting them as well? Oppression is one such force, I argue; it can damage someone's rational capacities so thoroughly that her ability to act rationally is severely, sometimes permanently, compromised. And oppressed people face restrictions on their ability to exercise their rational capacities even more frequently than they face full-fledged damage to these capacities. There are a number of different ways that oppression can affect our capacity for practical rationality. I discuss several of them next.

Oppression can cause self-deception

A classic form of practical irrationality occurs when someone acts irrationally because she is deceiving herself. Oppression can cause self-deceptive behaviour because oppressive social systems create incentives for oppressed people to believe certain falsehoods about themselves, contrary to their own evidence. A particularly interesting example of this is given by Elizabeth Anderson, who shows how contradictory sexist norms of femininity and sexuality can cause women to become "radically self-deceived" about their motivations for some of their actions.[11] Anderson focuses on the case of women who seek abortions after having failed to use contraception. Despite not wanting to become pregnant, these women do not use contraception, Anderson argues, because doing so would force them to see themselves as "sexually active, receptive to sexual advances from strange men, taking sexual initiatives, [and] exercising agency with respect to their sexual choices."[12] And these women do not want to see themselves in these ways because they are in the grip of other norms of femininity that are inconsistent with this picture of sexual agency. These women are "caught between contradictory norms of femininity: one that tells them it isn't nice to have sex without intimacy; another that tells them it isn't nice to refuse their date's sexual demands unless they have a good excuse; [they are thus] heteronomous agents self-destructively caught between contradictory external norms."[13] To put the point more concretely, these women deceive themselves about the likelihood that they will have sex and so do not take steps to provide for contraception. But this is irrational behaviour since they do not want to become pregnant and they also do not take abortion to be as good a method for dealing with unwanted pregnancy as contraception. This irrational behaviour is evidence that these women have undergone harm to their rational nature.

Oppression can harm capacities for rational deliberation

Another way oppression can harm people's capacity to act rationally is by harming their capacities for rational deliberation. This sort of harm can affect someone's capacity for determining which means will allow her to achieve the ends she has set, or it can affect her capacity for determining which ends to set in the first place.[14]

Harm to someone's capacity for instrumental rational deliberation could result, for example, from depriving her of the basic educational resources needed at key developmental stages to fully develop these skills.[15] This sort of harm could also result from the long-term cognitive damage that results from malnutrition – something possibly experienced by some of the Bengali women we considered earlier – or, in extreme cases, from language deprivation in early childhood. Members of oppressed groups are significantly more likely to be deprived of these various resources. The terror or trauma oppressed people can experience when they face violence, or even the threat of violence, can also impair their rational capacities. Harm to rational capacities can also result when someone is institutionalized, medicated, or lobotomized, or from extreme cases of depression. Oppressed people are more likely to face such adversities.[16]

Harm to an oppressed person's capacity to use means-ends reasoning could result if her independence is not fostered; if someone is always dependent on others to do things for her, her ability to figure out how to do things for herself can become impaired. If the means to your ends must always be to ask someone else to do it for you because you are unable to do it yourself, this could eventually permanently impair your capacity to determine how to do things on your own. And even in cases where one's rational capacities are not permanently damaged, insofar as this lack of independence places unfair limits on the means that are available to someone in the pursuit of her ends it is a restriction on the exercise of these capacities. When oppression takes the form of infantilization, these harms can happen all too easily.

Harm to someone's rational capacity to choose certain valuable ends in the first place can result from oppression because oppression can make it less likely that the oppressed will imagine or conceive of various choices as live options for people like them. This, we have seen, occurs when internalized oppression results in the problem of adaptive preferences. Internalized oppression can damage or restrict people's sense of self-worth, so they do not set certain worthwhile ends for themselves because they do not think they deserve them. This can also happen when someone internalizes social roles that rule out various lifestyle choices as inappropriate or undesirable for people like her. In a related manner, when an oppressed person has internalized the belief that she is inferior to others, she can be more likely to set ends that fail to protect her future well-being; such ends, many philosophers think, are irrational because it is a requirement of practical reason that people have prudential regard for their future well-being.[17]

Oppression can cause weakness of will

Weakness of will – *akrasia* – is a matter of deciding what one has reason to do in a given situation, deciding to do it, but then doing something else instead because one has given in to countervailing pressures that have been brought on by various nonrational considerations. One way oppression might cause someone to do this turns on the self-fulfilling prophecies that can result when people who are oppressed internalize derogatory stereotypes that depict people like them as lazy or impetuous or irresponsible. Someone who has internalized such stereotypes just might not hold herself to very high standards of rationality and thus might be more susceptible to succumbing to weakness of will in various circumstances. If you know that others expect people like you to succumb to certain temptations, you might eventually come to expect yourself to succumb, and it can be that much harder to resist such temptations when they arise.

Another example of how oppression can cause weakness of will can be found in the case of the abortion-seeking women we considered earlier.

At least some of these women consent to unwanted sex, Anderson claims, because they cannot see how to say 'no'. One explanation of what has gone on here is that they suffer from weakness of will inculcated by having internalized social norms that fail to teach women to stand up for themselves. These women recognize that they have good reason to refrain from having sex but succumb to their partners' sexual demands nevertheless. And engaging in this irrational behaviour is evidence that their rational nature has been harmed in some way.

An objection from standpoint theory

Before moving on, I would like to briefly consider an objection that is motivated by certain concerns that standpoint theorists have raised. The central insight behind standpoint theory is what Alison Wylie has called an "inversion thesis":

> those who are subject to structures of domination that systematically marginalize and oppress them may, in fact, be epistemically privileged in some crucial respects. They may know different things, or know some things better than those who are comparatively privileged (socially, politically), by virtue of what they typically experience and how they understand their experience.[18]

This inversion thesis suggests that people who live at the margins of society – people who are oppressed in virtue of, say, their class, race, gender, or sexual orientation – are actually better situated to know certain things. These people's marginalization makes them likely to be discredited epistemically because they are often seen to be uneducated, or uninformed, or unreliable. But marginalization can actually confer epistemic advantage, standpoint theorists argue. Living one's life at the margins of society can put someone in a position to know things that more privileged people usually do not know, or things they have a vested interest in not knowing, or things they have a vested interest in systematically ignoring or denying. This is especially true when it comes to knowledge about oppressive social structures. Because oppressed people do not have an interest in maintaining an oppressive status quo, it is easier for them to understand how oppression works.

Given the considerations brought to light by standpoint theorists, then, a critic might claim that my account has things exactly backwards. I have argued, remember, that the reason people have an obligation to resist their oppression is that oppression harms people's rational capacities.

This harm can make oppressed people act in practically irrational ways. But, if you take standpoint theory seriously, you might think it is not the members of *oppressed* groups who are in danger of acting irrationally; it is the members of *oppressor* groups.[19] Furthermore, it might be charged that, because my account focuses on the ways oppression can damage people's rational capacities, it is, in effect, guilty of carrying on the tradition of epistemically discrediting people who are oppressed.

To respond to these objections, I want to emphasize certain clarifications of standpoint theory that theorists such as Wylie have been careful to articulate. Early standpoint theorists often said things to suggest that marginalized standpoints are *universally* epistemically advantaged.[20] But it is a mistake, Wylie claims, to think that the epistemic advantages of marginalization are automatic, or that they are all-encompassing. While not denying that the marginalization that results from oppression can confer certain epistemic advantages, Wylie points out that oppression can sometimes put people at an epistemic disadvantage as well. Oppressed people often lack access to formal education, for example, and this deprivation can affect the kinds of information they have access to, the kinds of theoretical or explanatory tools they have at their disposal, and their ability to develop various analytical reasoning skills. Many of the harms to oppressed people's rational capacities discussed above can also be understood as examples of the ways that oppression can put oppressed people at an epistemic disadvantage. There are, in short, things that oppressed people will not be able to know because of the effects of oppression on their rational capacities.

In agreeing with Wylie here, I am perhaps just reasserting my claim that oppression harms people's rational capacities. But I am also insisting that this claim is not in conflict with the tenets of standpoint theory, properly understood. Standpoint theorists need not exaggerate the epistemic advantages of oppression. Focusing on the ways oppression harms oppressed people's rational capacities risks contributing to the tradition of epistemically discrediting these people, I will admit. But this is a risk I am willing to take, for the only alternative is to pretend that these harms are not really there. Ignoring these harms will not make them go away. But identifying them, and working to eradicate them, might.

Four objections from demandingness

We have just seen that oppression can damage or restrict one's capacity for practical rationality in a number of ways, and thus harm one's rational nature. Because there is an obligation to protect one's rational nature, in cases where oppression harms rational nature, one has an obligation to protect oneself from these harms. But what exactly does this obligation require? In most circumstances the most practical way to protect one's rational nature from the harms of oppression is to *resist* this oppression. What, then, is someone obligated to do when she is obligated to resist her own oppression, and when is she so obligated? Just how demanding is this obligation? Given the moral seriousness of these harms, there is good reason to think that someone is obligated to resist her oppression whenever she is oppressed. But, if this is the case, then, given the ubiquity of oppression and the resilience of the systems that produce it, the obligation to resist one's own oppression would be very demanding. Probably too demanding, in fact.

There is a real concern, I concede, that my account might be guilty of demanding too much of people. We just cannot be obligated to resist our oppression at *every available opportunity*, the thought might be. Nor can we be obligated to do *whatever it takes* to resist oppression. In many oppressive contexts, actively resisting oppression can be dangerous or counterproductive; resistance can be exhausting, victimizing, and can subject someone to retribution from others. In these sorts of cases, it looks like *not* resisting your oppression is a better way to protect your rational capacities from oppression's harms than resisting it is. In other cases, resistance might simply be impossible and, given the ubiquity of oppression, it is probably not logistically possible to resist its every manifestation; given the severity of some oppressive harms, a victim might be rendered incapable of resistance; given the social nature of oppression, resistance might require the cooperation of others who are unwilling to help; given the mystification of oppression, someone might not even realize she is oppressed and, as we all well know, if someone *cannot* do something then it cannot be that she *ought* to do it. And in virtually every case, defending an obligation to resist oppression seems to be tantamount to blaming the victim. If there is an obligation to resist oppression, after all, then it seems that those who fail to resist their oppression will be the appropriate subjects of blame. Finally, one might argue that resisting one's oppression is supererogatory rather than obligatory. Resisting one's own oppression is heroic, certainly, but it is simply not reasonable to say that failing to resist makes someone immoral or blameworthy.

These various objections can be classified into four broad categories: (1) *the objection from risk*; (2) *the objection from blaming the victim*; (3) *the objection from ought implies can*; and (4) *the objection from supererogation*. Let us now consider these four objections in more detail.

The objection from risk

According to the objection from *risk*, there cannot be a general obligation to resist oppression because resisting oppression can sometimes endanger the victim. The thought here is that, because in certain oppressive contexts taking action to protect one's rational capacities can be dangerous or counterproductive, *refraining* from acting to protect one's rational capacities might actually be the best way to *protect* them. Sometimes *not* resisting your oppression can be a better way to protect your rational capacities from oppression's harms than resisting it. The dangers of resisting oppression could take the form of harms that are purely mental, or they could take the form of mental harms that are physically induced. These dangers could come from being made to experience feelings of exhaustion or victimization, or they could come from facing the retribution of others. All of these possibilities have to do with this obligation's apparent requirement to resist oppression in every instance, whenever one is able.

For example, attempting to resist *every* instance of oppression – by, say, attempting to neutralize or dismantle every oppressive social institution, or by attempting to change the behaviour of every single oppressor – could be potentially exhausting or could lead to a sense of victimization that could leave oppressed people unable to appreciate their own potential for resisting oppression. Feelings of exhaustion or victimization could, in effect, damage oppressed people's rational capacities by leading to depression or feelings of helplessness that could undermine their ability to set or pursue their ends. This might be what Native Companion, who we considered in Chapter 3, has in mind when she expresses her desire to do nothing to resist her oppression at the hands of the carnies. Perhaps she recognizes on some level that, because oppressive situations like this one are so common, being required to mount resistance to every situation like it would be exhausting or victimizing. This exhaustion could, for example, make it difficult for someone to do what she judges to be best because she lacks the energy or inner strength to act effectively on her judgements; this kind of exhaustion would thus be conducive to a kind of practical irrationality. This victimization could, for example, make it difficult for someone to do what she judges to be best because her trust in her ability to make her own decisions has been undermined; this kind of victimization would thus be conducive to a kind of practical irrationality.

Perhaps what Native Companion is chafing against, then, is the implication that she could be obligated to do something that would subject her to these sorts of harms. In cases like this, it seems, resisting oppression does not necessarily protect one's rational capacities. So, because obligating people to resist their oppression would sometimes be obligating them to undergo a particular kind of harm to their rational capacities, and because the obligation here is supposed to be an obligation to *protect* these capacities, there cannot be a general obligation to resist oppression.

In addition to the harms that result from having to resist oppression in *every instance*, there are other harms that could result from attempting to resist certain *specific* instances of oppression. The cases I have in mind are those where resistance could expose oppressed people to severe physical harm, to death, or to expulsion from their only community. Should the Bengali women discussed above resist their oppression they could face serious consequences. If these women were to stand up for themselves – by, say, vocally demanding their fair share of the limited resources available to them – they could be perceived as disobedient or unruly and could face retribution from people keen to remind them of their place. They could risk beatings, expulsion from their community, even murder. Their external actions could subject their children to these risks. These retributive harms could, among other things, damage these women's rational capacities. So, again, because obligating people to resist their oppression would sometimes be obligating them to undergo harms to their rational capacities, and because the obligation here is supposed to be an obligation to *protect* these capacities, there cannot be a general obligation to resist oppression that is based on the obligation to defend one's rational capacities.

The objection from blaming the victim

According to the objection from *blaming the victim*, an obligation to resist oppression is unfair because the victim has not done anything wrong. Given that someone who has been oppressed has been subjected to a moral harm, I admit that it seems strange to suggest that this imposes moral obligations on the victim, instead of the perpetrator. After all, an oppressed person has already suffered harms in virtue of her oppression; obligating her to resist this oppression would seem to unfairly impose further burdens upon her. Anita Superson makes such an argument. She argues that women who acquiesce in their oppression by conforming to patriarchal gender roles ought not to be blamed for this acquiescence. Superson thinks this is the case even though she admits that this acquiescence contributes not only to the oppression of those who conform, but also to the oppression of all women. She argues that it is unfair to say that these women have an obligation to resist oppression because "their choice of lifestyle, and the values and beliefs accompanying it, ... takes place in the context of severe restrictions of their freedom caused mainly by patriarchy. Their lifestyle, in turn, significantly limits their choices further."[21] To say that they have an obligation to change is to "expect them to act in ways that restrict their choices even further," and would be tantamount to blaming the victim.

But what, exactly, is wrong with blaming the victim? Jean Harvey argues that all morally objectionable practices of blaming the victim share three features in common: first, someone (the victim) is harmed in some way; second, in attempting to explain the harm, the victim is focused on in an "inappropriate and typically unflattering way"; and third, the act of blaming the victim is itself damaging to the victim.[22] Victim-blaming can be morally objectionable in a number of ways, Harvey argues. It is morally objectionable to blame a victim who is innocent, for example, whether the accusation is one of negligence or something worse. It is morally objectionable to shift some or all of the moral accountability away from the perpetrator who has actually harmed the victim. It is morally objectionable to claim that some nonmoral failing on the victim's part played a major role in the situation. It is morally objectionable to pretend that a victim has the power to do something safely about the situation, when she does not. It is morally objectionable to urge a victim into problematic relationships with other people or into a diminished moral status within her community at large. And it is morally objectionable to urge a victim to do things that will ultimately diminish her self-respect.

If an obligation to resist oppression results in the victims of oppression being blamed in any of these morally objectionable ways, that would be reason to reject the existence of such an obligation. And there is certainly a danger of this happening. If there is an obligation to resist oppression, after all, then those who fail to resist their oppression will be the appropriate subjects of blame. This would be to blame the victims of oppression for failing to live up to certain of their obligations. The concern, then, is that failing to live up to the obligation to resist oppression would result in oppressed people being blamed in one or more of these morally objectionable ways.

The objection from ought implies can

According to the objection from *ought implies can*, the obligation to resist oppression founders on logistical considerations. In many different oppressive social situations, for any one of a number of different reasons, an oppressed person simply cannot resist her oppression. And, the argument goes, if someone *cannot* resist her oppression then it cannot be that she *ought* to.

One reason it might be logistically impossible to resist oppression has to do with how prevalent oppressive social institutions are. Frye's birdcage analogy, considered in Chapter 1, illustrates just how ubiquitous oppression is; the harms of oppression surround a victim like the wires in a cage. Oppression infects virtually every aspect of its victims' lives: it is present in institutional structures, in interpersonal interactions, and even in the very ways they are able to think, speak, and feel. Its effects are present in the family, in the academy, in religion, in popular culture, in the workplace. Given this ubiquity, one might hold that it is just not logistically possible for someone to resist oppression by attempting to neutralize or dismantle every oppressive social institution. There simply are not enough hours in the day. And so, if one cannot resist oppression then it cannot be that she ought to.

Another reason it is sometimes not logistically possible to resist oppression is that in some cases resisting oppression requires the cooperation of others. Sometimes there is literally nothing one can do to resist one's oppression unless other members of one's oppressed group are willing to resist as well. Cudd gives an example of this sort of case:

> If you are the only worker at the plant who is willing to strike, then it cannot be a duty for you to strike, since your action will likely be ineffective even in sending a message of revolt (for example, if you just look like a shirker). And if striking (when others strike) is the only course of resistance in this case, then it cannot be a duty to resist.[23]

Because an individual worker cannot strike alone – because her actions *will not count* as striking unless other people take similar actions – her successful resistance is, in an importance sense, contingent on the actions of others. The point here, to be clear, is not simply that *effective* resistance requires solidarity from others; the point is that regardless of how effective your actions are in affecting an oppressive institution, the actions will not even *qualify* as resistance unless others are resisting with you. In such a case, if others are unwilling to cooperate, then one cannot resist her oppression. So it cannot be that she ought to.

A final reason it is sometimes not logistically possible to resist oppression is that the harms of oppression can damage someone's rational capacities so severely that she is incapable of resisting. Severe harms to someone's capacity for rational deliberation, of the sort we considered above, could have this effect. Deprivation of the basic educational resources needed at key developmental stages; long-term cognitive damage resulting from malnutrition at key developmental stages; extreme dependence resulting from infantilization; internalized feelings of worthlessness; depression; incapacitation resulting from being institutionalized, medicated, or lobotomized: these, and other, effects of oppression could render someone literally unable to resist. Severe cases of oppression can so thoroughly damage an oppressed person's rational capacities that acts of resistance are not merely *difficult* for her but are actually *impossible*. And, again, if one cannot resist oppression then it cannot be that she ought to.

The objection from supererogation

According to the final objection I want to consider, resisting oppression is *supererogatory* rather than obligatory. The objection from supererogation shares with my account the recognition that resisting one's oppression is sometimes possible, and when so, is a morally good thing to do. But, instead of characterizing resisting oppression as an obligation, a proponent of this view contends that resisting oppression is, in general, better thought of as supererogatory. This is because such a proponent thinks there are various reasons to think that there cannot be a general obligation to resist oppression. The clearest proponent of the supererogatory view of resisting oppression is Cudd.[24] Cudd explicitly denies that resistance to oppression is always obligatory. Instead, she argues that one has an obligation to resist oppression *only* when failing to do so harms other members of one's oppressed group. When there is a duty to resist oppression, then, this is a duty one has to others, not a duty one has to oneself. In cases where acquiescing in one's oppression harms only oneself, resistance is *supererogatory* rather than obligatory.

Cudd's justification for finding it implausible that people could have an obligation to resist their own oppression appeals to certain practical considerations. Many of these considerations are actually versions of the other objections we have just considered. Cudd argues, for example, that because oppressed people are often not in a position to know that they are oppressed – because "it is often a part of their oppression that it is hidden from them under the guises of tradition or divine command or the natural order of things"[25,26] – it will be difficult for these people to know how to go about resisting their oppression. She also points out that the pervasiveness of oppression means that it is impossible for someone who is oppressed to resist all of it simultaneously. And, as we just saw, she points out that because effective resistance to oppression is sometimes only possible in concerted effort with others, individual members of oppressed groups are powerless to resist unless other members of their oppressed group act in solidarity with them. These are all versions of the objection from *ought implies can*. Furthermore, Cudd argues that the coercive nature of oppression – the fact that oppressed people are put in oppressive circumstances through no fault of their own – should mitigate oppressed people's responsibility to ameliorate the situation. This is a version of the objection from *blaming the victim*.

These practical considerations are sufficient to undermine the possibility of there being a general obligation to resist one's oppression, Cudd thinks. But she admits that resisting one's own oppression is usually still a good thing, despite being unwilling to argue that oppressed people are obligated to resist. In general, then, she thinks resisting one's oppression is, at most, *supererogatory*. There are certain cases of oppression, however, for which Cudd doesn't think the obligation to resist is merely supererogatory. The cases she has in mind are not those where failing to resist oppression harms oneself – these seem to be harms Cudd is willing to let people undergo willingly – but those cases where failing to resist oppression harms *others*:

> In [certain cases of] oppression ... the alternative to resistance is participation in the oppressive institution. *By participating in an oppressive situation, one lends some strength and stability to it, perhaps even legitimates it to some degree*. ... One has only two options in such cases: resist or strengthen the unjust institution. Thus, in [these] cases of oppression ... *failing to resist harms others*.[27]

Resistance to oppression in cases like these is not supererogatory, Cudd thinks. When failing to resist oppression amounts to participation in and legitimization of oppressive social structures that harm all members of an oppressed group, each individual member of that group has an obligation to resist. But it is important to notice that the obligation here is one oppressed people have to each other, not one they have to themselves. Insofar as an act of resisting oppression stands to benefit only the individual performing it, the resistance is perhaps morally praiseworthy but it is never morally required. So, even for the overlapping cases where both Cudd and I agree that people have an obligation to resist oppression, Cudd's account of *why* they have this obligation differs from mine. For her, the duty to resist oppression is a duty one has to prevent harms to others, not a duty to prevent harms to oneself. Cudd thinks resistance to one's own oppression is, in general, *supererogatory*.

To address these various lines of objection, in what follows I argue that the obligation to resist one's own oppression is an *imperfect duty* and that, as a result, someone is not obligated to do whatever it takes to resist her oppression; and it might be that she is not obligated to resist at every available opportunity either.

Imperfect duties

I will argue below that there are many different forms that resistance to oppression can take. Thinking about the obligation to resist one's oppression in this way – as an obligation that can be fulfilled by more than one kind of action – makes this obligation what Kantians call an *imperfect duty*. The distinguishing characteristic of imperfect duties is that they permit a wider range of acceptable actions in fulfilling them than is the case for perfect duties.[28] This is because (unlike perfect duties) imperfect duties are not, strictly speaking, duties to perform specific *actions*. Rather, imperfect duties are duties to adopt certain *general maxims*, or principles of action. These maxims can be satisfied by more than one action. Imperfect duties thus allow a latitude of choice that perfect duties do not. To say that the duty to resist one's oppression is imperfect, however, is not to suggest that it is less stringent or less important than other duties. Instead, calling this duty imperfect means there is a strict duty to set the end of resisting one's own oppression, but there can be more than one way to go about pursuing this end. What the imperfect duty to resist one's oppression rules out is the refusal to do anything to resist one's oppression. That is, it rules out acquiescing in one's own oppression.

That imperfect duties permit latitude in action is not a matter of dispute. But exactly how much and what kind of latitude these duties have is very much up in the air. Kant says that imperfect duties "cannot specify precisely in what way one is to act" (*MM* 6:390) and "cannot specify precisely...how much one is to do" (*MM* 6:390). This might lead us to think that there is nothing more specific to be said about the particular actions prescribed by the different imperfect duties or about how often we have to act or how much we have to do to fulfil them. What is clear is that there is no general story to be told about the latitude that various imperfect duties have. Instead, we have to look at the duties individually since different imperfect duties have different kinds and degrees of latitude.

In what follows, I will focus on two different kinds of latitude in action that can be permitted by imperfect duties.[29] One kind of latitude someone might have is latitude to decide between various different ways of acting in a particular situation to satisfy the maxim required by an imperfect duty. Call this kind of latitude *latitude in which action to take*. Someone could fulfil the imperfect duty to be beneficent, for example, by working at a soup kitchen or by donating to Planned Parenthood or by giving used clothing to the Goodwill. The duty of beneficence does not require any of these acts in particular; it just requires that one do *something* that is beneficent. Because imperfect duties are duties to adopt general maxims, not duties to perform specific actions, all imperfect duties permit this kind of latitude. A second kind of latitude someone might have is latitude to choose either to perform, or to refrain from performing, an action on a particular occasion, so long as she stands ready to perform the given sort of action on at least some other occasions. Call this kind of latitude *latitude in refraining from action*. Someone could count as fulfilling the imperfect duty to be beneficent, for example, even if she refrained from performing all of the above-mentioned beneficent actions on a given occasion, as long as she does not always refrain from acting beneficently.

Before we consider whether, and to what extent, the imperfect duty to resist oppression permits these two different kinds of latitude, I want to take a step back to consider a potential objection to my characterization of this duty as imperfect. Remember, I am characterizing the obligation to resist one's oppression as an obligation to protect one's rational capacities from the harms of oppression. Given that the obligation to respect these capacities is supposed to be the duty that grounds all others in the Kantian picture, it might come as a surprise that I characterize the duty to resist one's oppression as an *imperfect*, rather than a *perfect*, duty. One might think that the fundamental importance of rational nature should mean that we have a strict, exceptionless duty to protect it.

It is fairly clear that Kant himself would insist that the duty to respect humanity is perfect. In the *Doctrine of Virtue*, for example, he says that we have a perfect duty to ourselves to preserve our animal nature, that is, to avoid "*depriving* oneself (permanently or temporarily) of one's *capacity* for the natural (and so indirectly for the moral) *use* of one's powers (*MM* 6:421)." This duty to not deprive yourself of your rational capacities is a *perfect* duty, Kant says. Allowing your rational capacities to be damaged is a kind of self-mutilation, which is a failing akin to suicide. This passage alone fairly definitively rules out the possibility that Kant himself would be happy to call the duty to resist one's oppression (as I have characterized it, as a duty to protect one's rational capacities) an imperfect rather than a perfect duty. Depriving yourself of the capacity for the use of your rational powers is, for all intents and purposes, the very harm we have been concerned with here: it is letting your rational capacities be damaged. A second example that bolsters the case for thinking that Kant would characterize the duty to resist oppression as perfect rather than imperfect can be found in what he says about the duty to avoid servility. The vice of servility, remember, amounts to a public and systematic willingness to disavow one's equal moral status; I argued in Chapter 2 in favour of a duty to resist these failures of self-respect that are brought about under oppression. Kant says explicitly that the duty to avoid the vice of servility is perfect (*MM* 6:434–436). Given that Kant is so clear about both these points, I am forced to concede that Kant would think the duty to resist one's oppression is a perfect duty. Nevertheless, while Kant himself would characterize this duty as perfect, I hope to make a case for a Kant*ian* to be able to characterize it as imperfect.

The first consideration that supports interpreting this duty as imperfect has to do with how Kant characterizes the difference between perfect and imperfect duties. Much of what Kant says suggests that he thinks of the difference between perfect and imperfect duties as a matter of *degree* rather than *kind*. Kant compares various duties as wider or narrower relative to each other. He says, for example, that the duty to respect others is "*narrow* in comparison with the duty of love, and it is the latter that is considered a *wide* duty" (*MM* 6:449–450). He also says, for example, that, "[t]he wider the duty,...the more imperfect is a man's obligation to action" (*MM* 6:390). In general, Kant speaks of duties as "wid*er*" and "narrow*er*," not "wide" or "narrow." This picture is one where duties fall on a scale of wideness and narrowness and where the line between perfect and imperfect is not necessarily a clean one. Certain duties are clearly perfect and permit no latitude in action; others are clearly imperfect and permit a great deal of latitude. But some duties are somewhere in between. Given that I will end up characterizing the duty to resist oppression as a relatively narrow imperfect duty – permitting quite a bit of latitude in which actions fulfil it, but relatively little latitude in refraining from action – my account of this duty should count as Kantian, even if Kant himself would characterize things slightly differently. Interpreting the difference between perfect and imperfect duties as one of degree rather than kind means that the difference between Kant's perfect duty to protect one's rational capacities from mutilation and my relatively narrow imperfect duty to protect these capacities from the harms of oppression need not amount to a repudiation of my Kantian approach.

A second consideration that supports interpreting this duty as imperfect has to do with what Kant says about other imperfect duties we have toward rational nature. While we cannot avoid interpreting Kant as saying we have a perfect duty *not to harm* rational capacities, we can still, at the same time, interpret him as saying we have an imperfect duty to *foster* these capacities. We just saw that Kant says we have a perfect duty not to harm our rational capacities; he thinks depriving oneself of the capacity to use one's rational powers is akin to murdering oneself and that we have a perfect duty to ourselves not to let this happen (*MM* 6:421). Elsewhere, however, Kant says that we have various *imperfect* duties with respect to our rational capacities: an imperfect duty to perfect these capacities in ourselves (*MM* 6:387, 393, 445–447); and an imperfect duty to beneficently encourage the development of these capacities in others (*MM* 6:388, 449–450). The imperfect duties of self-perfection and beneficence can be thought of as duties to *foster* rational capacities, in ourselves and others. We can thus show that the duty to resist oppression can be an imperfect duty by showing that *protecting* rational capacities is closer, in terms of the latitude it permits, to *fostering* them than it is to *not harming* them.

We can interpret beneficence as a duty to foster the rational capacities of others by focusing on how it requires taking the ends of another as your own (*MM* 6:449–450). Taking another's ends as your own – being concerned with their happiness and well-being – involves helping them achieve whatever it is they have decided they want to achieve (*MM* 6:388). But this is usually, among other things, to help them foster their rational capacities.[30] We saw above that Kant characterizes the duty of beneficence as a *wide* imperfect duty that permits latitude in which actions to take (because which actions you take to fulfil this duty will depend, in part, on what the other person's ends are) and in not having to act in every instance (because, at the very least, one is not bound by beneficence to expend so many of his resources that "he himself would finally come to need the beneficence of others" (*MM* 6:454)). If the duty of beneficence is, in part, a duty to foster others' rational capacities, then it follows that Kant thinks that our duty to foster others' rational capacities is imperfect. From this, we can infer that he could agree that our duty to *protect* others' rational capacities – at least in cases where only a small, incremental harm is at stake – is similarly imperfect. For the same reasons that he thinks there should be many ways we can act to fulfil the duty to foster others' rational capacities, and for the same reasons that he thinks we do not have to act in every instance to fulfil the duty to foster others' rational capacities, Kant could agree that the duty to protect others' rational capacities permits these kinds of latitude. But I will leave this claim undefended, because the duties we are most interested in are duties one has to oneself. It is enough here to notice that there is room for a Kantian to defend the view that the duty to protect other people's rational nature permits as much latitude in action as the duty to foster their rational nature.

Let us move on, then, to consider what Kant says about the duties we have to foster our own rational nature. It is reasonable to think that the imperfect duty of self-perfection includes, as one aspect, a duty to foster one's own rational capacities. This interpretation makes sense if we think of the duty of self-perfection as a matter of cultivating our various powers for the sake of our rational nature. Kant says there are two kinds of duties of self-perfection: the duty to perfect our *natural talents* and the duty to increase our *moral perfection*. The duty to perfect our natural talents requires us to develop our mental and physical capacities – everything from analytical skills, memory, and imagination, to powers of the body – so that we are as well-prepared as possible to do that which makes us distinctively valuable (that is, to set ends) (*MM* 6:392, 445). The duty to increase our moral perfection requires us to strive to act always from duty – to have the incentive of our actions be only the moral law, to do what is right for its own sake (*MM* 6:393). Kant characterizes both of these duties of self-perfection as imperfect, and thus both as permitting latitude in action. When it comes to the duty to develop our natural talents, we have latitude in which action to take because which capacities we cultivate will depend on which ends we have, and we have latitude in refraining from action because we do not need to act in every possible instance to cultivate our powers (*MM* 6:392, 446). When it comes to the duty to increase our moral perfection, we might not have much latitude in refraining from action, but we have at least some latitude in which action to take because there is no one way to go about becoming a better person that will work for all people (*MM* 6:393, 447).

If this interpretation of the duty of self-perfection as, in part, a duty to foster our rational capacities fits plausibly within a Kantian framework, then a Kantian can characterize our duty to foster our rational capacities as imperfect. This opens up the possibility that our duty to *protect* our rational capacities could be similarly imperfect. Just as the imperfect duties of *fostering* our rational capacities can permit latitude both in which action to take and which to refrain from, the imperfect duty of *protecting* our rational capacities can permit a similar degree and kind of latitude. I will argue next that there are many different ways to protect our rational capacities in oppressive contexts, and thus many different actions that count as fulfilling the duty to protect them. There might even be reason to think that we can protect rational capacities in oppressive contexts without acting in every instance, and can thus fulfil the duty to protect them while refraining from action on occasion.

Latitude in which action to take

What are the different sorts of actions one could take to fulfil the obligation to resist oppression? One could resist oppression by participating in some form of *activism* intended to engage with, and ultimately change, the social norms, roles, and institutions that make up an oppressive system. In at least some cases oppressed people can directly confront the individuals who are actively oppressing them. Oppressed people can also give time or money to organizations that are dedicated to dismantling oppressive social institutions. Sometimes oppressed people can both empower themselves and undermine the effectiveness of oppressive social roles by reappropriating derogatory stereotypes or language. People have attempted to do this (not uncontroversially[31]) with words like "bitch," "nigger," and "faggot." In some cases oppressed people can take part in oppressive social institutions in ways that demonstrate that such institutions need not necessarily be oppressive. One could, for example, enter into a marriage of mutual respect (one where both partners were committed to ensuring that each partner had an equal opportunity to pursue meaningful life projects and that the inevitable sacrifices and compromises of family life did not unfairly disadvantage one partner over the other) and thereby show that the institution of marriage itself is not necessarily oppressive, even if its most conventional forms function to entrench sexist oppression. In other cases activist resistance can take the form of sabotage from within an oppressive institution. Activism can also be a matter of publicly refusing to accept humiliation from one's oppressors, as in the following incident described by Nelson Mandela about the beginning of his incarceration at the hands of the apartheid South African government:

> As we walked toward the prison, the guards shouted "Two – two! Two – two!" – meaning we should walk in pairs.... I linked up with Tefu. The guards started screaming, "Haas!...Haas!" The word haas means 'move' in Afrikaans, but it is commonly reserved for cattle.
>
> The wardens were demanding that we jog, and I turned to Tefu and under my breath said that we must set an example; if we give in now we would be at their mercy....
>
> I mentioned to Tefu that we should walk in front, and we took the lead. Once in front, we actually decreased the pace, walking slowly and deliberately. The guards were incredulous [and said]...we will tolerate no insubordination here. Haas! Haas! But we continued at our stately pace. [The head guard] ordered us to halt and stood in front

of us: "Look, man, we will kill you, we are not fooling around.... This the last warning. Haas! Haas!

To this I said: "You have your duty and we have ours." I was determined that we would not give in, and we did not, for we were already at the cells.[32]

Activist resistance such as this not only preserves one's dignity by refusing to accept the subhuman identity imposed by one's oppressors; it can also set an example for others.

Another way to resist oppression is to *opt out* of oppressive social norms, roles, and institutions. Oppressed people could boycott an oppressive institution, for example. Or they could opt out of oppressive social norms by refusing to conform to conventional modes of dress or behaviour as, for example, when someone refuses to identify with conventional gender norms and instead presents herself as androgynous or as opposite to the gender she has been assigned. Another option for oppressed people is to isolate themselves from their oppressors to foster solidarity with other members of their oppressed group. This sort of opting out could be as radical as lesbian separatism or as moderate as creating a women's-only space on a college campus. Opting out can also occur when oppressed people refuse to behave in ways considered appropriate to their social group such as, for example, when women are assertive, confident, or opinionated. Opting out like this can be particularly effective for women, since many of the kinds of practical irrationality to which many women are especially prone in virtue of their oppression are those that involve a lack of confidence, or a lack of willingness to make a scene, or a lack of willingness to make someone else uncomfortable.

Both engaging in activism and opting out are *external* forms of resisting oppression. But resistance to oppression could be *internal* as well; someone could, at least theoretically, fulfil the obligation to respect her rational nature by becoming the sort of person whose rational nature was simply not damaged by oppression, perhaps by building up mental walls against many of the harms. She could educate herself about the potential risks of these harms and be wary of their effects. She could simply refuse to believe what oppressive social messages were telling her about the character or worth of people like her. Insofar as these and other forms of internal resistance succeed in protecting one's rational capacities from the harms of oppression, they would qualify as actions that successfully fulfil the obligation to resist one's oppression. And insofar as these and other forms of internal resistance manifest self-respect, they are probably morally required for other reasons as well, many of which we considered in Chapter 1.

In some cases, when every other form of resistance would subject her to harm (or the serious risk of harm), some form of internal resistance might be the only resistance available to an oppressed person. The Bengali widows we saw earlier could be an example. If risks like the ones faced by these women are attached to resisting externally, one has every reason not to resist externally. But even if these women would be risking harm by resisting oppression externally, they could still tell themselves that they *deserve* the food they are giving up as much as anyone else does and that their survival is as important as anyone else's.

In some cases, there might be nothing an oppressed person can do to resist her oppression other than simply *recognizing that something is wrong* with her situation. This is, in a profound sense, better than nothing. It means she has not acquiesced to the innumerable forces that are conspiring to convince her that she is the sort of person who has no right to expect better. It means she recognizes that her lot in life is neither justified nor inevitable. It means she has resisted internalizing her oppression and resisted forming badly adaptive preferences. There is something importantly self-respecting about engaging in internal resistance, and the possibility of this sort of resistance captures the intuition that there are actions someone can engage in to fulfil the duty to resist oppression even when external resistance is imprudent or impossible.

Admittedly, in many cases it might be difficult to tell whether someone is resisting her oppression internally. Consider the case of Native Companion that we looked at in Chapter 3. Native Companion, remember, argued that there was no point in confronting the carnival workers who harassed her:

> "So if I noticed or I didn't, why does it have to be *my* deal? What, because there's assholes in the world I don't get to ride on The Zipper? I don't get to ever spin? Maybe I shouldn't ever go to the pool or ever get all girled up, just out of fear of assholes?"...
>
> "Assholes are just assholes. What's getting hot and bothered going to do about it except keep me from getting to have fun?"...
>
> "They might ought to try just climbing on and spinning and ignoring assholes and saying Fuck 'em. That's pretty much all you can do with assholes."[33]

The question is how we should best understand Native Companion's responses here. Is she claiming that she has no obligation to resist her oppression in this situation? Or, by refusing to let the carnies get to her, is she actually resisting her oppression internally? We could argue that by refusing to feel humiliated, by refusing to let the carnies dictate when and how she can have fun, and by refusing to believe that their sexually objectifying her demeans her moral status as a person in any way, Native Companion is protecting her rational capacities from the harms of oppression and so is, in effect, resisting her oppression internally. This is a plausible interpretation of what has gone on in this situation, I think. Native Companion is portrayed in this story as someone who is feisty, confident, and self-secure; there is every reason to think she is the sort of person whose rational capacities are not endangered by an isolated incident of sexual harassment.

But an alternative interpretation of what has gone on here that is just as plausible, I think, is that Native Companion is exhibiting either bad faith or ignorance resulting from internalized oppression. She might be unaware of how the systematic nature of oppression means that its harms are likelier to occur corrosively than discretely, and thus that the full extent of its harms cannot be appreciated when looking only at isolated incidents. She might resist characterizing herself as oppressed because she does not want to think of herself as a victim or the men in her life as victimizers. She might be unwilling to give up the few benefits afforded to her by the oppressive status quo. She might have simply accepted the sexist status quo – a status quo where men are free to objectify and harass women and face relatively few consequences – as not merely inevitable but actually not unjust. Native Companion's hypothetical ignorance or bad faith here might be blameless. But she would be mistaken, nevertheless. If this interpretation of the situation is the right one, then Native Companion is not resisting her oppression internally by refusing to let the carnies get under her skin. Rather, she is exhibiting exactly the bad faith or ignorance that we should expect of someone in her circumstances.

The point here is that the very nature of oppression can make it difficult or impossible to tell whether someone is resisting internally or is acquiescing. So, if the only resistance someone is putting up is internal, we might have no way of knowing whether she is fulfilling the obligation to resist her oppression. There will be a fact of the matter here, but we might not have access to it. (To be clear: this is an epistemic point about whether we can know that internal resistance has taken place, not a metaphysical point about whether internal resistance has in fact taken place.) Notice that this possibility holds not only when attempting to determine whether someone else is resisting her oppression; it also holds when attempting to determine whether we ourselves are resisting. You might think that you are resisting your oppression internally – or, if, like

Native Companion, you are not inclined to think about things in terms of oppression, you might think you are being self-respecting or some such thing – but you could be fooling yourself. You could be engaging in *self-deception*, one of the forms of practical irrationality encouraged by oppression. This oppressive harm to our rational capacities can make it difficult to know whether we are fulfilling the obligation to resist oppression if we only resist internally. This gives us good reason to err on the side of caution, to not necessarily trust our gut when we think we are resisting internally, and to resist oppression externally whenever possible, to be sure we are successfully fulfilling this obligation.

Furthermore, internal resistance might be able to protect one's rational nature from the harms of oppression, but it would leave oppressive social structures intact. As I argued above, there are good reasons to think that someone who is oppressed has obligations to other members of her oppressed group to not acquiesce in oppressive social structures, even if these structures are not currently harming her personally. This means that internal resistance, even if successful in protecting one's own rational nature, would usually be insufficient to fulfil every moral obligation of resistance an oppressed person has.

On top of all this, it is psychologically implausible to suggest that successfully protecting one's rational nature solely by means of engaging in internal resistance is a live possibility for most oppressed people. Most people's psychologies are simply not oppression-proof. This is why the harms of oppression are so extensive. So, again, while the obligation to respect one's rational nature in the face of oppressive harms could theoretically be satisfied solely by resisting oppression internally rather than externally, there are epistemic, moral, and practical reasons to think that, in all but the most extreme cases, some degree of external resistance to oppression will remain necessary.

Insofar as these different forms of resistance – internal and external – function to protect one's rational nature while destabilizing or undermining oppressive social structures, they all count as resisting one's oppression. They are thus *sufficient* to fulfil the obligation to resist one's own oppression. (By calling these actions 'sufficient' I do not mean to imply that someone merely has to perform one of them and then she will have successfully fulfilled her obligation to resist her oppression and can go on her merry way and never have to bother resisting ever again. Rather, I mean that they count as one sort of action which, when performed in conjunction with other actions of this sort, successfully fulfil this obligation.) But are any of these forms of resistance *necessary*? Does the obligation to resist one's oppression *require* any of these actions? I contend that, while each of these actions counts as resisting one's oppression, none of these actions in particular is required by the obligation to resist.

Latitude in refraining from action

We have just seen that the imperfect duty to resist oppression permits a great deal of latitude in which action one can take to fulfil it. The question now is whether this obligation ever permits latitude in refraining from acting at all. All imperfect duties have the kind of latitude just discussed; because they are specified quite generally, there will always be more than one action someone can undertake to fulfil an imperfect duty. But some imperfect duties also have a different kind of latitude; it is sometimes permissible to refrain from acting to fulfil some imperfect duties, as long as one does not refrain all the time. The paradigm cases of imperfect duty found in Kant – beneficence and developing one's talents – have this kind of latitude (*MM* 6:392–394, 444–446). But Kant thinks other imperfect duties – respecting others and increasing one's moral perfection – do not have this latitude (*MM* 6:393–394, 446–447). The question here, then, is whether the imperfect duty to resist one's oppression has this kind of latitude. The question is whether, just as someone counts as fulfilling the duty of beneficence even if she does not act to fulfil this duty at every available opportunity, she also counts as fulfilling the duty of resisting her oppression if she does not act to fulfil this duty at every available opportunity. The question, in other words, is whether it is permissible to sometimes sit by and let oneself be oppressed.

To see why a Kantian might think the imperfect duty to resist one's oppression should permit latitude in refraining from action, think for a moment about the erosive effects of water dripping on stone. Just as individual droplets of water that seem not to have any effect on a piece of stone can cumulatively wear it away, rational nature can be harmed in almost invisible increments. So too for oppression. What might seem to be merely the harmless slights or annoyances or inconveniences of oppression can have a cumulative effect on people's rational nature. This analogy illustrates not only how the effects of oppression are as likely to be gradual and cumulative as they are discrete; it also presents us with a case for arguing that people are not obligated to resist *every* instance of their oppression. If you have a piece of stone that has to be protected only from *detectable* erosion, then you obviously cannot let water run over it for any period of time, but any individual drop splashing on it here and there will not be a problem as long as you are careful to not let it happen for too long or too often. So too for the corrosive effects of oppression on one's rational nature; many individual instances of oppression can be borne without discernibly harming one's rational nature, but eventually they will accumulate and discernible harm will occur. This means that the obligation to protect one's rational nature from being harmed by oppression could allow one to refrain from resisting at least once in a while. Because rational nature is so valuable, one needs to err on the side of caution, obviously, and be careful not to let the corrosive effects of oppression accumulate. But it is compatible with an obligation to protect one's rational nature to occasionally fail to resist individual instances of oppression that would end up harming one's rational nature were one to fail to resist them all the time. None of us is so fragile that we cannot bear the stress of an occasional instance of oppression.

This result suggests that the obligation to resist one's oppression might permit at least some latitude in refraining from action. Remember, imperfect duties are duties to adopt a general principle of action, not duties to perform a particular action; this generality means that one can fulfil some imperfect duties without necessarily acting on them at every available opportunity. And it looks like the obligation to resist one's oppression might allow this sort of latitude. Someone can protect her rational nature, and thus fulfil the obligation to protect it, without resisting her oppression at every opportunity, so long as she does not do this so often that the corrosive effects of oppression are allowed to accumulate. This means, for example, that someone like Native Companion could, on occasion, be morally permitted to not do everything in her power to resist her oppression. She could be morally permitted to do nothing in this instance; she could not bother confronting the carnies, and even not bother reporting the incident to their boss. If the erosion analogy is apt, it turns out that "climbing on and spinning and ignoring assholes and saying Fuck 'em,"[34] might be okay, at least once in a while. Maybe sometimes it is true that this is "pretty much all you can do with assholes."[35] The erosion analogy suggests that Native Companion's imperfect duty to resist her oppression should permit her at least some latitude in refraining from action.

To be clear, what this duty does not permit her to do is resist so rarely that the harms of oppression accumulate and damage her rational nature. Because rational nature is so fundamentally valuable, the duty to protect it by resisting one's oppression would obviously have less of this sort of latitude than imperfect duties like the duty of beneficence and the duty to develop one's talents. But unlike, say, the imperfect duty to increase one's moral perfection, which Kant says permits no latitude in refraining from action, it is possible that the imperfect duty to resist one's oppression *could* permit *some* latitude in refraining from action. And, to be clear, this latitude is a possibility because the obligation here is not merely to *respect* one's rational nature, but to *protect* it.

To determine whether the obligation to resist oppression should permit latitude in refraining from action, we need to examine why Kant thinks some other imperfect duties permit this latitude. Kant points out that there are countless ways to fulfil the imperfect duties of beneficence and of developing one's talents, and so we must recognize that our finite, limited nature forces us to choose among these options. It is simply impossible to pursue all the different ways in which we might develop our talents, and if we were to attempt to pursue every one of them we would fail to succeed at developing any of our talents at all. So too for beneficence; we could not successfully act beneficently were we to attempt to help every single other person achieve their ends in every instance. These two imperfect duties permit latitude in refraining from action because the possibility of successfully fulfilling them actually *requires* not acting at every available opportunity. The imperfect duties of respecting others and increasing our moral perfection, on the other hand, do not permit latitude in refraining from action because it *is* possible to successfully fulfil them while acting at every available opportunity.

Is the obligation to resist oppression like this? Is it impossible to fulfil this obligation if we must act on it at every available opportunity? What most strongly motivates the attractiveness of thinking that the obligation to resist oppression should permit latitude in refraining from action, I think, is the very same line of thinking that motivated the *objection from risk* that we considered above, that is, a recognition that there are situations where resisting one's oppression in the wrong way can be dangerous (or at least counterproductive). Because certain actions taken to protect rational capacities can be dangerous or counterproductive if they are taken all the time or in the wrong circumstances, *refraining* from acting to protect one's rational capacities might actually be the best way to *protect* them in certain circumstances. Fair enough. But it would be a mistake to categorize the latitude in question here as latitude in refraining from action. This is because the explanation for why someone is not required to *act* (or is permitted to not act) in these sorts of circumstances is that successfully fulfilling the duty to protect one's rational capacities requires (or permits) that one *not act* in these circumstances. One's failure to act here is thus actually better described as a failure to act *outwardly* or *externally*. One is still acting, in the relevant sense. One has still set the maxim to protect one's rational capacities, and one's behaviour is still in accord with this maxim. It is just that in these circumstances the best way to achieve this end is to refrain from doing anything outward. One recognizes this, and acts accordingly. One is, in short, resisting one's oppression *internally*. It is latitude in which action to take to fulfil the duty to protect rational capacities – the *other* kind of latitude – that explains why one is required (or permitted) to fulfil this duty by refraining from acting externally in these circumstances. Were this to be a case of latitude in refraining from action, one would set the maxim to protect her rational capacities, recognize that the best way to achieve this end in these circumstances would be to take a certain course of action, but then *refrain* from taking this course of action. And that is not what one has done here.

The possibility of internal resistance means that, unlike the imperfect duties of beneficence and developing one's talents, practical considerations do not make the obligation to resist one's oppression impossible to fulfil if acted on at every opportunity. Perhaps this should lead us to say that, because internal resistance is always a possibility, the duty to resist oppression permits *no* latitude in refraining from action.

But why, exactly, must we say that the duty to resist oppression always requires at least internal resistance? Why can we not say that refraining from even internal resistance is sometimes permissible? The erosion analogy establishes as a possibility that there could be cases where someone may not have to do *anything* to resist her oppression because it shows that many individual instances of oppression can be borne without discernibly damaging one's rational nature. But, given that we can account for the most intuitive cases of when it seems that resistance should not be required with the possibility of engaging in internal resistance, the burden of proof is on the person who wants to claim that not even internal resistance is required in a given circumstance. Notice that any argument attempting to claim that not even internal resistance is required in a given circumstance is, in effect, going to be an argument for why someone does not have to be self-respecting in this circumstance. This will not be an easy argument to make. Saying, "I just don't feel like it," or, "It's just not that big a deal," is nowhere near sufficient to establish that one should not have to be self-respecting.

Think again of the other imperfect duties that permit latitude in refraining from action. Even when one permissibly refrains from engaging in a particular action that would fulfil the imperfect duties to be beneficent or to develop one's talents, one must retain a latent recognition that engaging in such an action is a possibility for oneself and that insofar as it would fulfil the duty it would be a good thing to do. One must not deny that such an action would fulfil the duty (even if someone chooses not to volunteer at a soup kitchen she must be willing to recognize that doing so would fulfil the duty of beneficence). And, importantly, one must not deny that the duty is important and that one remains subject to it (even if someone chooses not to be beneficent in this particular instance she must be willing to recognize that beneficence is important and that she is still bound by the duty).

So, if the obligation to resist one's oppression permits latitude in refraining from action, someone who avails herself of this latitude must still be willing to recognize the importance of the obligation to protect her rational nature from the harms of oppression. She must recognize that she remains subject to this obligation. And she must recognize that various actions are open to her to fulfil this obligation, and that they would be good to do, even if she chooses not to engage in them in a particular instance.

Take the case of Native Companion. If her expressed desire to do nothing to resist her oppression at the hands of the carnies is actually a form of internal resistance – perhaps because she recognizes on some level that being required to mount external resistance to every situation like this would be exhausting or victimizing – then she is in the clear. She is fulfilling the duty to protect her rational nature by reserving her energy for more important matters. She is respecting herself by resisting her oppression internally. If, on the other hand, by doing nothing to resist her oppression she is actually refraining from engaging in any sort of resistance, then if this is to be a permissible instance of latitude in refraining from action she must be willing to uphold the importance of resisting oppression, she must recognize that she is subject to the obligation to resist oppression, and she must recognize that the actions she is choosing not to engage in would count as fulfilling this obligation. So, if Native Companion wants to do nothing here because she is unwilling to recognize that she has been subject to oppression, because she is unwilling to recognize that she has an obligation to resist her oppression, or because she is unwilling to recognize the importance of resisting oppression, then this is not a permissible instance of latitude in refraining from action and she has not fulfilled the obligation to resist her oppression. If these are her reasons for refraining from action in this oppressive situation, she is likely to make a similar judgement about the permissibility of refraining from action in other oppressive situations.

Taking claims such as, "I just don't feel like it," or, "It's just not that big a deal," to be good reasons to refrain from action is evidence that one does not properly appreciate the gravity of the situation; it is evidence that one does not properly appreciate the value of her rational nature or the risks her rational nature faces under oppression. And failing to appreciate this will inevitably lead to harms to one's rational capacities. Refraining from internal resistance is thus likely to result in erosive harms to one's rational nature because it is likely that an unwillingness to resist oppression, at least internally, manifests either as a lack of appreciation of the seriousness of the moral harms of oppression or, worse, a lack of self-respect. Cases where one is permitted latitude in refraining from internal resistance will thus be exceedingly rare.

In spite of the evocativeness of the erosion analogy, it is extremely difficult to find practical cases where the imperfect duty to resist one's oppression does permit latitude in refraining from action. Here are a few final possibilities, all motivated by the considerations we looked at above in the objection from *ought implies can*. This objection, remember, contends that the obligation to resist oppression cannot accommodate certain logistical considerations. One of these logistical considerations has to do with how prevalent oppressive social situations are. Given this prevalence, it is simply impossible to resist oppression by attempting to neutralize or dismantle every oppressive social institution. Another consideration is that resisting oppression can be impossible when it has already severely damaged one's rational capacities to the point where acts of resistance are not merely difficult but are actually impossible. Yet another arises when we consider that the obligation to resist oppression seems to require that one is aware of her oppression and of the harm that it poses to her rational nature; in cases where someone does not have this knowledge, then, ignorance of one's oppression should presumably vitiate the obligation to resist it.[36] A proponent of the *ought implies can* objection claims that if one cannot resist her oppression then it cannot be that she ought to resist it. Perhaps these are the sorts of cases where the obligation to resist oppression might permit latitude in refraining from action.

The first logistical consideration – that it is impossible for any one person to single-handedly dismantle oppression – can be dispensed with relatively quickly. This is because the obligation to resist oppression, as I have characterized it here, is not an obligation to dismantle oppression. Rather, the obligation here is to protect one's rational capacities from the harms of oppression. And, while it might not be logistically possible for one person to fix every oppressive institution, it *is* possible for her to at least attempt to protect her rational capacities from the harms of these institutions.

The problem with the next consideration – that oppression can harm people's rational capacities to the point where it is not merely difficult but impossible for them to resist – is illustrated by a concern that Boxill raises about Frye's birdcage metaphor. What is wrong with this metaphor, he argues, is that it can encourage us to think of the victims of oppression as completely incapable of resisting their oppression.

> All similes and metaphors have their limitations and this one is no exception. Birds in a cage flutter futilely against its bars until they drop in exhaustion. The simile invites us to think of the oppressed like those birds, fluttering piteously against their bars until they too drop in exhaustion. Like those birds they can do nothing to resist their oppression and consequently there is no point in posing the question whether they have a responsibility to resist it. But oppressed people are not really like birds in a cage. Perhaps caged birds are condemned to dash themselves against the bars of their cage until they give up, but humans are not.[37]

Instead, people can, and often do, resist their oppression. Of course, we should concede that if severely oppressed people, such as the Bengali women, have had their rational capacities harmed to the point where they are actually *incapable* of resisting their oppression, then clearly it cannot be that they have an obligation to resist. But we need to be careful not to arrive too quickly at the judgement that an individual is incapable of resistance. For example, the case of the Bengali women comes from a larger body of work in which Nussbaum shows how many oppressed people *do* resist their oppression, despite the tremendous odds. Much of Nussbaum's work focuses on highlighting the ways that even severely oppressed people can band together successfully to resist their oppression. Nussbaum concludes, in response to these sorts of cases, that oppressed people can "overcome the greatest of obstacles, showing an amazing courage and resourcefulness."[38] Because they *can* resist, even many people who are severely oppressed are obligated to resist. Of course, we should willingly concede that resistance is not always possible in severe cases of oppression, and if someone is so oppressed that she is literally *incapable* of resisting then she cannot be obligated to do so. But this is a virtue of my account, for it fits with the intuition both that we should hold people responsible for fulfilling their obligations when they are able to fulfil them, and that we should not hold them responsible when they are unable.

The possibility of this consideration vitiating the obligation to resist oppression is further undermined in light of a discussion from Marcia Baron. People often misinterpret Kant's point of the "ought implies can" doctrine, Baron claims. According to her, "ought implies can" does not mean that morality ought not require too much of us; instead, it means that anything that morality requires of us is something we *are able* actually to do. This fits well with a familiar theme in Kant's ethics, that we are often far too quick to find excuses for making exceptions of ourselves from the requirements of morality.

> Kant's famous principle is often cited as support for a claim that we must not regard too much as our duty, but his point was not the contraposition of the dictum – that if we cannot do x, we have no duty to do x – but rather that if we ought to do it, we *can* do it. "When the moral law commands that we *ought* now to be better men, it follows inevitably that we must *be able* to be better men" (R 50–51/46).... Far from endorsing the assumption that acts that are very difficult for us should be regarded as optional, Kant's principle emphasizes that *difficult* does not mean *impossible*.[39]

Baron warns against thinking of acts that are *difficult* for us to perform as if they are *impossible* for us to perform because doing so threatens to undermine our freedom. If we pretend as if our particular inclinations – our "fears, desires, and aversions" – make it utterly impossible for us to perform certain acts, then we are acting as if we are not free. This is clearly something Kant would be loath to accept. Baron refers here to a passage where Kant discusses a person whose Sovereign threatens to kill him unless he makes

> "a false deposition against an honourable man whom the ruler wished to destroy under a plausible pretext: 'that it would be possible for him [to refuse] he would certainly admit without hesitation. He judges, therefore, that he can do something because he knows that he ought, and he recognizes that he is free – a fact which, without the moral law, would have remained unknown to him'" (*CPR* 5:30).

Knowing that we *ought* to do something can be what tells us that we are *able* to do it, Kant thinks. We should not pretend, then, that acts that are difficult for us are actually impossible for us. This further undermines the objection that acts that are difficult for us cannot be required by duty. 'Ought implies can' means not that morality ought not be too demanding, but that it ought not be too lenient. So, then, as long as it has been established that an individual is actually *capable* of resisting her oppression, the mere fact that this resistance will be *difficult* for her is, by itself, insufficient to excuse her from the obligation or to permit latitude in refraining from action to fulfil it.

The final consideration – that if someone does not know that she is oppressed, then it cannot be that she is obligated to resist – also fails to permit latitude in refraining from action to fulfil the obligation to resist oppression. Ignorance of an obligation does not make that obligation disappear. However, this does not prevent us from saying that at least some of the people who are ignorant of their oppression should not have to resist it. Notice that saying that someone who is ignorant of her oppression "should not have to resist it" does not necessarily mean that she is not *obligated* to resist. It might mean, instead, that she has an *excuse* for failing to fulfil this obligation. She might, as we saw in Chapter 3, not be *culpable* for this failure. The obligation to resist one's oppression exists whether someone is aware of her oppression or not. Ignorance of one's oppression can, however, affect whether someone is blameworthy for failing to fulfil the obligation to resist. This is a familiar moral phenomenon – when an agent does something wrong but, for one reason or another, we do not hold her culpable for her offense – and it shows that failing to fulfil the obligation to resist one's oppression does not necessarily mean that one is blameworthy for such a failure. To be clear, the latitude in refraining from action that characterizes some imperfect duties does not amount to permission to fail to fulfil these duties in situations where one *should* fulfil them. We should not try to explain these failures to fulfil the obligation to resist oppression that result from ignorance as permissible instances of latitude in refraining from action. Instead, we should explain failures to resist that result from nonculpable ignorance as cases of nonculpable failure to fulfil the obligation, and failures to resist that result from culpable ignorance as cases of culpable failure to fulfil the obligation. So, for example, if Native Companion's ignorance of her oppression is not her fault, then neither is it her fault that she fails to resist this oppression. But her lack of blameworthiness for failing to fulfil this obligation does not mean the obligation itself goes away. It just means she should not be held morally responsible for her failure to fulfil it.

The erosion analogy shows that it might be compatible with an obligation to protect one's rational nature to occasionally fail to resist individual instances of oppression that would end up harming one's rational nature were one to fail to resist them all the time. But I think it is clear that if the erosion analogy is apt it gets us a really quite limited amount of latitude in refraining from action: because rational nature is so fundamentally valuable one needs to be very careful to not let the corrosive effects of oppression accumulate. This discussion emphasizes just how little latitude in refraining from action this duty should permit. Because the most compelling cases that seem to require latitude in refraining from action are actually addressed by the possibility of internal resistance, even if this duty does permit some of this latitude there is not much reason to want it to permit much of it. Still, because there are many different ways to protect our rational capacities in oppressive contexts, and thus many different actions that count as fulfilling the obligation to protect them, this obligation permits a great deal of latitude in which action to take.

Conclusion

My goal in this chapter was to establish that oppressed people have an obligation to resist their oppression. I set out to do this first by defending the Kantian tenet that the fundamental moral importance of our rational nature means we have an obligation to protect it from harm. Then I showed how the systemic harms of oppression can damage people's rational natures, and showed how this often happens in nearly invisible increments. So, I argued, that under oppressive social circumstances the obligation to protect our rational nature translates into an obligation to resist oppression. And, if we understand this obligation as one that permits different kinds of latitude in action, we need not worry that imposing it on oppressed people would be too onerous.

Notes

1. There might be other ways of explaining the results of this survey; I am merely speculating that the Bengali women held these beliefs about their relative worth. But, given that at least some oppressed people do internalize their oppression in this way – and, as we have seen, this phenomenon is so ubiquitous that most people internalize at least some aspects of their oppression – this speculation is unfortunately neither unreasonable nor unrealistic. There is a philosophical issue here, I contend, regardless of whether my speculations are right in this particular case.
2. See Sen, "Gender Inequality and Theories of Justice," and "Rights and Capabilities."
3. This, of course, is not to suggest that it is *worse* to fail to resist one's own oppression than it is to oppress others. I mean only to argue that it is a moral failing to fail to resist one's own oppression.

4. For example, as we will see in more detail below, Ann Cudd argues that what is wrong when women acquiesce in their own oppression is that doing so strengthens sexist institutions that harm all women. See Cudd, *Analyzing Oppression*, 198–200. Also see her "Strikes, Housework, and the Moral Obligation to Resist," and her "Oppression by Choice."
5. Thanks to an anonymous reviewer for this second point.
6. Wollstonecraft, "Of the Pernicious Effects which Arise from the Unnatural Distinctions Established in Society," 235.
7. Elizabeth Cady Stanton, cited in Judith Nies, *Nine Women: Portraits from the American Radical Tradition* (Los Angeles: University of California Press, 2002), 67.
8. de Beauvoir, *The Second Sex*, xvii.
9. Hill, "Servility and Self-Respect," 95.
10. It might be that Kant himself would not accept the idea that our practical rationality as such is something that admits of improvements or impairments. After all, the very idea suggests that one is not metaphysically free. If this is right, then my view differs from Kant's in this respect; I contend that practical rationality itself can be both harmed and improved. These harms and improvements are analogous to harms and improvements to our memory, imagination, and so on.
11. Elizabeth Anderson, "Should Feminists Reject Rational Choice Theory?," *A Mind of One's Own: Feminist Essays on Reason and Objectivity*, Antony and Witt (eds) (Boulder: Westview, 2002), 369–397.
12. Anderson, "Should Feminists Reject Rational Choice Theory?," 385.
13. Anderson, "Should Feminists Reject Rational Choice Theory?," 386.
14. In characterizing rationality as a matter that concerns not merely the means one uses to achieve one's ends, but also what one's ends themselves are, I am committing myself to the view that certain ends are intrinsically rational and others intrinsically irrational. For an account of how this sort of reason can be involved in determining what ends we set, see Henry Richardson, *Practical Reasoning About Final Ends* (Cambridge: Cambridge University Press, 1997). One implication of committing myself to this view is that my account of rationality is set apart from those that would equate rationality with adaptive behaviour. Such adaptive accounts of rationality would suggest that members of the oppressed act rationally when they "play along" with their own subjugation. The ethical point I would like to advance, however, maintains that such complicity can compromise our rationality by undermining our capacity to set ends for ourselves and to pursue these ends in a purposeful manner.
15. There is evidence to suggest that various factors that bear on people's capacity for rational deliberation – things such as people's talents and their ability to see the value in delayed gratification – are highly dependent on education or training in one way or another. See, for example, J. Currie, "Early Childhood Education Programs," *Journal of Economic Perspectives* 15 (2001): 213–238; J. Currie and D. Thomas, "Does Head Start Make a Difference?," *American Economic Review* 85 (1995): 341–364; E. Zigler and S. J. Styfco (eds) *The Head Start Debates*, (Baltimore: Brookes, 2004). For evidence that what is generally thought of as inborn talent is often actually highly socially determined, see Ericsson (ed.) *Cambridge Handbook of Expertise and Expert Performance* (New York: Cambridge University Press, 2006).

156 *Kantianism, Liberalism, and Feminism*

16. For example, performing the kind of work that women are traditionally held responsible for – work such as routine, repetitive housework – is associated with higher rates of depression. See, for example, R.C. Barnett and Y. C. Shen, "Gender, High- and Low-Schedule-Control Housework Tasks, and Psychological Distress," *Journal of Family Issues* 18 (1997): 403–428; J. Glass and T. Fukimoto, "Housework, Paid Work, and Depression among Husbands and Wives," *Journal of Health and Social Behavior* 35 (1994): 179–191; R. W. Larsen, M. H. Richards, and M. Perry-Jenkins, "Divergent Worlds: The Daily Emotional Experience of Mothers and Fathers in the Domestic and Public Spheres," *Journal of Personality and Social Psychology* 67 (1994): 1034–1046. For discussions of how being oppressed increases one's likelihood of institutionalization, see, for example, R.T. Roth and J. Lerner, "Sex-Based Discrimination in the Mental Institutionalization of Women," *California Law Review* 62 (1974): 789–815; Licia Carlson, "Cognitive Ableism and Disability Studies: Feminist Reflections on the History of Mental Retardation," *Hypatia* 16 (2001): 124–146, and *The Faces of Intellectual Disability: Philosophical Reflections* (Bloomington: Indiana University Press, 2009).
17. See, for example, Thomas Nagel, *The Possibility of Altruism* (Princeton: Princeton University Press, 1970).
18. Alison Wylie, "Why Standpoint Matters," *Science and Other Cultures: Issues in Philosophies of Science and Technology,* Figueroa and Harding (eds) (London: Routledge, 2003), 39.
19. Thanks to members of the audiences at the University of Dayton's 2008 Richard R. Baker Colloquium on the topic of "Building Coalitions Across Difference," and the Society for Analytical Feminism's 2008 conference at the University of Kentucky, for raising versions of this objection.
20. Marxist standpoint theorists, for example, argued that one's social position with respect to material labour necessarily determines one's epistemic position, and the marginalized position of the proletariat gives them epistemic advantages over the bourgeoisie because their ability to understand their exploitation is not clouded by a motivation to maintain a status quo from which they do not benefit. Feminist standpoint theorists, such as Nancy Hartsock, argued that women's experiences surrounding childrearing and other forms of domestic labour result in epistemic perspectives that are systematically different between men and women, and that women's is one that universally confers epistemic advantages in understanding patriarchal institutions. See Nancy Hartsock, "The Feminist Standpoint: Developing the Ground for a Specifically Feminist Historical Materialism," *Discovering Reality: Feminist Perspectives on Epistemology, Metaphysics, Methodology, and the Philosophy of Science,* Harding and Hintikka (eds) (Dordrecht: D. Reidel, 1983), 283–310.
21. Superson, "Right-Wing Women," 40.
22. Jean Harvey, *Civilized Oppression* (Lanham: Rowman and Littlefield, 1999), 79–80.
23. Cudd, *Analyzing Oppression,* 199.
24. Cudd, *Analyzing Oppression,* 187–221.
25. Cudd, *Analyzing Oppression,* 198.
26. Cudd clearly has in mind here something like Sandra Bartky's concept of *mystification,* "the systematic obscuring of both the reality and agencies of

psychological oppression so that its intended effect, the depreciated self, is lived out as destiny, guilt, or neurosis." See Bartky, "On Psychological Oppression," 23.

27. Cudd, *Analyzing Oppression*, 199–200.
28. Kant says imperfect duties leave "a [wiggle-room] (*latitudo*) for free choice in following (complying with) the law, that is, that the law cannot specify precisely in what way one is to act and how much one is to do by the action for an end that is also a duty" (*MM* 6:390).
29. Thomas Hill's account of the different kinds of latitude that could be permitted by Kant's imperfect duties is probably the best accepted in the literature. The two kinds of latitude I focus on here are both articulated by Hill. See Thomas Hill, "Kant on Imperfect Duty and Supererogation," *Dignity and Practical Reason in Kant's Moral Theory* (Ithaca: Cornell University Press, 1992), 147–175.
30. In certain circumstances, helping someone else might actually harm her rational capacities, by encouraging dependence or a lack of self-confidence, for example. Nevertheless, the existence of such cases does not undermine the more general point that, in most cases, the result of beneficently helping other people is that their rational capacities are fostered.
31. There are a number of reasons why this way of resisting oppression could be problematic. One is that attempts at reappropriation might just *reinforce* derogatory stereotypes. Another is that it might be difficult to tell whether someone has really reappropriated derogatory stereotypes, or whether they have merely *internalized* (and thus endorsed) them. A third is that the use of epithets like these might be harmful to other members of the oppressed groups who are either not aware of, or take issue with, the ironic way in which the terms are being used. Thanks to an anonymous reviewer for these suggestions.
32. Nelson Mandela, *A Long Walk to Freedom: The Autobiography of Nelson Mandela* (London: Little Brown, 1994), 297–299. As cited in Morton Deutch, "Overcoming Oppression with Power," March, 2005 http://www.beyondintractability.org/bi-essay/oppression-power (Accessed 24 January 2013).
33. Wallace, "Getting Away from Already Pretty Much Being Away From it All," 101.
34. Wallace, "Getting Away from Already Pretty Much Being Away From it All," 101.
35. Wallace, "Getting Away from Already Pretty Much Being Away From it All," 101.
36. Thanks to two anonymous reviewers for pressing me to answer versions of this question.
37. Boxill, "The Responsibility of the Oppressed to Resist Their Own Oppression," 7.
38. Nussbam, *Sex and Social Justice*, 18.
39. Baron, *Kantian Ethics Almost Without Apology*, 44–45.

5
Respect-Worthiness and Dignity

I hope to have established by now that people who are oppressed have an obligation to resist their oppression. What I want to consider now is what we are to make of people who fail to do so. I have argued that such people are guilty of failing to fulfil an important moral obligation; this makes their behaviour immoral. The question now is whether it is possible for these failures to reach a point where the person committing them no longer deserves moral respect. If this is possible, then there is a concern that past failures to fulfil the obligation of self-respect could vitiate future instances of this obligation. Someone who fails to respect herself might literally become unworthy of respect.

The questions I will take up here are whether someone's self-loathing or servile behaviour can ever undermine the obligations others have toward her, or whether it can undermine the obligations she has toward herself. These are broader, more general, versions of the question of whether people who behave immorally by acquiescing in their oppression risk losing their right to be respected. This more general problem is raised by the issues of oppression that I have been focusing on, but it is a problem, I contend, for anyone committed to a Kantian moral framework, according to which, most scholars argue, it is a person's capacity for moral decision-making that both gives her dignity and makes her deserve moral respect. Whether or not we can solve this problem is, I believe, a deal-breaker for Kantian feminism. The same intuitions that motivate the recognition that it is morally problematic to blame the victim should make us extremely wary of endorsing a moral framework in which acquiescing in oppression could undermine one's right to be not oppressed.

The brief details of my alternative Kantian proposal are as follows. People are worthy of the sort of respect that constrains how they may be treated (that is, in Kantian terms, they are *ends in themselves*, or, are *respect-worthy*) in virtue of something very minimal: their capacity to set and pursue ends according to reason (that is, in Kantian terms, their *humanity*). People have unconditional and incomparable value (that is, in Kantian terms, they have *dignity*), however, only insofar as they successfully exercise this capacity in a particular way, that is, insofar as they act morally (that is, in Kantian terms, insofar as they have *personality*, or *autonomy*). Because Kant is notoriously inconsistent in his terminology, Kant scholars have long puzzled over how best to understand Kant's views on the relationship between respect-worthiness and dignity. What is novel about this interpretation is that respect-worthiness and dignity actually can be separated, and while people have the former merely in virtue of possessing certain quite minimal rational capacities, they have the latter only insofar as they manage successfully to use these capacities in the right way. The view that respect-worthiness and dignity are functionally coextensive has been articulated by such varied commentators as Richard Dean, Paul Guyer, Thomas Hill, Christine Korsgaard, and Allen Wood, among others.[1]

My interpretation flies in the face of all of these views. In effect, I intend to chart a middle ground between the standard Kantian view that a person's dignity is grounded in her rational nature (which view is made problematic after the recognition that Kant himself clearly suggests that a person can lose her dignity), and the more radical view that a person deserves no respect whatsoever unless she is a good person. This interpretation is required, I contend, if we are to offer a satisfactory moral explanation of what is going on when people damage their rational capacities but still warrant our ethical regard. This interpretation also helps make sense of certain provocative passages in the *Metaphysics of Morals* and *Lectures on Ethics* where Kant appears to have different conceptions of the sort of respect he thinks people are owed.

But let us begin with an example of the sort of case I have in mind. "Tralala," one of the short stories in Hubert Selby's *Last Exit to Brooklyn*, is the story of a young woman, Tralala, who lives in Brooklyn in the 1940s.[2] The story begins when Tralala is 15 and discovers that if she has sex with the neighbourhood boys they will buy her cigarettes and take her to the movies. This progresses to helping the boys rob neighbourhood drunks, then to helping them rob soldiers on leave. Tralala often acts as bait, leading these men off to a dark alley or abandoned lot where the boys can jump them. Some of these robberies are brutal. They hit the men over the head with bricks and leave them for dead. Eventually, many of the neighbourhood boys are arrested and Tralala tires of sharing her take with the others, so she starts out on her own. She picks up johns – usually drunken soldiers on leave – waits until they pass out (or hits them over the head with a bottle to speed up the process), and then steals their money. She is young and beautiful and has her pick of the men in the bars she frequents. Months pass, then years. Things spiral downward. She stops having her pick of the drunks in the nicer bars. She loses her fancy clothes. She gets kicked out of the nicer bars. And then the not-so-nice ones. She stops bathing, starts drinking constantly, and will have sex with anyone who will give her a place to sleep for the night. Still she goes on, stealing what she can from whoever she can. One night she finds herself back at the bar where she had started out. The story ends there with a horrifying depiction of Tralala being brutally gang-raped.

Let me tip my hand for the forthcoming discussion of self-respect: there is *nothing* Tralala could have done to deserve this. Certainly, she has behaved immorally on many occasions. In one of the story's most memorable scenes, for example, she laughs at and spits on a sobbing man she has just robbed and whom her friends have just beaten to within an inch of his life. She is callous and heartless; she preys on men who are naïve, weak, and vulnerable. In addition to behaving immorally toward others, we might even think she has behaved immorally toward herself, that she has failed to respect herself by allowing her life to spin out of control, by trading sex for movie tickets, cigarettes, and beer money. But nothing she has done – nothing she *could* do – could justify being gang-raped and left for dead.

The story of Tralala motivates two thoughts, I think. The first is that when someone fails to respect herself she can degrade herself to the point where she has lost something that is of great value. The second is that no matter what someone does, no matter how immoral or degraded she has become, she is still owed a certain kind of respect. I think almost everyone would intuitively chafe against the suggestion that there is anything anyone could do to make it such that we had *no* moral obligations toward her. Even the vilest of people do not forfeit their moral rights. This is because the judgement that someone has acted immorally by failing to respect herself does not, we usually think, undermine the basic moral obligations we have toward her. This much is a moral platitude.

But, I will argue, a surprising implication of the received interpretation of Kant's practical philosophy – where most commentators agree that it is a person's capacity to act rationally that gives her moral value and thus makes her deserve moral respect – is that people who fail to respect themselves can actually fail to deserve moral respect. Though defenders of this received view would be reluctant to concede this, I will demonstrate that it follows from their interpretation that people who fail to act morally can lose whatever value it is that makes them deserve the respect that would constrain others' behaviour toward them. This, clearly, will not do. So I intend to offer an alternative interpretation of Kant's views.

According to this alternative interpretation, the feature of people in virtue of which they have unconditional and incomparable value is not the same feature in virtue of which they are owed the respect that constrains our treatment of them. This means, among other things, that a Kantian can maintain both (1) that someone loses an important sort of value when she acts in certain immoral, self-disrespecting ways; and (2) that no matter how immoral someone is she cannot lose whatever it is that forbids us from treating her however we might like to. Because the reasons in virtue of which people are valuable and that they are owed respect apply in the same way to oneself as they do to other people, this implication applies to the obligations we have to ourselves as well as the obligations we have to others. When someone fails to act morally toward herself, this does not vitiate her obligation to respect herself, even though at the same time her failure to do so does make her lose a certain kind of value. This means that, even though someone who fails to resist her own oppression fails to respect herself in the right way, and even though this failure to fulfil the obligation of self-respect makes her lose a certain kind of value, her obligation to resist her oppression does not go away.

Let me make explicit that I think the analysis I will provide here probably also applies in a straightforward manner to immorality that is directed toward others, not merely to immorality that is self-directed. But, both because I think the problem at hand is most intuitively strong when it comes to self-directed immorality, and because, as we will see, Kant himself seems to think the problem is most acute with respect to self-directed immorality, my central focus will be on failures to treat oneself in a morally acceptable manner, not on failures to treat others acceptably. I should also say that I think the value of what I say here does not hang entirely on whether I can conclusively defend my interpretation of Kant himself. I think something very much like this point was intended by Kant, and I attempt to show that his usage of certain key terms maps on to the distinctions I am making. Still, even if I am wrong and this is not what Kant had in mind, the account I offer here allows a Kant*ian* to explain the intuition that someone's failure to respect herself does not undermine our basic moral obligations to her.

Respect-worthiness and dignity

My Kantian proposal is this. People are worthy of the sort of respect that constrains our treatment of them (that is, they are *respect-worthy*) in virtue of something very minimal: their capacity for setting and pursuing ends according to reason. People have unconditional and incomparable value (that is, they have *dignity*), however, only insofar as they successfully exercise this capacity in a particular way, that is, insofar as they act morally. What is novel about this proposal is that I am suggesting that respect-worthiness and dignity should come apart, and that while people have the former merely in virtue of possessing certain, quite minimal, rational capacities, they have the latter only insofar as they manage to use these capacities in the right way.

Something very much like this idea is behind a distinction that Stephen Darwall has articulated. Darwall distinguishes two very different kinds of respect that can be owed to persons: (1) *recognition respect*, which is a matter of properly recognizing the fundamental features of a person in virtue of which she is owed basic moral respect and respecting her accordingly by being willing to constrain one's behaviour toward her; and (2) *appraisal respect*, which is a matter of evaluating a person's conduct or character and respecting her insofar as she measures up to certain standards of human excellence.[3] Appraisal respect is owed to persons only insofar as they earn it through what they do or who they are and so is a sort of respect that one can lose or have in degrees; by contrast, recognition respect is owed to persons just in virtue of their being persons and so can be neither lost nor had in degrees.

I contend that something very much like this idea – that merely having certain capacities calls for a certain type of treatment and attitudes, while having exercised these capacities calls, in addition, for certain other attitudes and treatment – is actually intended by Kant himself. According to the interpretation I want to put forward, the relevant bits of Kantian jargon that map onto these distinctions are: *humanity* for the relevant capacities; *personality* (or *autonomy*) for the state of those who have exercised them successfully; *end in itself*-hood for the sort of value that calls for recognition respect; and *dignity* for the sort of value that calls for appraisal respect. Kant says that our humanity is an end in itself, and he says that we have dignity insofar as we act morally. Let us look at these claims more closely.

Humanity is an end in itself

Kant's account of humanity explains both why people must be respected and what this respect entails. Humanity, for Kant, is not the whole of human nature, but is, rather, a particular subset of characteristics that are often associated with human nature, specifically, those having to do with *rational* nature. As we will see below, I think it best to understand Kantian humanity in a relatively thin sense as the bare capacity to set and pursue ends. Remember, Kant's Formula of Humanity commands: *"So act that you use humanity, whether in your own person or in the person of any other, always at the same time as an end, never merely as a means"* (G 4:429). And the ground, or explanatory justification, of this moral principle is that *"[r]ational nature exists as an end in itself"* (G 4:429).

The value of humanity, according to Kant, is that it is an end in itself. One of the ways Kant explains what he means in calling humanity an end in itself is by calling it an *objective end*.[4] Objective ends, according to Kant, are "a supreme limiting condition in the use of all means" (G 4:438); they place limits both on what other ends we may set and on what means we may use to pursue them. And the demands that objective ends make on us are necessary; they apply regardless of whether we actually want the end in question. To say that humanity is an objective end, then, is to say that it makes demands on us irrespective of how we feel about it. So one implication of humanity being an end in itself is that there are limits on the ways that beings who possess humanity can be treated. Translating this point into Darwall's terminology, to say that humanity is an end in itself, in the sense of being an objective end, is to say that humanity demands *recognition respect*. The recognition that someone possesses rational nature brings with it an obligation to respect her by constraining our behaviour toward her in certain ways.

When Kant says that humanity is an end in itself, he means to attribute a very particular sort of value to our rational nature, a value that makes it worthy of a kind of respect that places limits on the acceptable ways we can act toward those who have it. But this respect-worthiness is not the only kind of value we have, Kant thinks. We also have what he calls *dignity* or *absolute worth*. As I will argue next, Kant attributes this other kind of value to us not merely insofar as we have humanity, but insofar as we use the capacities that comprise our humanity in a particular way.

Personality has dignity

I just argued that Kant thinks humanity is our capacity to act rationally. Many commentators have argued that Kant means to include in his conception of humanity not just our rational capacities but also the successful exercise of these capacities that culminates in moral behaviour.[5] I want to argue that this way of interpreting Kant conflates important distinctions that are better kept separate.

To see why this is the case, first notice that, despite its potentially misleading label, humanity is just one aspect of human nature. Kant thinks human nature also includes two other distinct elements: *animality* and *personality*.[6] We have animality simply in virtue of being living motile beings; our animality is what explains our instinctual drives. We have personality insofar as we respect the moral law and act from duty alone; as we will see below, personality is what Kant associates with autonomy of the will. Essentially, animality is our capacity to be motivated by instinct;[7] humanity is our capacity to be motivated by reason in general;[8] and personality is what we have when we are motivated by the moral law in particular.[9,10] It is the last two capacities that concern us most here.

When it comes to our moral nature Kant is far less consistent with his terminology than he is with that for our animal and rational natures. We have just seen that Kant refers to our moral nature as our *personality*, but in many other places he identifies our moral nature with our *autonomy*.[11] The will is autonomous, for Kant, when a rational being's capacity to set and pursue his or her own ends results in a form of self-legislation whereby there are certain moral ends that he or she must set for him- or herself.[12,13] We are autonomous, Kant thinks, only when we manage to act morally, when our free wills set and pursue ends that are in accordance with the laws of morality (and are in accordance with our inclinations only contingently, if at all).[14] Many commentators, however, prefer to understand things slightly differently, interpreting Kantian autonomy as the capacity we have to *set* laws for ourselves independent of inclination, without reference to whether we actually choose to *act* on such laws.[15] On such a view, a person can choose to act immorally, against the laws that her autonomous will has set for herself, but still retain the capacity to set these laws and thus retain her autonomy. The problem with this interpretation, I contend, is that it is not clear how a Kantian can make sense of the idea that someone could regard herself as bound by a law that she sometimes chooses not to follow, yet still count as autonomous. If someone really has adopted a principle of action, and really does regard herself as bound by it, then on a Kantian conception of motivation she simply could not fail to follow this maxim and still count as autonomous. That is, in not following the principle she has set for herself, she would show herself to be acting heteronomously rather than autonomously. And thus, although a layperson outside the sphere of Kant interpretation might understand autonomy as mere freedom of the will, I do not think there is sufficient evidence to support the view that Kant himself understood autonomy in this way. Interpreting autonomy to require success in acting morally means, admittedly, that Kantian autonomy ends up as very different from what we might ordinarily think of as autonomy.[16] But there is, I think, a great deal of textual evidence to support this interpretation. We are autonomous, for Kant, when we *actually act* rationally (and thus morally), not just when we have the capacity to do so. Kant says that autonomy is "the will's property of being a law to itself" (G 4:447), and that "the principle of autonomy is...to choose only in such a way that the maxims of your choice are also included as universal law in the same volition" (G 4:440). Being able to universalize the maxims of your actions is, of course, the test of whether your actions are moral: "*[m]orality* is...the relation of actions to the autonomy of the will, that is, to a possible giving of universal law through its maxims" (G 4:439). Autonomy, for Kant, is not the mere *capacity* to choose rationally; rather, autonomy is the *successful exercise* of this capacity, which is possible for us to achieve, but is something we can and do fail to achieve all the time. Autonomy is something we must strive for, not something we merely possess in virtue of our rational powers.[17]

I do not intend to give a detailed analysis of exactly what the difference between the concepts of autonomy and personality amounts to. These terms will be, for my purposes here, interchangeable. What I want to highlight is that Kant consistently uses both of these terms to refer to our moral nature, that he uses both of these terms to refer to the idea that acting morally requires acting independently of inclination, and that he uses both of these terms to support the idea that, insofar as we act morally, we have a particular sort of value. For clarity's sake, in what follows I will impose some consistency by using the term "personality" to refer to our moral nature. And I will argue that it is our personality, understood as success in acting morally, that Kant thinks gives us dignity.

Kant attributes to us a very special kind of value – *dignity*, or *absolute worth* – insofar as we act morally.[18] What has dignity is of *unconditional* worth (it is valuable even if no one happens to value it) and *incomparable* worth (it is literally priceless).[19] Because we have dignity, Kant thinks we are valuable even if no one values us, and he thinks we cannot rationally be traded away for anything else.[20] Dignity is a sort of value that exists over and above the value of being worthy of treatment-constraining respect. Things that have dignity are also always respect-worthy, because the rational capacities that give someone respect-worthiness are required in order to be able to engage in the moral behaviour that gives someone dignity. But it would be a mistake to collapse the two values into one. Claims about the unconditional and incomparable worth we have in virtue of our dignity have implications for how we may permissibly be treated, to be sure. But an attribution of dignity is also a value-ascription in its own right, independent of considerations of how this value affects how its bearer may be treated.[21]

It is crucial to note, for the interpretation I am putting forward, that Kant does not, strictly speaking, usually ascribe dignity to *humanity*, or rational nature in general. Instead, Kant ascribes dignity to rational nature only insofar as it is moral – that is, insofar as it has *personality* or *autonomy*.

> Now, morality is the condition under which alone a rational being can be an end in itself, since only through this is it possible to be a lawgiving member in the kingdom of ends. **Hence morality, and humanity insofar as it is capable of morality, is that which alone has dignity** (*G* 4:435). (Emphasis mine.)

This point has been recognized, but treated very differently, by other commentators.[22] What I want to emphasize is that Kant is relatively consistent in ascribing dignity to *personality* rather than to humanity, and in saying that it is *humanity*, not personality, that is an end in itself.

The view I am suggesting here distinguishes being an end in itself from having dignity. The former – *end in itself*-hood – is what imposes an obligation to respect someone; the latter – *dignity* – is what gives someone unconditional and incomparable value. One is an end in herself in virtue of her humanity; one has dignity in virtue of her personality. Humanity is our rational nature, our capacity to set and pursue ends on the basis of reason and independently of our desires. Personality, on the other hand, is not the mere *capacity* to set and pursue ends on the basis of reason; personality is, rather, the *successful exercise* of this capacity. We achieve personality, then, only when we manage to act morally, when our free wills set and pursue ends that are in accordance with the laws of morality.

More textual evidence

Further evidence in favour of this interpretation of Kant's moral framework comes from considering what he says about the possibility of losing one's dignity and whether he thinks a loss of this dignity translates into a loss of the right to demand respect. Would Kant be willing to attribute dignity to even the most self-disrespecting of persons, or does he think it is possible to treat oneself in ways that could cause one to lose so much of one's dignity that one is no longer deserving of respect?

Kant does sometimes speak as if someone *can* lose her dignity if she fails to treat her humanity in certain ways. In fact, almost all of the places where Kant says that one is in danger of losing one's dignity are not those where one behaves immorally toward others, but rather those where one behaves immorally toward *oneself*.[23,24,25,26] Kant insists that a person "who violates duties toward himself...throws away his humanity" that "humanity in our own person must be highly esteemed, since without this, man is an object of contempt, which is an absolute fault, since he is worthless, not only in the eyes of others, but also in himself," and that "self-regarding duties...are founded on a certain love of honour consisting in the fact that a man values himself, and in his own eyes is not unworthy that his actions should be in keeping with humanity" (*LE* 27:341, 343, 347). These and other passages suggest that Kant does think that one can put herself in danger of losing her dignity by acting in certain ways toward herself; one risks losing her dignity by failing to respect her own humanity.[27,28]

Even in those places where Kant says that one loses one's dignity by acting in certain ways towards *others*, the loss of dignity ultimately comes from a failure to fulfil obligations to the self. For example, in the *Doctrine of Virtue* Kant argues that lying is a "renunciation by the speaker of his personality...[that makes] such a speaker...a mere deceptive appearance of a human being, not a human being himself" (*MM* 6:429). A liar, Kant thinks, "has even less worth than if he were a mere thing," and "throws away and, as it were, annihilates his dignity as a human being" (*MM* 6:429). What is wrong with lying, however, is that it is a misuse of one's natural powers of communication; it is a violation of an obligation one has to *oneself*, not one that one has to others. Furthermore, Kant argues that lying to oneself is even worse than lying to others, because one who is guilty of this "makes himself contemptible in his own eyes and violates the dignity of humanity in his own person" (*MM* 6:430).

It seems clear, then, that Kant *does* think that one can lose dignity, at least by failing to respect one's own humanity. The next question to ask is whether Kant thinks that a loss of dignity can bring with it a loss of respect-worthiness. When it comes to the dignity one might lose by behaving immorally toward others, it is clear that Kant does not think this loss means that one is owed any less respect. He is insistent that even the most immoral and vicious of people can still make demands on how he is permitted to be treated.[29] No matter how criminal someone's behaviour, we are still constrained in how we may treat him or her.[30]

There is, of course, a sense in which Kant thinks we are permitted to look down on, or think less of, people who act immorally toward others. He is not asking us to pretend that it is not the case that some people's actions are better than others or that some people's characters are more virtuous than others. We are certainly permitted to make these sorts of judgements about people. And it is tempting to think of this as a sense in which Kant thinks we are permitted to fail to *respect* people who act immorally toward others. But it is important to notice that this sense in which we are permitted to refrain from respecting people who act immorally toward others is only the sense in which we are permitted to refrain from according them *appraisal respect*. We may evaluate such a person's conduct and find it despicable or evaluate her character and find it lacking. These judgements may make us lose a certain kind of respect for someone. But the respect that is permissibly lost in such cases is appraisal respect. It is not the sort of respect that constrains our treatment of those to whom it is owed. We are never permitted to refrain from according someone treatment-constraining *recognition respect*. Whatever loss of dignity might come from behaving immorally toward others, Kant does not think that this loss of dignity ever means one is worth less of the sort of respect that constrains the ways in which one may be treated. And Kant's (infamously) retributivist views on punishment bear this point out. Kant believes respecting someone who has committed an immoral deed is compatible with extremely harsh punishment. But, because a wrongdoer is always still worthy of respect, his punishers are constrained in how they may punish him.

But what about a loss of dignity that results from immoral behaviour directed toward the self? We have just seen that Kant seems to regard this kind of immorality as far more grave than immorality directed toward others, at least insofar as it threatens the perpetrator with a loss of dignity. Might he believe, then, that self-directed immorality, unlike other-directed immorality, could make one lose so much dignity that it could translate into a loss of treatment-constraining respect-worthiness? Can someone who fails to respect herself – someone like Tralala – eventually lose the right to demand respect from others (or from herself)? It seems not, in these cases as well. While Kant clearly thinks that one *can* lose some of her dignity by failing to fulfil one's obligations to oneself, he also insists that one cannot lose *all* of it.[31] Even someone who fails to fulfil the obligations she has to herself does not become unworthy of respect. It is simply not possible for someone to degrade herself to the point where she is no longer worthy of the respect that forbids this degradation. As long as someone is alive and has minimally functional rational capacities she is both author of and subject to the moral law, and this is what makes her worthy of the sort of respect that constrains how she may be treated. This, then, is why it is important to endorse a relatively thin, minimal conception of Kantian humanity as the bare capacity to set and pursue ends, because, short of brain death, this capacity is next to impossible for a person to lose and, as long as a person retains her humanity, she retains her respect-worthiness. If we interpret Kant in this way we can accommodate fully the moral intuition that has been motivating us here, the thought that just because someone has been immoral does not mean that we are thereby permitted to treat her however we would like. Since humanity (rather than personality) is an end in itself, we are obligated to respect people – that is, to have recognition respect for them and thus constrain our behaviour toward them – regardless of how they happen to act.[32]

Motivations and potential objections

In addition to its textual plausibility, a significant motivation for this interpretation is that without it Kant's account would be subject to an extremely unintuitive conclusion: if people were to be treated as ends in themselves in virtue of their acting morally, rather than in virtue of their capacity to be rational, then people who acted immorally would be less worthy of being treated as ends in themselves. Admittedly, this is not a conclusion that would be happily accepted by commentators who conflate those distinctions I have been at pains to argue that Kant really intended to keep separate. But it is nevertheless, I contend, a conclusion to which these commentators are committed. That is, defenders of the received views of what Kant means by humanity, autonomy, dignity, and respect-worthiness are committed to the conclusion that people who act immorally are worthy of less respect. While there might be a sense in which people are less worthy of respect insofar as they act immorally, this kind of respect – the sort one can gain or lose depending on what she does – is what Darwall would call *appraisal respect*. This is not the sort of respect that is supposed to attach to humanity, as Kant sees it, inasmuch as he calls humanity an *objective end* (an end that places limits both on what other ends we may set and on what means we may use to pursue any of our ends). Appraisal respect does not constrain our behaviour toward one to whom it is owed; it is merely an evaluation of one's conduct or character. Darwall's *recognition respect*, on the other hand, makes no reference to a person's actions and does constrain our behaviour toward those to whom it is owed. As we have seen, this is the sort of respect that Kant means to require when he calls humanity an end in itself, particularly insofar as he calls humanity an *objective end*.

This interpretation fits well with the intuitive thought that our behaviour toward other people is constrained in certain ways simply in virtue of the fact that they are persons, regardless of the immorality of their deeds. It also fits well with the intuitive thought that a person loses a very important kind of value by treating herself (or letting herself be treated) in certain ways, and so there is a sense in which such a person has less dignity. But, at the same time, whatever this loss of value is, it does not, ever, translate into a loss of a person's right to be treated in certain ways, simply in virtue of the fact that she is a certain sort of being.

Notice how this implication applies to the obligations a person has to *herself*. Even if someone like Tralala loses some of her dignity by failing in her obligation to herself to respect her humanity, she nevertheless remains subject to the obligation to respect her humanity. Because this obligation applies to the self as well as to others, and because it hinges on one's capacity for rationality, not on how morally well one actually exercises this capacity, the obligation of self-respect is not vitiated by a failure to fulfil it. Someone who fails to respect her rational capacities is still morally required to take the steps necessary to respect these capacities, even though at the same time her failure to do so makes her lose a certain kind of worth.

So much for the various motivations for this view; on now to some potential objections. One potential objection is that while this interpretation might solve one problem it seems to create another. Making humanity rather than personality an end in itself ensures that immoral people are still owed the sort of respect that constrains our behaviour toward them, but making personality rather than humanity be what gives people dignity means that immoral people are in danger of losing their unconditional and incomparable worth. Remember, for Kant, people lose personality when they behave badly. Since people have dignity in virtue of their personality, failing to act morally thereby makes people lose dignity. This seems counterintuitive, to say the least. This sort of value might intuitively seem like the sort of thing that people have, regardless of what they do. It seems strange to say that unconditional and incomparable worth can be revoked for bad behaviour. This interpretive strategy might seem especially egregious when it comes to *unconditional* worth – after all, what is making the attribution of dignity contingent on one's acting the right way, if not imposing a condition upon this worth?

But notice that what Kant says is unconditional in this case is the *value* of personality, not the *attribution* of personality to particular individuals with humanity. It is personality itself that has unconditional worth, not the individual beings who contingently possess it. So we can say that personality, qua something with the unconditional worth of dignity, has value even if no one happens to value it and at the same time say that the attribution of personality to individual people is a matter of degree and depends upon the extent to which an individual succeeds in conforming her behaviour to the universalizable maxims of morality.

It is admittedly counterintuitive to claim that ascribing dignity to personality rather than to humanity means that one who fails to act morally risks losing some of her dignity. But it is the bullet we must bite to solve the interpretive dilemma to which I contend the majority of Kantian commentators are committed. It seems strange, to be sure, to suggest that one's dignity is something that could come and go according to whether one acts according to one's inclinations instead of according to universalizable maxims. But, remember, the respect owed to people is not contingent upon their actions, because people are ends in themselves in virtue of their humanity rather than their personality. Because of this, we can retain the intuitive thought that our behaviour toward others is constrained regardless of how they act.

Another potential problem for the interpretation I am offering here is that we are left without grounds for the respect-worthiness of humanity. I am arguing, remember, that rational nature is respect-worthy regardless of whether it has dignity, that is, regardless of whether someone uses her rational nature to act morally. But then what is the justification for this respect-worthiness? If rational nature is not, in itself, unconditionally and incomparably valuable, then why must it always be treated with respect? The received interpretation of Kant's views on this matter has it that the respect our humanity is owed derives straightforwardly from the dignity it has, so this interpretation is not subject to this problem. But, because I propose to separate the features in virtue of which someone is owed respect from the features in virtue of which she has dignity, and because I argue that someone can be worthy of respect even if she behaves in ways that make her lose dignity, a critic might argue that I am left without a way to explain or justify why someone's rational nature must be respected regardless of what she does with it.

There is, however, a straightforward solution to this problem. As I discussed above, rational nature is a necessary precondition for the possibility of someone acting morally. Rational nature is the one thing you

172 *Kantianism, Liberalism, and Feminism*

need to have if you are even going to be in the running for having that value which is most morally important (that is, dignity).[33] So, humanity is always worthy of (treatment-constraining) respect because it is what makes morality *possible*. I contend that the best way to interpret the connection between respect-worthiness and dignity is that our rational capacities must be respected because they are what make it possible for us to act morally, and insofar as we succeed in acting morally we have the highest possible value.

Some textual counterevidence

My suggestion here, remember, is that Kant means to separate the dignity people have from the respect they are owed and that he does not think that a loss of the former can affect the latter. There are good reasons for adopting this interpretation, I have argued. But I will admit that this interpretation faces what appears to be considerable textual counterevidence. For example, in one place Kant explicitly says that "morality is an end in itself" (*MM* 6:422–423), and in several other places he refers to the "dignity of humanity" (*G* 4:439; *MM* 6:420, 440, 449) and to "humanity in its proper dignity" (*CPR* 5:88). I will admit that my interpretation is controversial, that it certainly does not fit with everything in Kant's texts, and that it is not impossible to come up with examples of passages where Kant says things that cut against my interpretation, where he says things other than that it is autonomy that has dignity and humanity that is an end in itself. It is also relatively easy to come up with examples of passages where Kant says things that alternately support and cut against my interpretation. I want to examine several such cases now.

The first example of a passage that alternates between supporting and undermining my interpretation comes from the *Critique of Practical Reason*. Here, Kant runs together the four distinctions I have been at pains to keep apart:

> The moral law is *holy* (*inviolable*). A human being is indeed unholy enough but the *humanity* in his person must be holy to him. In the whole of creation everything one wants and over which one has any power can also be used *merely as a means*; a human being alone, and with him every rational creature, is an *end in itself*: by virtue of the autonomy of his freedom is he the subject of the moral law, which is holy (*CPR* 5:87).

First he says here that it is in virtue of someone's humanity that she, and every other rational creature, is an end in herself. This is precisely the line I have been pushing. But then Kant says that

> [j]ust because of this every will, even every person's own will directed to himself, is restricted to the condition of agreement with the *autonomy* of the rational being, that is to say, such a being is not to be subjected to any purpose that is not possible in accordance with a law that could arise from the will of the affected subject himself; hence this subject is to be used never merely as a means but as at the same time an end (*CPR* 5:87).

Here he has said that it is the *autonomy* of rational beings (which, remember, I am interpreting as the successful exercise of one's rational capacities, that is, as actually acting morally) that means they must "be used never merely as a means but as at the same time an end." I have been arguing that the successful exercise of someone's rational capacities is what gives her dignity, not what means she must always be treated as an end in herself. And he goes on to say that

> [w]e rightly attribute this condition even to the divine will with respect to the rational beings in the world as its creatures, inasmuch as it rests on their *personality*, by which alone they are ends in themselves (*CPR* 5:87).

He has said here that rational creatures are ends in themselves in virtue of their personality; again, this is exactly what I am arguing is not the case.

A second example of a passage that alternately supports and undermines my interpretation comes from the *Doctrine of Virtue*:

> The *respect* that I have for others or that another can require from me (*observantia aliis praestanda*) is therefore recognition of a *dignity* (*dignitas*) in other human beings (*MM* 6:462).

This immediately subverts my interpretation. Kant has said that respect is required by the recognition that someone has *dignity*, whereas I have been arguing that respect is required by the recognition that someone is an *end in itself*. Then Kant tells us that

> [h]umanity itself is a dignity; for a human being cannot be used merely as a means by any human being (either by others or even

by himself) but must always be used at the same time as an end (*MM* 6:462).

Again, not good. Humanity is not supposed to have dignity, autonomy is. What is worse, Kant implies that this dignity is what makes someone an end in herself. But then Kant turns around and says that

> [i]t is just in this that his dignity (personality) consists, by which he raises himself above all other beings in the world that are not human beings and yet can be used, and so over all *things* (*MM* 6:462).

This sits much better with the interpretation I am putting forward. Here, he once again associates dignity explicitly with personality. Unfortunately, he immediately goes on to associate dignity with humanity:

> But just as he cannot give himself away for any price (this would conflict with his duty of self-esteem), so neither can he act contrary to the equally necessary self-esteem of others, as human beings, that is, he is under obligation to acknowledge, in a practical way, the dignity of humanity in every other human being (*MM* 6:462).

It is not possible to explain this particular instance away. Were my interpretation to be completely uncontroversial, Kant would have had to say that it is the dignity of the *personality* in others that we must acknowledge. Kant goes on to say that it follows from this "dignity of humanity" that

> [h]ence there rests on him a duty regarding the respect that must be shown to every other human being (*MM* 6:462).

Notice that it is ambiguous here whether we owe other people respect because they have humanity (which fits with my interpretation) or because they have dignity (which does not).

A third example of a passage that similarly alternates between supporting and undermining my interpretation is found in what Kant says about the vice of lying in the *Doctrine of Virtue*. He starts off by saying that

> [t]he greatest violation of a human being's duty to himself regarded merely as a moral being (the humanity in his own person) is the contrary of truthfulness, *lying* (*MM* 6:429).

If Kant were consistent in using the terminological distinctions I am advocating, a duty to oneself "regarded merely as a moral being" would be to the *autonomy* in one's own person, not to the *humanity* in one's own person, as he says here. He goes on to say that when someone lies to himself,

> he makes himself contemptible in his own eyes and violates the dignity of humanity in his own person (*MM* 6:429).

Now he has gone and said that the humanity in one's own person has *dignity*. But I have been suggesting that dignity attaches to *autonomy*, not to humanity. Humanity is supposed to be what makes one an *end in itself*, not what gives one dignity. None of this bodes well for my suggested interpretation. Kant then tells us that lying does not merely violate one's dignity, it actually destroys it:

> By a lie a human being throws away and, as it were, annihilates his dignity as a human being (*MM* 6:429).

At least here he has not said what the dignity in a human being attaches to. This particular line is consistent with dignity attaching to either the humanity or the autonomy in a person. (Though given that this line follows straightaway the line where he has said that dignity attaches to humanity, we should probably not put too much stock in this ambiguity. There is no real reason to think he has changed his mind so quickly about what dignity attaches to.) Kant goes on to explain exactly what is wrong with lying:

> A human being who does not himself believe what he tells another...has even less worth than if he were a mere thing; for a thing, because it is something real and given, has the properly of being serviceable so that another can put it to some use. But communication of one's thoughts to someone through words that yet (intentionally) contain the contrary of what the speaker thinks on the subject is an end that is directly opposed to the natural purposiveness of the speaker's capacity to communicate his thoughts, and is thus a renunciation by the speaker of his **personality**, and such a speaker is a mere deceptive appearance of a human being, not a human being himself (*MM* 6:429). (Emphasis mine.)

Here, finally, we have some support for my interpretation. Lying is, in effect, a perversion of someone's capacity to communicate. This amounts to a renunciation of one's personality, Kant thinks. Personality is what we have when we actually successfully behave morally, remember. Lying is a renunciation of this because it is a failure to do what the moral law requires of us. The ultimate problem with lying, then, boils down to a matter of its effect on one's *personality*, not one's humanity. This explains why it results in a loss of dignity (which, I am suggesting, attaches to personality instead of humanity).

Fourth and fifth examples from the *Doctrine of Virtue* are similarly ambiguous. Here, Kant says that

> a human being's duty to himself as a moral being only (without taking his animality into consideration) consists in what is formal in the consistency of the maxims of his will with the dignity of humanity in his person (*MM* 6:420).

He then goes on to say that

> [t]he dignity of humanity consists precisely in this power of giving universal law, though only on condition of also being subject to this same lawgiving (*MM* 6:440).

In both of these passages, Kant supports various aspects of my interpretation. In the first passage he affirms an important distinction between different aspects of our nature (in this case, our moral nature and our animal nature) and associates the duties we have to ourselves in virtue of our moral nature with the special value of dignity. In the second passage he affirms that dignity attaches to our moral capacity to formulate and subject ourselves to universal laws. Unfortunately, however, these are also both passages where Kant locates dignity in humanity rather than personality. As I admitted above, there are a few problematic phrases that unequivocally cut against my interpretation; these are two of them.

Finally, a sixth example, also from the *Doctrine of Virtue*, that both supports and undermines my interpretation:

> [A] human being regarded as a *person*, that is, as the subject of a morally practical reason, is exalted above any price; for as a person (*homo noumenon*) he is not to be valued merely as a means to the ends of others or even to his own ends, but as an end in itself, that is, he possesses a *dignity* (an absolute inner worth) (*MM* 6:434).

So far it looks as if my interpretation is correct. Kant is clearly saying that dignity attaches to personality, that it is properly ascribed to people insofar as they behave morally. But he goes on immediately to say, this dignity is that

> by which [this person]...exacts *respect* for himself from all other rational beings in the world (*MM* 6:434).

This fits much less well with my interpretation. Respect-worthiness, I am arguing, is supposed to attach to humanity, not personality. We are able to make claims on the way others are permitted to treat us in virtue of our *humanity*, I am arguing. It seems that Kant has just denied this and has said instead that it is the dignity we have in virtue of our *personality* that gives us the right to be respected by others. But then he goes on to say just the reverse:

> Humanity in his person is the object of the respect which he can demand from every other human being, but which he must also not forfeit (*MM* 6:435).

Thus Kant ends up saying just what we would expect him to say if my interpretation is the correct one. Once again, it is *humanity* that grounds the respect that is owed from others, not personality.

As these passages show, my interpretation does not fit seamlessly with the entire Kantian corpus. In a number of places Kant uses the terms "humanity" and "personality" as if they were interchangeable. And he is not always consistent in attributing dignity to personality and end-in-itself-hood to humanity. I do not know how to make these differing strains in Kant completely consistent, and I am not aware of a single passage that settles this issue conclusively. However, even if the textual kinks here cannot be ironed out completely, I want to foreground both Kant's consistent characterization of humanity as an *objective end* – an end that places limits on how beings with humanity can be treated – and foreground the fact that he usually attributes dignity to autonomy or personality instead of humanity. Doing this suggests that we have reason to think that, at least according to my interpretation of Kant's most considered view, "humanity" and "personality" are *not* interchangeable, and that the former is what is owed treatment-constraining respect while the latter is what has dignity.

Conclusion

In the interpretation I have put forward here, Kant ascribes dignity to personality rather than humanity, and he ascribes respect-worthiness to humanity rather than personality. I recognize that I am implying here that someone who fails to respect herself risks losing her dignity. But I am also suggesting that, even if someone loses some of this worth, we are still constrained in how we are permitted to treat her. It is admittedly a bit strange to be forced to admit that the dignity (the unconditional and incomparable worth) one has in virtue of one's personality can be lost through bad behaviour (and thus that it can come in degrees). But I think this is a far more attractive bullet to bite once we realize that, because the constraints upon the way one can be treated are a matter of one's humanity, not personality, the respect one is owed in virtue of one's humanity cannot be done away with, regardless of how one acts.

We came to this problem, remember, because of the worry that failing to fulfil the Kantian obligation to protect one's rational nature might actually vitiate future instances of this obligation. I have responded to this objection by defending a novel interpretation of Kant's views on the relation between the value we have and the respect we are owed. I have argued, contra the received view among Kant scholars, that the feature in virtue of which someone has unconditional and incomparable value is not the same feature in virtue of which she is owed the respect that constrains how she may be treated. So, even though someone who fails to attempt to protect her rational nature fails to respect herself in the right way, and even though this moral failing does make her lose a certain kind of value, her obligations to respect herself do not go away. One can become less valuable insofar as she abuses, defiles, dishonours, or fails to develop aspects of her moral *agency*, but this loss of value *never* threatens her moral *patiency*.

We came to this problem, remember, because an implication of the Kantian account I have been defending seemed to be that if oppression harms rational nature, and if the value of rational nature is what grounds the obligation to resist oppression, then a person whose rational nature has been harmed by oppression will at some point no longer be obligated to resist it. The worry was that failing to fulfil the obligation to protect one's rational nature from the harms of oppression might actually vitiate future instances of this obligation. I have responded to this concern by defending a novel interpretation of Kant's views on the relation between the value we have and the respect we are owed. I argue, contra the received view among Kant scholars, that the feature in virtue of which someone has intrinsic value is not the same feature in virtue of which she is owed the respect that constrains how she may be treated (by herself or others). So, even though someone who fails to resist her own oppression fails to respect herself in the right way, and even though this moral failing does make her lose a certain kind of value, her obligations to respect herself and to resist her oppression never go away.

Notes

1. Richard Dean collapses the distinction between respect-worthiness (that is, end-in-itself-hood) and dignity in his rather idiosyncratic interpretation of Kantian humanity: "Kant begins the *Groundwork* with the claim that only a good will is good without qualification, and that only a good will has incomparably high value, or dignity. Later in the *Groundwork*, he says that only humanity is an end in itself, and only humanity has a dignity. A thorough analysis of these claims reveals that something that has an incomparably high value, and is valuable without qualification, must also be an end in itself. So good will must be the end in itself." See Richard Dean, *The Value of Humanity in Kant's Moral Theory* (New York: Oxford University Press, 2006), 8. Paul Guyer's interpretation is more conventional, but he also ends up equating respect-worthiness and dignity when he says, for example, that "the idea of humanity as an end in itself...is identical to the idea of the incomparable dignity of human autonomy or freedom governed by the law that we give to ourselves." See Guyer, *Kant on Freedom, Law, and Happiness*, 9–10. Thomas Hill does the same when he says, for example, that "humanity in each person has dignity, no matter how immoral the person may be.... Autonomy is said to be the ground of dignity, and this is a property of the will of every rational being." See Thomas Hill, "Humanity as an End in Itself," *Dignity and Practical Reason in Kant's Moral Theory* (Ithaca: Cornell University Press, 1992), 47. Christine Korsgaard collapses this distinction when, for example, she argues that dignity attaches to the capacity for acting morally (which she elsewhere characterizes as humanity, which is an end in itself): "If we regard ourselves as having the power to justify our ends,...we must regard ourselves as having an inner worth [(that is, dignity)] – and we must treat others who can also place value on their ends in virtue of their humanity as having the same inner worth." See Christine Korsgaard, "Two Distinctions in Goodness," *Creating the Kingdom of Ends* (Cambridge: Cambridge University Press, 1996), 273. Allan Wood initially appears to distinguish respect-worthiness from dignity when he says, "[i]f being an *end in itself* constitutes the worth of *humanity* – in the technical Kantian sense, which is the capacity to set ends according to reason – then having *dignity* constitutes the worth of *personality* – which is the capacity to give oneself moral laws and obey them." But, because he characterizes personality as the *capacity* to act morally (rather than the successful exercise of this capacity) Wood immediately goes on to say that "Kant nevertheless frequently speaks of the 'dignity of humanity' as well as the dignity of personality. Kant usually writes as if humanity and personality were coextensive." This move, in effect, collapses the distinction

between respect-worthiness and dignity. See Allan Wood, *Kantian Ethics* (Cambridge: Cambridge University Press, 2008), 94.
2. Hubert Selby, "Tralala," *Last Exit to Brooklyn* (New York: Grove Press, 1957).
3. Darwall, "Two Kinds of Respect."
4. "[R]ational beings are called *persons* because their nature already marks them out as an end in itself, that is, as something that may not be used merely as a means, and hence so far limits all choice (and is an object of respect). These, therefore, are not merely subjective ends, the existence of which as an effect of our action has a worth *for us*, but rather *objective ends*, that is, beings the existence of which is in itself an end, and indeed one such that no other end, to which they would serve *merely* as means, can be put in its place, since without it nothing of *absolute worth* would be found anywhere; but if all worth were conditional and therefore contingent, then no supreme practical principle for reason could be found anywhere" (*G* 4:428).
5. See, for example, Dean, *The Value of Humanity in Kant's Moral Theory*; Hill, *Dignity and Practical Reason in Kant's Moral Theory*; and Mark Timmons, *Moral Theory: An Introduction* (Lanham: Rowman and Littlefield, 2002).
6. Kant distinguishes the three "elements of the determination of the human being" in the following way: "(1) The predisposition to the *animality* of the human being, as a *living being*; (2) To the *humanity* in him, as a living and at the same time *rational* being; (3) To his *personality*, as a rational and at the same time *responsible* being." Immanuel Kant, *Religion within the Boundaries of Mere Reason*, Wood and Giovanni (ed. and trans.) (Cambridge: Cambridge University Press, 1998 [1793]), 6:26. '*R*' in parenthetical documentation hereafter refers to this work.
7. "Our duties to ourselves on the animal level are to preserve ourselves, preserve the species, and preserve our capacity to enjoy life" (*MM* 6:420).
8. "The capacity to set oneself an end – any end whatsoever – is what characterizes humanity (as distinguished from animality)" (*MM* 6:392).
9. "It is nothing other than personality, that is, freedom and independence from the mechanism of the whole of nature, regarded nevertheless as also a capacity of being subject to special laws – namely pure practical laws given by his own reason, so that a person as belonging to the sensible world is subject to his own personality insofar as he also belongs to the intelligible world; for, it is then not to be wondered at that a human being, as belonging to both worlds, must regard his own nature in reference to his second and highest vocation only with reverence, and its laws with the highest respect" (*CPR* 5:86–87).
10. "A *person* is a subject whose actions can be *imputed* to him. Moral personality is therefore nothing other than the freedom of a rational being under moral laws (whereas psychological personality is merely the ability to be conscious of one's identity in different conditions of one's existence). From this it follows that a person is subject to no other laws than those he gives to himself (either alone or at least along with others)" (*MM* 6:224).
11. "*Morality* is ... the relation of actions to the autonomy of the will, that is, to a possible giving of universal law through its maxims. ... Our own will insofar as it would act only under the condition of a possible giving of universal law through its maxims ... is the proper object of respect; and the dignity of humanity consists just in this capacity to give universal law, though

with the condition of also being itself subject to this very lawgiving" (*G* 4:439–440).
12. "[W]hat, then, can freedom of the will be other than autonomy, that is, the will's property of being a law to itself?" (*G* 4:447).
13. "For, this moral law is based on the autonomy of the will, as a free will which, in accordance with its universal laws, must necessarily be able at the same time *to agree* to that to which it is to *subject* itself" (*CPR* 5:132).
14. "Autonomy of the will is the property of the will by which it is a law to itself (independently of any property of the objects of volition). The principle of autonomy is, therefore: to choose only in such a way that the maxims of your choice are also included as universal law in the same volition" (*G* 4:440).
15. See, for example, Anne Margaret Baxley, "Autonomy and Autocracy," *Kant-Studien* 94 (2003): 1–23; Lara Denis, "Freedom, Primacy, and Perfect Duties to Oneself," *Kant's Metaphysics of Morals: A Critical Guide* (Cambridge: Cambridge University Press, 2010), 171–172; Hill, "The Hypothetical Imperative," *Dignity and Practical Reason in Kant's Moral Theory*, 34–35; and Timmons, *Moral Theory: An Introduction.*
16. For a careful consideration of many other ways in which the Kantian conception of autonomy differs from other conceptions, see Hill, "The Kantian Conception of Autonomy."
17. This way of understanding Kantian autonomy is not unprecedented. Stephen Engstrom, for example, argues that "the concept of self-legislation, or autonomy, implies [that] in a rational being the law in accordance with which its (rational) capacities are exercised and the representation of that law are the same." See Stephen Engstrom, "Happiness and the Highest Good in Aristotle and Kant," *Aristotle, Kant, and the Stoics: Rethinking Happiness and Duty* (Cambridge: Cambridge University Press, 1996), 115. Guyer argues that autonomy is "the aim that a person with free will must adopt if he is to preserve and promote his freedom of choice and action..., which is something such an agent ought to do, and can do, but does not necessarily do." See Paul Guyer, "Kant on the Theory and Practice of Autonomy," *Social Philosophy and Policy* 20 (2003), 71. Korsgaard supports a similar view, arguing that "[w]hen you are motivated autonomously, you act on a law that you give to yourself; when you act heteronomously, the law is imposed on you by means of a sanction – you are provided with an interest in acting on it." See Christine Korsgaard, "Ethical, Political, and Religious Thought," *Creating the Kingdom of Ends* (Cambridge: Cambridge University Press, 1996), 22.
18. "For, nothing can have a worth other than that which the [universal] law determines for it. But the lawgiving itself, which determines all worth, must for that very reason have a dignity, that is, and unconditional, incomparable worth; and the word *respect* alone provides a becoming expression for the estimate of it that a rational being must give. *Autonomy* is therefore the ground of the dignity of human nature and of every rational nature" (*G* 4:436).
19. "The *respect* that I have for others or that another can require from me...is therefore recognition of a *dignity*...in other human beings, that is, of a worth that has no price, no equivalent for which the object...could be exchanged" (*MM* 6:462).

20. This understanding of dignity is very much in line with how most other commentators understand the concept. See, for example, Guyer, *Kant on Freedom, Law, and Happiness*, 153–154; Hill, *Dignity and Practical Reason in Kant's Moral Theory*, chapters 2 and 10, and *Respect, Pluralism, and Justice: Kantian Perspectives*, (New York: Oxford University Press, 2000), 24–26; Herbert James Paton, *The Categorical Imperative* (London: Hutchison and Co., 1947), 189; Allan Wood, *Kant's Ethical Thought* (Cambridge: Cambridge University Press, 1999), 115. One notable exception to this agreement is Oliver Sensen, who argues that Kantian dignity is not best understood as our absolute inner value, but rather as a "sublimity" that indicates that, in virtue of our capacity for moral action, we are "raised up" above all other creatures. See Oliver Sensen, "Kant's Conception of Human Dignity," *Kant-Studien* 100 (2009): 309–331.
21. Some commentators interpret value ascriptions in the Kantian moral framework as, in effect, nothing over and above prescriptions about how a thing may permissibly be treated. This would, of course, have the effect of collapsing the distinction between respect-worthiness and dignity. This interpretive move is undermined, however, by a distinction Kant makes between two kinds of respect: *Reverentia* and *Observantia*. *Reverentia* is the feeling of respect that is elicited by our recognition of the moral law and a person who is successfully acting upon it, "in terms of which he is above any price and possesses an inalienable dignity" (*MM* 6:436). *Observantia* is "respect in a practical sense," a respect which constrains our treatment of others and is owed to them in virtue of their humanity (*MM* 6:459, 463). I am arguing that we should read Kant as telling us that, strictly speaking, *Reverentia* is owed to personality and *Observantia* is owed to humanity. Because *Reverentia* is a subjective feeling, not a treatment, and Kant tells us explicitly that it, like all feelings, cannot be a duty and is instead the subjective condition of the possibility of being susceptible to duty (*MM* 6:402), we have here a particular response to a recognition of the value of something that cannot be reduced to a prescription about how it must be treated. This means that value ascriptions cannot be reduced to prescriptions about permissible treatment.

   In any case, I think it is sufficiently unclear whether Kant himself held respect-worthiness and dignity to be co-extensive or distinct to render an interpretation that holds them distinct at least plausible, but I recognize that other Kantians might beg to differ. Thanks to an anonymous reviewer for pressing me on this point; thanks to Robin Dillon for helpful discussion on this point.
22. See, for example, Guyer, "Kant on the Theory and Practice of Autonomy;" Hill, "Humanity as an End in Itself," *Dignity and Practical Reason in Kant's Moral Theory*; Korsgaard, "Ethical, Political, and Religious Thought," *Creating the Kingdom of Ends*; and Wood, *Kantian Ethics*.
23. "Nor can persons give themselves up to satisfying the desires of another – even if they might thereby at once save parents and friends from death – without casting their person away. If someone does it to satisfy their own inclination, that is still, indeed, natural, though it is very lacking in virtue and runs counter to morality; but if done for money, or any other purpose, it throws away the worth of one's humanity, in that it allows one to be used as a tool. ... Suicide is the supreme violation of the duties to oneself" (*LE* 27:342).
24. "So far from these duties being the lowest, they actually take first plae, and are the most important of all; for ... we may ask how, if a man degrades his own

person, anything can be demanded of him? He who violates duties toward himself, throws away his humanity, and is no longer in a position to perform duties to others. Thus a person who has performed his duties to others badly, who has not been generous, kindly or compassionate, but has observed the duty to himself, and lived in a seemly fashion may still in himself possess a certain inner worth. But the man who has violated the duties to himself has no inner worth. Thus the infringements of self-regarding duties takes all his worth from a man, and the infringement of duties to others deprives him of worth only in that respect. Hence the former are the condition under which the others can be observed" (*LE* 27:341).

25. "Self-regarding duties...are independent of all advantage, and pertain only to the worth of being human. They rest on the fact that in regard to our person we have no untrammelled freedom, that humanity in our own person must be highly esteemed, since without this, man is an object of contempt, which is an absolute fault, since he is worthless, not only in the eyes of others, but also in himself. The self-regarding duties are the supreme condition and *principium* of of all morality, for the worth of the person constitutes moral worthl the worth of skill relates only to one's circumstances" (*LE* 27:343–344).

26. "The self-regarding duties are negative, and restrict our freedom in regard to the inclinations that are directed to our well-being. Just as the precepts of the law restrict our freedom in our dealings with other people, so the self-regarding duties restrict our freedom with respect to ourselves. All such duties are founded on a certain love of honour consisting in the fact that a man values himself, and in his own eyes is not unworthy that his actions should be in keeping with humanity. To be worthy in his eyes of inner respect, the treasuring of approval, is the essential ingredient of the duties to onself" (*LE* 27:347).

27. Very much in line with this, Denis argues that we should understand Kant as holding that "the preservation, expression, and furtherance of each agent's freedom depends more fundamentally on her compliance with perfect duties to herself than with her compliance with other duties or on others' compliance with their duties toward her. [Perfect duties to the self] concern the protection of basic conditions of agency to an extent unrivaled by other duties.... The agent is in a unique position to impair her inner freedom and autocracy; to undermine her sense of herself as a being with dignity and a subject of the moral law; to forfeit her standing as an honourable human being in the eyes of herself and others; and to imperil the grounds of her virtue. [Perfect duties to the self] are the only duties that forbid actions, vices, or maxims that threaten freedom in these profound and distinctive ways." See Denis, "Freedom, Primacy, and Perfect Duties to Oneself," *Kant's Metaphysics of Morals: A Critical Guide*.

28. Departing somewhat from many interpretations of Kant, I contend that we should think of humanity as an ordinary human capacity, as susceptible to harm as many other human capacities. Our humanity can be harmed both when damage is done to our capacity to set and pursue ends according to reason, and also when we face illegitimate restrictions on the full and proper exercise of this capacity. The former sort of harm occurs when one's rational capacities are prevented from functioning in a way that also threatens their future functioning; the latter sort of harm occurs when one encounters an

unfair temporary interference with the full exercise of one's rational capacities. The line between these two sorts of harm will not always be completely clear, but this vagueness is unimportant given our purposes here because Kant clearly believes that both sorts of harm are capable of threatening one's dignity.

29. "To be *contemptuous* of others (*contemnere*), that is, to deny them the respect owed to human beings in general, is in every case contrary to duty; for they are human beings. At times one cannot, it is true, help but inwardly *looking down* on some in comparison with others (*despicatui habere*); but the outward manifestation of this is, nevertheless, an offense.... I cannot deny all respect to even a vicious man as a human being; I cannot withdraw at least the respect that belongs to him in his quality as a human being, even though by his deeds he makes himself unworthy of it. So there can be disgraceful punishments that dishonour humanity itself (such as quartering a man, having him torn by dogs, cutting off his nose and ears). Not only are such punishments more painful than loss of possessions and life to one who loves honor (who claims the respect of others, as everyone must); they also make a spectator blush with shame at belonging to the species that can be treated that way.... The censure of vice ... must never break out into complete contempt and denial of any moral worth to a vicious human being; for on this supposition he could never be improved, and this [is] not consistent with the idea of a *human being*, who as such (as a moral being) can never lose entirely his predisposition to the good" (*MM* 6:463–464).

30. "Since men are objects of well-liking love, in that we should love the humanity in them, even judges, in punishing crime, should not dishonour humanity; they must, indeed, penalize the evil-doer, but not violate his humanity by demeaning punishments; for if another dishonours a man's humanity, the man himself sets no value on it; it is as if the evil-doer had himself so demeaned his humanity, that he is no longer worthy of being a man, and must then be treated as a universal object of contempt" (*LE* 27:418).

31. "A human being cannot renounce his personality as long as he is a subject of duty, hence as long as he lives; and it is a contradiction that he should be authorized to withdraw from all obligation, that is, freely to act as if no authorization were needed for this action" (*MM* 6:422–423).

32. I have argued that failing to respect oneself never threatens one's respect-worthiness. Michael J. Meyer acknowledges this point, but does not defend any particular Kantian interpretation of it in detail, when he states that "[t]he fact that anyone engages in undignified behaviour or fails to have an appropriate sense of dignity gives no individual moral licence to treat him – even while he is doing so – as if he has no dignity. While we might say of someone who degrades himself that he has 'lost his dignity', we nonetheless recognize that this 'loss' is not complete in this important sense: it does not provide others with the privilege to treat him like an object or deprive him of the status of a human being." See Michael J. Meyer, "Dignity, Rights, and Self-Control," *Ethics* 99 (1989): 529.

I have also argued that the Kantian moral framework needs certain distinctions: that we need to be able to capture the idea that merely having certain capacities calls for a certain type of treatment and attitudes, while having exercised these capacities calls, in addition, for certain other attitudes and

treatment. Hill has also recognized the need for similar distinctions in Kant. But because Hill's ways of understanding Kantian humanity, personality, dignity, and respect-worthiness are all different from mine, his interpretative solution to this dilemma is completely different. See Hill, "Must Respect be Earned?" *Respect, Pluralism, and Justice: Kantian Perspectives*, and "Kant on Imperfect Duty and Supererogation," *Dignity and Practical Reason in Kant's Moral Theory*.
33. See, for example, G 4:428.

Selected Bibliography

Ruth Abbey, "Back toward a Comprehensive Liberalism? Justice as Fairness, Gender, and Families," *Political Theory* 35 (2007): 5–28.

———, *The Return of Feminist Liberalism* (Montreal and Kingston: McGill-Queen's University Press, 2011).

Kathryn Pyne Addelson, *Moral Passages: Toward a Collectivist Moral Theory* (New York: Routledge, 1994).

Linda Alcoff, "Phenomenology, Post-structuralism, and Feminist Theory on the Concept of Experience," *Feminist Phenomenology*, Fisher and Embree (eds) (Norwell: Kluwer Academic Publishers, 2000), 39–56.

Elizabeth Anderson, *Value in Ethics and Economics* (Cambridge: Harvard University Press, 1993).

———, "Should Feminists Reject Rational Choice Theory?," *A Mind of One's Own: Feminist Essays on Reason and Objectivity*, Antony and Witt (eds) (Boulder: Westview, 2002), 369–397.

———, "Toward a Non-Ideal, Relational Methodology for Political Philosophy: Comments on Schwartzman's Challenging Liberalism," *Hypatia* 24 (2009): 130–145.

———, "Epistemic Justice as a Virtue of Social Institutions," *Social Epistemology* 26 (2012): 163–173.

Louise Antony, "Natures and Norms," *Ethics* 111 (2000): 5–36.

Amy Baehr, (ed.) *Varieties of Feminist Liberalism* (Lanham: Rowman and Littlefield, 2004).

Annette Baier, "What Do Women Want in a Moral Theory?," *Nous* 19 (1985): 53–63.

———, "The Need for More than Justice," *Science, Morality and Feminist Theory*, Hanen and Nielsen (eds) (Calgary: University of Calgary Press, 1987).

———, *Moral Prejudices: Essays on Ethics* (Cambridge: Harvard University Press, 1995).

Marcia Baron, "The Alleged Moral Repugnance of Acting from Duty," *Journal of Philosophy* 81 (1984): 197–220.

———, "Servility, Critical Deference and the Deferential Wife," *Philosophical Studies* 48 (1985): 393–400.

———, *Kantian Ethics Almost Without Apology* (Ithaca: Cornell University Press, 1995).

———, "Kantian Ethics and Claims of Detachment" *Feminist Interpretations of Kant*, Schott (ed.) (University Park: Pennsylvania State University Press, 1997), 145–172.

Linda Barclay, "What Kind of Liberal is Martha Nussbaum?," *SATS – Nordic Journal of Philosophy* 4 (2003): 5–24.

Sandra Bartky, "On Psychological Oppression," *Femininity and Domination: Studies in the Phenomenology of Oppression* (New York: Routledge, 1990), 22–32.

Simone de Beauvoir, *The Second Sex*, Parshely (trans.) (Harmondsworth: Penguin, 1984 [1949]).

Seyla Benhabib, "The Generalized and the Concrete Other," *Women and Moral Theory*, Kittay and Meyers (eds) (Totowa: Rowman and Littlefield, 1987).
____, *Situating the Self: Gender, Community and Postmodernism in Contemporary Ethics* (Cambridge: Polity Press, 1992).
Paul Benson, "Freedom and Value," *Journal of Philosophy* 84 (1987): 465–486.
Isaiah Berlin, "Two Concepts of Liberty," *Four Essays on Liberty* (London: Oxford University Press, 1969), 118–172.
Bernard R. Boxill, "Self-Respect and Protest," *Philosophy and Public Affairs* 6 (1976): 58–96.
____, *Blacks and Social Justice* (Totowa: Rowman and Allanheld, 1984).
____, "The Responsibility of the Oppressed to Resist Their Own Oppression," *Journal of Social Philosophy* 41 (2010): 1–12.
Elizabeth Brake, "Rawls and Feminism: What Should Feminists Make of Liberal Neutrality?," *Journal of Moral Philosophy* 1 (2004): 293–309.
Samantha Brennan, "Reconciling Feminist Politics and Feminist Ethics on the Issue of Rights," *Journal of Social Philosophy* 30 (1999): 260–275.
____, "The Liberal Rights of Feminist Liberalism," *Varieties of Feminist Liberalism*, Baehr (ed.) (Lanham: Rowman and Littlefield, 2004), 85–102.
____, "Feminist Ethics and Everyday Inequalities," *Hypatia* 24 (2009): 141–159.
Wendy Brown, *States of Injury: Power and Freedom in Late Modernity* (Princeton: Princeton University Press, 1995).
Sarah Buss, "Justified Wrongdoing," *Noûs* 31 (1997): 337–369.
Judith Butler, *Gender Trouble: Feminism and the Subversion of Identity* (New York: Routledge, 1990).
Claudia Card, *The Unnatural Lottery: Character and Moral Luck* (Philadelphia: Temple University Press, 1996).
John Christman, "Liberalism and Individual Positive Freedom," *Ethics* 101 (1991): 343–359.
____, "Feminism and Autonomy," *Nagging Questions: Feminist Ethics in Everyday Life*, Bushnell (ed.) (Savage: Rowman and Littlefield, 1995), 17–39.
____, "Relational Autonomy, Liberal Individualism, and the Social Constitution of Selves," *Philosophical Studies* 117 (2004): 143–164.
Lorraine Code, *What Can She Know? Feminist Theory and the Construction of Knowledge* (Ithaca: Cornell University Press, 1991).
Margaret A. Crouch, "Sexual Harassment in Public Places," *Social Philosophy Today* (2010).
Ann Cudd, "Oppression by Choice," *Journal of Social Philosophy* 25 (1994): 22–44.
____, "Psychological Explanations of Oppression," *Theorizing Multiculturalism: A Guide to the Current Debate*, Willett (ed.) (Malden: Blackwell, 1998), 187–215.
____, "Strikes, Housework, and the Moral Obligation to Resist," *Journal of Social Philosophy* 29 (1998): 20–36.
____, "The Paradox of Liberal Feminism: Preference, Rationality, and Oppression," *Varieties of Feminist Liberalism*, Baehr (ed.) (Lanham: Roman and Littlefield, 2004): 37–62.
____, *Analyzing Oppression* (New York: Oxford University Press, 2006).
Stephen Darwall, "Two Kinds of Respect," *Ethics* 88 (1977): 36–49.
Partha Dasgupta, *An Inquiry into Well-being and Destitution* (Oxford: Clarendon Press, 1993).

Richard Dean, *The Value of Humanity in Kant's Moral Theory* (New York: Oxford University Press, 2006).
Lara Denis, "Kant's Ethics and Duties to Oneself," *Pacific Philosophical Quarterly* 78 (1997): 321–348.
——, "Kant's Ethical Duties and their Feminist Implications," *Feminist Moral Philosophy: Canadian Journal of Philosophy Supplementary* 28 (2002): 157–187.
——, "Freedom, Primacy, and Perfect Duties to Oneself," *Kant's Metaphysics of Morals: A Critical Guide* (Cambridge: Cambridge University Press, 2010), 170–191.
Robin Dillon, "Care and Respect," *Explorations in Feminist Ethics: Theory and Practice*, Cole and Coultrap-McQuin (eds) (Bloomington: Indiana University Press, 1992).
——, "How to Lose your Self-Respect," *American Philosophical Quarterly* 29 (1992): 125–139.
——, "Respect and Care: Toward Moral Integration," *Canadian Journal of Philosophy* 22 (1992): 105–132.
——, "Toward a Feminist Conception of Self-Respect," *Hypatia* 7 (1992): 52–69.
——, "Self-Respect: Moral, Emotional, Political," *Ethics* 107 (1997): 226–239.
——, "'What's a Woman Worth? What's Life Worth? Without Self-Respect!': On the Value of Evaluative Self-Respect," *Moral Psychology: Feminist Ethics and Social Theory*, DesAutels and Walker (eds) (Lanham: Rowman and Littlefield, 2004): 47–66.
Enrique Dussel, *Ethics and Community*, Knoll (trans.) (New York: Orbis Books, 1988).
——, *Twenty Theses on Politics*, Ciccariello-Maher (trans.) (Durham: Duke University Press, 2008).
Jane Flax, "A Constructionist Despite Herself? On Capacities and their Discontents," *Controversies in Feminism*, Sterba (ed.) (Lanham: Rowman and Littlefield, 2001), 47–57.
Elizabeth Fox-Genovese, *Feminism Without Illusions: A Critique of Individualism* (Chapel Hill: University of North Carolina Press, 1991).
Marilyn Friedman, "Moral Integrity and the Deferential Wife," *Philosophical Studies* 47 (1985): 141–150.
——, "Autonomy and Social Relationships: Rethinking the Feminist Critique," *Feminists Rethink the Self*, Meyers (ed.) (Boulder: Westview Press, 1997), 40–61.
——, *Autonomy, Gender, Politics* (New York: Oxford University Press, 2003).
Marilyn Frye, *The Politics of Reality* (Freedom, CA: The Crossing Press, 1983).
——, "History and Responsibility," *Hypatia* 8 (1985): 215–216.
Carol Gilligan, *In a Different Voice: Psychological Theory and Women's Development* (Cambridge: Harvard University Press, 1982).
Jean Grimshaw, "Autonomy and Identity in Feminist Thinking," *Feminist Perspectives in Philosophy*, Griffiths and Whitford (eds) (Bloomington: Indiana University Press, 1988): 90–108.
Paul Guyer, *Kant on Freedom, Law, and Happiness* (Cambridge: Cambridge University Press, 2000).
——, "Kant on the Theory and Practice of Autonomy," *Social Philosophy and Policy* 20 (2003): 70–98.
Jean Hampton, "Should Political Philosophy by Done without Metaphysics?" *Ethics* 99 (1989): 791–814.

——, "Contract and Consent," *A Companion to Contemporary Political Philosophy* 2 (1993): 478–492.

——, "Feminist Contractarianism," *A Mind of One's Own: Feminist Essays on Reason and Objectivity*, Antony and Witt (eds) (Boulder: Westview Press, 1993), 227–256.

——, "Selflessness and the Loss of Self," *Social Philosophy and Policy* 10 (1993): 135–165.

——, "The Common Faith of Liberalism," *The Intrinsic Worth of Persons: Contractarianism in Moral and Political Philosophy* (New York: Cambridge University Press, 2007).

Nancy Hartsock, "The Feminist Standpoint: Developing the Ground for a Specifically Feminist Historical Materialism," *Discovering Reality: Feminist Perspectives on Epistemology, Metaphysics, Methodology, and the Philosophy of Science*, Harding and Hintikka (eds) (Dordrecht: D. Reidel, 1983), 283–310.

——, *Money, Sex, and Power* (Boston: Northeastern University Press, 1988).

Jean Harvey, *Civilized Oppression* (Lanham: Rowman and Littlefield, 1999).

Sally Haslanger, "Gender and Race: (What) Are They? (What) Do We Want Them To Be?," *Nous* 34 (2000): 31–55.

——, "Oppressions: Racial and Other," *Racism, Philosophy and Mind: Philosophical Explanations of Racism and Its Implications*, Levine and Pataki (eds) (Ithaca: Cornell University Press, 2004), 97–123.

——, "Changing the Ideology and Culture of Philosophy: Not by Reason (Alone)," *Hypatia* 23 (2008): 210–223.

Virginia Held, "Feminism and Moral Theory," *Women and Moral Theory*, Kittay and Meyers (eds) (Totowa: Rowman and Littlefield, 1987), 111–128.

——, *Feminist Morality: Transforming Culture, Society, and Politics* (Chicago: University of Chicago Press, 1993).

——, *The Ethics of Care: Personal, Political, and Global* (New York: Oxford University Press, 2006).

Barbara Herman, "On the Value of Acting from the Motive of Duty," *Philosophical Review* 90 (1981): 359–382.

——, "Integrity and Impartiality," *Monist* 66 (1983): 233–250.

——, "Could it be Worth Thinking about Kant on Sex and Marriage?," *A Mind of One's Own: Feminist Essays on Reason and Objectivity*, Antony and Witt (eds) (Boulder: Westview Press, 2002), 53–72.

Tracy Higgins, "Gender, Why Feminists Can't (Or Shouldn't) be Liberals," *Fordham Law Review* 72 (2004): 1629–1641.

Thomas Hill, "Servility and Self-Respect," *The Monist* 57 (1973): 87–104.

——, "Self-Respect Reconsidered," *Tulane Studies in Philosophy* 31 (1982): 129–137.

——, "The Importance of Autonomy," *Women and Moral Theory*, Kittay and Meyers (eds) (Totowa: Rowman and Littlefield, 1987), 129–138.

——, *Autonomy and Self-Respect* (New York: Cambridge University Press, 1991).

——, *Dignity and Practical Reason in Kant's Moral Theory* (Ithaca: Cornell University Press, 1992).

——, *Respect, Pluralism, and Justice: Kantian Perspectives* (New York: Oxford University Press, 2000).

Linda Hirshman, *Get to Work: A Manifesto for Women of the World* (New York: Viking Penguin, 2006).

Sarah Hoagland, "Some Thoughts about 'Caring,'" *Feminist Ethics*, Card (ed.) (Lawrence: University Press of Kansas, 1991), 246–263.

———, "Some Concerns About Nel Noddings' Caring," *Hypatia* 5 (1990): 109–114.

Barbara Houston, "Caring and Exploitation," *Hypatia* 5 (1990): 115–119.

Alison Jaggar, *Feminist Politics and Human Nature* (Totowa: Roman and Allanheld, 1983 repr. 1988).

Immanuel Kant, *Observations on the Feeling of the Beautiful and Sublime*, Frierson and Guyer (eds) (Cambridge: Cambridge University Press, 2011 [1764]). 'O' in parenthetical documentation refers to this work.

———, *Groundwork of the Metaphysics of Morals*, Gregor (ed. and trans.) (Cambridge: Cambridge University Press, 1998 [1785]). 'G' in parenthetical documentation refers to this work.

———, *The Critique of Practical Reason*, Gregor (ed. and trans.) (Cambridge: Cambridge University Press, 1997 [1788]). 'CPR' in parenthetical documentation refers to this work.

———, *Religion within the Boundaries of Mere Reason*, Wood and di Giovanni (ed. and trans.) (Cambridge: Cambridge University Press, 1998 [1793]). 'R' in parenthetical documentation refers to this work.

———, *The Metaphysics of Morals*, Gregor (ed. and trans.) (Cambridge: Cambridge University Press, 1996 [1797]). 'MM' in parenthetical documentation refers to this work.

———, *Anthropology from a Pragmatic Point of View*, Louden (trans.) (Cambridge: Cambridge University Press, 2006 [1798]). 'A' in parenthetical documentation refers to this work.

———, *Lectures on Ethics*, Heath (ed. and trans.) (Cambridge: Cambridge University Press, 2001). 'LE' in parenthetical documentation refers to this work.

Jean Keller, "Autonomy, Relationality, and Feminist Ethics," *Hypatia* 12 (1997): 152–164.

Andrew Kernohan, *Liberalism, Equality, and Cultural Oppression* (New York: Cambridge University Press, 1999).

Eva Feder Kittay, "Human Dependency and Rawlsian Equality," *Feminists Rethink the Self*, Meyers (ed.) (Boulder: Westview Press, 1997), 219–266.

———, *Love's Labor: Essays on Women, Equality, and Dependency* (New York: Routledge, 1998).

———, "When Caring is Just and Justice is Caring," *The Subject of Care: Feminist Perspectives on Dependency*, Kittay and Feder (eds) (Lanham: Rowman and Littlefield, 2002), 257–276.

Pauline Kleingold, "The Problematic Status of Gender-Neutral Language in the History of Philosophy: The Case of Kant," *Philosophical Forum* 24 (1992–1993): 134–150.

Christine Korsgaard, *Creating the Kingdom of Ends* (Cambridge: Cambridge University Press, 1996).

Chandran Kukathas, "Liberalism, Multiculturalism and Oppression," *Political Theory: Tradition and Diversity* (Cambridge: Cambridge University Press, 1997): 132–153.

———, "Is Feminism Bad for Multiculturalism?," *Public Affairs Quarterly* 15 (2001): 83–98.

———, *The Liberal Archipelago* (Oxford: Oxford University Press, 2003).

Will Kymlicka, *Liberalism, Community and Culture* (Oxford: Clarendon Press, 1989).

―――, "Liberal Complacencies," *Is Multiculturalism Bad for Women?* Cohen, Howard, and Nussbaum (eds) (Princeton: Princeton University Press, 1999), 31–34.
Linda LeMoncheck, "What's Wrong with Being a Sex Object?" *Living with Contradictions: Controversies in Feminist Social Ethics*, Jaggar (ed.) (Boulder: Westview Press, 1994): 199–206.
―――, "The Power of Sexual Stereotypes and the Sexiness of Power," *Sexual Harassment: Issues and Answers*, LeMoncheck and Sterba (eds) (New York: Oxford University Press, 2001), 264–269.
Genevieve Lloyd, *The Man of Reason* (Minneapolis: University of Minnesota Press, 1981).
Catriona Mackenzie and Natalie Stoljar, (eds) *Relational Autonomy: Feminist Perspectives on Autonomy, Agency, and the Social Self* (New York: Oxford University Press, 2000).
Catharine MacKinnon, *Sexual Harassment of Working Women: A Case of Sex Discrimination* (New Haven: Yale University Press, 1979).
―――, *Feminism Unmodified: Discourses on Life and Law* (Cambridge: Harvard University Press, 1987).
―――, and Andrea Dworkin, *In Harm's Way: The Pornography Civil Rights Hearings* (Cambridge: Harvard University Press, 1987).
―――, *Toward a Feminist Theory of State* (Cambridge: Harvard University Press, 1991).
Nelson Mandela, *A Long Walk to Freedom: The Autobiography of Nelson Mandela* (London: Little Brown, 1994).
Bonnie Mann, "Dependence on Place, Dependence in Place," *The Subject of Care: Feminist Perspectives on Dependency*, Kittay and Feder (eds) (Lanham: Rowman and Littlefield, 2002), 348–368.
―――, *Women's Liberation and the Sublime: Feminism, Postmodernism, Environment* (New York: Oxford University Press, 2006).
―――, "Creepers, Flirts, Heroes, and Allies: Four Theses on Sexual Harassment," *APA Newsletter on Feminism and Philosophy* 11 (2012): 24–31.
Karl Marx, *Grundrisse*, trans. Nicolaus (Harmondsworth: Penguin Books, 1973).
Susan Mendus, "'An Honest but Narrow-Minded Bourgeois'?" *Essays on Kant's Political Philosophy*, Williams (ed.) (Chicago: University of Chicago Press, 1992), 166–190.
Diana T. Meyers, "Personal Autonomy and the Paradox of Feminine Socialization," *Journal of Philosophy* 84 (1987): 619–628.
―――, *Self, Society, and Personal Choice* (New York: Columbia University Press, 1989).
―――, "Feminism and Women's Autonomy: The Challenge of Female Genital Cutting," *Metaphilosophy* 31 (2000): 469–491.
―――, "Intersectional Identity and the Authentic Self: Opposites Attract," *Relational Autonomy: Feminist Perspectives on Autonomy, Agency, and the Social Self*, MacKenzie and Stoljar (eds) (New York: Oxford University Press, 2000), 151–180.
―――, *Being Yourself: Essays on Identity, Action, and Social Life* (Lanham: Rowman and Littlefield, 2004).
John Stuart Mill, "The Subjection of Women," in J.S. Mill and Harriet Taylor Mill, *Essays on Sex Equality*, Rossi (ed.) (Chicago: University of Chicago Press, 1970 [1869]).

Sarah Clark Miller, "A Kantian Ethic of Care?," *Feminist Interventions in Ethics and Politics: Feminist Ethics and Social Theory*, Andrew, Keller, & Schwartzman (eds) (Lanham: Rowman and LIttlefield, 2005), 111–127.
Charles Mills, and Carole Pateman, *Contract and Domination* (Malden: Polity Press, 2007).
——, "Schwartzman vs. Okin: Some Comments on *Challenging Liberalism*," *Hypatia* 24 (2009): 164–177.
——, "Occupy Liberalism! Or, Ten Reasons Why Liberalism Cannot be Retrieved for Radicalism (And Why They're All Wrong)," *Radical Philosophy Review* 15 (2012): 305–323.
Kurt Mosser, "Kant and Feminism," *Kant-Studien* 90 (1999): 322–353.
Herta Nagl-Docekal, "Feminist Ethics: How It Could Benefit from Kant's Moral Philosophy," Morgenstern (trans.), *Feminist Interpretations of Kant*, Schott (ed.) (University Park: Pennsylvania State University Press, 1997), 101–124.
Uma Narayan, "Minds of Their Own: Choices, Autonomy, Cultural Practices, and Other Women," *A Mind of One's Own: Feminist Essays on Reason and Objectivity*, 2nd edition, Antony and Witt (eds) (Boulder: Westview Press, 2002), 418–432.
Jennifer Nedelsky, "Reconceiving Autonomy: Sources, Thoughts, and Possibilities," *Yale Journal of Law and Feminism* 1 (1989): 7–36.
Nel Noddings, *Caring: A Feminine Approach to Ethics and Moral Education* (Los Angeles: University of California Press, 1984).
Martha Nussbaum, "Aristotelian Social Democracy," *Liberalism and the Good*, Douglass, Mara, and Richardson (eds) (New York: Routledge, 1990), 203–252.
——, "Human Functioning and Social Justice," *Political Theory* (1992) 20: 202–246.
——, "Objectification," *Philosophy and Public Affairs* 24 (1995): 249–291.
——, "Public Philosophy and International Feminism," *Ethics* 108 (1998): 762–796.
——, "Interview," *Key Philosophers in Conversation*, Pyle (ed.) (London: Routledge, 1999), 239–256.
——, *Sex and Social Justice* (New York: Oxford University Press, 1999).
——, *Women and Human Development: The Capabilities Approach* (Cambridge: Cambridge University Press, 2000).
——, "Aristotle, Politics and Human Capabilities: A Response to Antony, Arneson, Charlesworth and Mulgan," *Ethics* 111 (2000): 102–140.
——, "Political Liberalism and Respect: A Response to Linda Barclay," *SATS – Nordic Journal of Philosophy* 4 (2003): 25–44.
——, "The Future of Feminist Liberalism," *Varieties of Feminist Liberalism*, Baehr (ed.) (Lanham: Rowman and Littlefield, 2004), 103–132.
——, *Frontiers of Justice: Disability, Nationality, and Species Membership* (Cambridge: Belknap Press, 2007).
——, *Creating Capabilities: The Human Development Approach* (Cambridge: Belknap Press, 2011).
Susan Moller Okin, *Justice, Gender, and the Family* (New York: Basic Books, 1989).
——, "Gender Inequality and Cultural Differences," *Political Theory* 22 (1994): 5–24.
——, "Feminism and Multiculturalism: Some Tensions," *Ethics* 108 (1998): 661–684.

———, "Recognizing Women's Rights as Human Rights," *American Philosophical Association Newsletter on Philosophy and Law* 97 (1998): 99–102.
———, "Reply," *Is Multiculturalism Bad for Women?* Cohen, Howard, and Nussbaum (eds) (Princeton: Princeton University Press, 1999), 115–132.
——— and Brooke Ackerly, "Feminist Social Criticism and the International Movement for Women's Rights as Human Rights," *Democracy's Edges*, Shapiro and Hacker-Cordon (eds.) (Cambridge: Cambridge University Press, 1999), 134–162.
———, "Mistresses of Their Own Destiny: Group Rights, Gender, and Realistic Rights of Exit," *Ethics* (2002) 112: 205–30.
———, "Justice and Gender: An Unfinished Debate," *Fordham Law Review* (2004): 1537–1546.
———, "Multiculturalism and Feminism: No Simple Question, No Simple Answers," *Minorities within Minorities: Equality, Rights and Diversity* (Cambridge: Cambridge University Press, 2005): 67–89.
Marina Oshana, "Autonomy and Free Agency," *Personal Autonomy: New Essays on Personal Autonomy and Its Role in Contemporary Moral Philosophy,* Taylor (ed.) (Cambridge: Cambridge University Press, 2005), 183–204.
Lina Papadaki, "What is Objectification?" *Journal of Moral Philosophy* 7 (2010): 16–36.
Carole Pateman, *The Problem of Political Obligation: A Critique of Liberal Theory* (Berkeley: University of California Press, 1979).
———, *The Sexual Contract* (Stanford: Stanford University Press, 1988).
———, "Self-Ownership and Property in the Person: A Tale of Two Concepts," *The Journal of Political Philosophy* 10 (2002): 20–53.
——— and Charles Mills, *Contract and Domination* (London: Polity Press, 2007).
John Rawls, *A Theory of Justice* (Cambridge: Belknap Press, 1971).
———, *Political Liberalism* (New York: Columbia University Press, 1993).
———, *Justice as Fairness: A Restatement* (Cambridge: Belknap Press, 2001).
———, *The Law of Peoples* (Cambridge: Harvard University Press, 2001).
Joseph Raz, *The Morality of Freedom* (Oxford: Clarendon Press, 1986).
———, "Facing Diversity: The Case of Epistemic Abstinence," *Philosophy & Public Affairs* 19 (1990): 3–46.
Janice Richardson, "On Not Making Ourselves the Prey of Others: Jean Hampton's Feminist Contractarianism," *Feminist Legal Studies* 15 (2007): 33–55.
Sara Ruddick, *Maternal Thinking: Towards a Politics of Peace* (Boston: Beacon Press, 1989).
Michael Sandel, *Liberalism and the Limits of Justice* (Cambridge: Cambridge University Press, 1981).
———, "The Procedural Republic and the Unencumbered Self," *Political Theory* 12 (1984): 81–96.
———, *Democracy's Discontent: America in Search of a Public Philosophy* (Cambridge: Harvard University Press, 1996).
Naomi Scheman, "Individualism and the Objects of Psychology," *Discovering Reality: Feminist Perspectives on Epistemology, Metaphysics, Methodology, and Philosophy of Science,* Harding and Hintikka (eds) (Dordrecht, Holland: D. Reidel, 1983).
———, *Engenderings: Constructions of Knowledge, Authority, and Privilege* (New York: Routledge, 1993).

Lisa Schwartzman, *Challenging Liberalism: Feminism as Political Critique* (University Park: Pennsylvania State University Press, 2006).
———, "Non-Ideal Theorizing, Social Groups, and Knowledge of Oppression: A Response," *Hypatia* 24 (2009): 177–188.
Sally Sedgwick, "Can Kant's Ethics Survive the Feminist Critique?" *Pacific Philosophical Quarterly* 71 (1990): 60–79.
Hubert Selby, "Tralala," *Last Exit to Brooklyn* (New York: Grove Press, 1957).
Amartya Sen, "Rights and Capabilities," *Resources, Values, and Development* (Oxford and Cambridge: Blackwell and MIT Press, 1984), 307–324.
———, *The Standard of Living* (Cambridge: Cambridge University Press, 1989).
———, "Gender and Co-operative Conflicts," *Women and World Development*, Tinker (ed.) (New York: Oxford University Press, 1990), 123–149.
———, *Inequality Reexamined* (Cambridge: Harvard University Press, 1992).
———, *The Quality of Life*, Nussbaum and Sen (eds) (New York: Oxford University Press, 1993).
———, "Gender Inequality and Theories of Justice," *Women, Culture, and Development*, Glover and Nussbaum (eds) (New York: Oxford University Press, 1995), 259–274.
———, *Women, Culture, and Development* (New York: Oxford University Press, 1995).
———, *Commodities and Capabilities* (Oxford: Oxford University Press, 1999).
Ayelet Shachar, *Multicultural Jurisdictions: Cultural Differences and Women's Rights* (Cambridge: Cambridge University Press, 2001).
Marcus G. Singer, "Duties and Duties to Oneself," *Ethics* 73 (1963): 133–142.
Jeff Spinner-Halev, "Feminism, Multiculturalism, Oppression and the State," *Ethics* 112 (2001): 84–115.
Cynthia Stark, "The Rationality of Valuing Oneself: A Critique of Kant on Self-Respect," *Journal of the History of Philosophy* 35 (1997): 65–82.
Anita Superson, "A Feminist Definition of Sexual Harassment," *Journal of Social Philosophy* 24 (1993): 46–64.
———, "Right-Wing Women: Causes, Choices, and Blaming the Victim," *Journal of Social Philosophy* 24 (1993): 40–61.
———, "Privilege, Immorality, and Responsibility for Attending to the 'Facts about Humanity,'" *Journal of Social Philosophy* 35 (2004): 34–55.
———, "Deformed Desires and Informed Desire Tests," *Hypatia* 20 (2005): 109–112.
———, "The Deferential Wife Revisited: Agency and Moral Responsibility," *Hypatia* 25 (2010): 253–275.
James Stacey Taylor, "Autonomy, Responsibility, and Women's Obligation to Resist Sexual Harassment," *International Journal of Applied Philosophy* 21 (2007): 55–63.
Elizabeth Telfer, "Self-Respect," *Philosophical Quarterly* 18 (1968): 114–21.
Joan Tronto, *Moral Boundaries: A Political Argument for an Ethic of Care* (New York: Routledge, 1993).
Margaret Urban Walker, *Moral Understandings: A Feminist Study in Ethics*, 2nd Edition (New York: Oxford University Press, 2007).
David Foster Wallace, "Getting Away from Already Pretty Much Being Away From it All," *A Supposedly Fun Thing I'll Never Do Again* (Boston: Little, Brown, 1997), 83–137.

Susan Wendell, "Oppression and Victimization: Choice and Responsibility," *Hypatia* 5 (1990): 15–46.
Andrea Westlund, "Selflessness and Responsibility for Self: Is Deference Compatible with Autonomy?" *The Philosophical Review* 112 (2003): 483–523.
——, "Rethinking Relational Autonomy," *Hypatia* 24 (2009): 26–49.
Susan Wolf, "Asymmetrical Freedom," *The Journal of Philosophy* 77 (1980): 151–166.
——, "Moral Saints," *The Journal of Philosophy* 79 (1982): 419–439.
——, *Freedom and Reason* (New York: Oxford University Press, 1990).
Mary Wollstonecraft, *A Vindication of the Rights of Woman* (Cambridge: Cambridge University Press, 1995 [1792]).
Allan Wood, *Kant's Ethical Thought* (Cambridge: Cambridge University Press, 1999).
——, *Kantian Ethics* (Cambridge: Cambridge University Press, 2008).
Alison Wylie, "Why Standpoint Matters," *Science and Other Cultures: Issues in Philosophies of Science and Technology*, Figueroa and Harding (eds) (London: Routledge, 2003), 26–48.
Iris Marion Young, *Justice and the Politics of Difference* (Princeton: Princeton University Press, 1990).
Kimberly Yuracko, *Perfectionism and Contemporary Feminist Values* (Bloomington: University of Indiana Press, 2003).

Index

abstraction, 39
  critiques of liberal, 13, 20–1
  defences of liberal, 21–3
absolute worth, 85, 163, 165, 180
  see also dignity
acquiescence, *see* oppression, acquiescence in
adaptive preferences, 10, 19, 22, 32, 72, 73, 75, 93, 100, 108, 117, 125, 142, 155
  see also deformed desires
agency, xi, 6, 10, 20, 71, 89, 93, 99, 100–1, 103, 124, 178, 183
akrasia, 125–6
amoralism, 64
androcentrism, 15
animals, 52–3, 54–5, 57, 63, 80, 81
animality, 52–3, 54–6, 80, 81, 82, 86, 136, 164, 176, 180
anti-colonialism, *see* colonialism
anti-racism, *see* race
Antony, Louise, xiii, 48
appraisal respect, *see* respect, appraisal vs. recognition
Aristotelianism, 33, 39
assimilationism, Liberal, 20–1
autonomy
  critiques of liberal, 1, 11, 15–18, 20, 24
  defences of liberal, viii, ix, 10, 18–19, 25, 29, 30, 34–5, 36, 37, 42, 43, 45, 48, 87
autonomy, Kantian, viii, 78, 80, 159, 164–6, 169, 172–3, 174, 175, 177, 179, 180, 181
  see also personality
autonomy, moral
  effects of oppression on, x, 71, 73, 91, 92, 93, 95, 97–8, 100–1, 106–9, 111, 112–13
  global vs. local, 107–8, 116
  obligation to protect, x, 89, 99–106

relational, 24, 41, 42, 43, 44–5
relationship to responsibility, x, 91, 99, 102, 106–13, 118

bad faith, 74, 119–20, 143–4
Baron, Marcia, 78, 82, 87, 152–3, 157
Bartky, Sandra, 73, 88, 92–3, 96, 115, 156
de Beauvoir, Simone, 72–3, 74, 88, 119–20, 155
beneficence, duty of, *see* imperfect duties, duty of beneficence
Bengali widows, 117–18, 124, 130, 142, 151, 154
blame-worthiness, 70, 71, 110–13, 121, 128, 130, 131, 143, 153
blaming the victim, 101, 104, 105, 158
  objection from, xi, 128, 130–1
Boxill, Bernard, 44, 113–15, 116, 151, 157
Brennan, Samantha, 35, 41, 48, 87
Butler, Judith, 42, 44
bystanders, 105–6, 116

capabilities approach, 32–5, 41, 43, 47, 48, 49, 154
care, ethics of, 15–16, 41, 42, 44, 53–4, 56, 57–8, 61, 77–8, 79, 80, 82, 88
children, 30–1, 36, 47, 53–4, 59–60, 73, 77, 80, 105, 107, 119, 124, 130, 156
civic republicanism, 27, 45
civil inattention, 96, 115
class, 17, 21, 23, 24, 71, 105, 126
colonialism, ix, 1, 12, 26–8, 32, 45–6
communitarianism, 13–14, 16–17, 23, 26, 27–8, 41, 45, 46
confrontation, x, 89–91, 99–100, 101–4, 113–15, 140, 142, 146

consent, 3, 9–10, 30, 32, 119, 126
consequentialism, *see* utilitarianism
contractarianism, 12, 43
Critique of Practical Reason, 83, 86, 172–3, 180–1
Crouch, Margaret, 91, 96, 98, 103, 115, 116
Cudd, Ann, xiii, 9, 41, 43, 44, 46, 73, 88, 132, 133–4, 154–5, 156, 157
culpability, 105, 107, 153
  vs. responsibility, 109, 110–13

Darwall, Stephen, 83, 162, 163, 169, 180
Deferential Wife, 70, 79, 87, 88, 116
deformed desires, *see* adaptive preferences
dependency, 16–17, 22, 23, 53–6, 57–9, 61, 77–8, 79, 124–5, 133, 157
develop one's talents, duty to, *see* imperfect duties, duty to develop one's talents
difference, 13–14, 20–1, 22–3, 39, 44
dignity, xi, 21, 35, 52–3, 69, 80, 141, 158, 165, 180–1, 182, 183
  as conferring unconditional and incomparable worth, xi, 159, 162, 165–6, 170–1, 182
  as distinct from respect-worthiness, 159, 162, 171–9, 180, 182, 185
  loss of, 166–9, 170, 175, 178, 184
  see also individualism, individual as intrinsically valuable; personality, as conferring dignity
Dillon, Robin, xiii, 42, 70–2, 78, 83, 88, 122, 182
disability, 53–4, 55–6
Doctrine of Virtue, see *Metaphysics of Morals*
duty
  acting in accordance with, 54–5, 57–60, 82–3, 85, 87, 164, 182

  perfect vs. imperfect, 134–9, 145–54, 157; *see also* imperfect duties
  of self-respect, *see* self-respect, Kantian duty of
  wide vs. narrow, 137–9
  to the self, 74, 81, 86, 118–19, 132–4, 139, 141, 174–7, 183, 184; *see also* self, possibility of duties to

education, 18, 36, 47, 55, 124, 127, 132–3, 155
embodiment, 33
  objection to Kantianism ix, 50, 52–6, 61–2, 78, 79–80
emotions, 81, 152, 164–5, 171, 182, 183
  contingency of, 54–5, 57, 60, 63, 80, 82–3, 84, 85
  historical association with women, 50–1, 57, 61
  objection to Kantianism, ix, 50, 56–62, 78
end-in-itself-hood, 63–5, 68, 80–1, 85, 86, 121, 162–3, 166, 169–70, 172–6, 179, 180
equality, 2, 11–12, 20, 22, 23, 26, 28, 32, 34, 35, 37, 38, 39, 52, 72, 94, 103
erosion analogy, 145–6, 148, 150, 153–4
exploitation, 39–40, 50, 54, 56, 61, 74–8, 88, 156

feminism, viii, ix, 10, 15–17, 27, 30, 35, 36–7, 39–49, 50–8, 60–2, 70–8, 78–80, 82, 87–8, 89–109, 112–13, 115–16, 117–35, 140–54, 154–7, 158
flourishing, 31–4, 38, 77
freedom, 7, 12, 17–19, 37–9, 52, 67, 92, 94, 98, 100, 101, 107–8, 131
  Kantian, 80, 84, 86–7, 152, 164, 172, 179, 180, 181, 183
  see also liberty
Frye, Marilyn, 40, 98, 104, 116
  birdcage metaphor, 7, 97, 109, 132, 151

gender essentialism, 58
gendered dominance and submission, 2–3, 95, 97, 103
Groundwork of the Metaphysics of Morals, 63, 64, 65, 80–6, 121, 163, 165, 166, 172, 179–81, 185
groups, 2, 3–6, 7–9, 12, 13, 14, 22–32, 40, 72, 73, 76–7, 93, 94, 98, 119, 124, 127, 132–4, 141, 144, 157
  rights of, 30–1

Hampton, Jean, 36–9, 43, 46, 49, 74, 79, 88
harm principle, 24, 36
Harvey, Jean, xiii, 116, 131
Haslanger, Sally, xiii, 8–9, 40, 41, 73, 88
heteronomy, 124, 164, 181
Hill, Thomas, 67–72, 82, 83, 85, 87, 116, 121–2, 155, 157, 159, 179, 180, 181, 182, 185
human condition, *see* human nature
human nature, 33–4, 37, 39, 48, 52–4, 62–3, 80, 162–4, 181
humanity
  as an end-in-itself, 86, 159, 162–3, 166, 169, 170–4, 179, 180
  as an objective end, 163, 169–70, 177
  formula of, 63, 64, 120–1, 162–3
  Kant's definition of, 62–3, 84–5, 162–4, 169, 179–81
  requirements of respect, 65–6, 82, 86, 167–72, 175–9, 182, 183, 184
  value of the individual in virtue of, 63–5, 69, 120–1, 136, 162, 166, 171, 172, 174–9, 182, 183
  see also rational nature

identity, 16, 22–5, 71, 141, 180
ignorance, 9, 70, 143, 150, 153
  Rawlsian veil of, 20, 23, 25
implicit bias, 9, 40–1, 94
impartiality, 20–1, 59–60
imperfect duties
  definition of, 86–7, 135–6, 145–6, 153, 157
  duty of beneficence, 136, 138, 145–9
  duty to develop one's talents, 138–9, 145–9
  duty to increase one's moral perfection, 138–9, 145, 147
  duty to resist one's oppression, xi, 134–9, 145–50, 153–4
  duty to respect others, 138, 145, 147
imperialism, 1, 12, 26, 28, 32, 35
inclinations, *see* emotions
increase one's moral perfection, duty to, *see* imperfect duties, duty to increase one's moral perfection
independence, 15, 16–17, 52, 54, 58, 61, 77, 80, 93–4, 119, 124–5, 180
individualism
  critiques of liberal, 1, 10, 11, 13–15, 16, 17, 20, 23–4, 41–9, 52–4, 77
  defences of liberal, 41–9, 77–8, 118–19
  individual as basic unit of social reality, 12, 15, 23, 24–6, 30, 32, 76
  individual as intrinsically valuable, viii, 38, 39, 63–6, 74, 179
  individual as locus of value, 12, 23, 24–6
instrumental value, 64–5
interests, 4–6, 10–14, 20–1, 24–6, 30, 32, 40, 59–60, 70, 74–8, 94, 100, 117–19
intrinsic value, *see* individualism, defences of liberal, individual as intrinsically valuable
irrationality, practical, xi, 123–7, 129, 141, 144, 155

Kant, Immanuel, viii–xi, 17, 39, 46, 49, 50–88, 99, 103, 116, 118, 120–1, 122, 123, 135–9, 145, 147, 152, 154, 155, 157, 158–85
  feminist critiques of, ix; *see also* emotions, objection to Kantianism; embodiment, objection to Kantianism

latitude in action, 51, 135–54, 157
  latitude in refraining from action, 136–9, 145–54
  latitude in which action to take, 135–9, 140–5
Lectures on Ethics, 80, 159, 167, 182–4
liberalism, viii–ix, 1–49
  comprehensive vs. political, ix, 28–31, 34–9, 48
  critiques of, *see* abstraction, critiques of liberal; autonomy, critiques of liberal; individualism, critiques of liberal; pluralism, critiques of liberal
  defences of, *see* abstraction, defences of liberal; autonomy, defences of liberal; individualism, defences of liberal; pluralism, defences of liberal
  definition of, 1, 11–15
  historical failures of, viii, ix, 12–15, 61
liberty, 1, 2, 11–12, 15–19, 26, 42–3, 120
  positive vs. negative, 16–19, 20, 27–8, 42
  see also autonomy; freedom

maxim, 62, 80, 83, 135–6, 148, 164–5, 171, 176, 180–1, 183
Mandela, Nelson, 140–1, 157
Marx, Karl, 13, 17, 42, 156
Metaphysics of Morals, 51–2, 66–7, 69, 79–86, 135–9, 145, 157, 159, 167, 172–7, 180–4
Mill, John Stuart, 1, 2–3, 9, 14, 36, 39, 46, 72, 88
Mills, Charles, xiii, 41, 44, 46
multiculturalism, 1, 12, 27, 30–1, 47, 48

Narayan, Uma, 45, 100–1, 116
Native Companion, 89–102, 112–14, 129–30, 142–4, 146, 149–50, 153
neutrality with respect to competing conceptions of the good, 18, 26–31, 31–9, 43–9
Nussbaum, Martha, 32–5, 39, 41–9, 52–3, 79–80, 95, 115, 151

objectification, 92, 94–7, 115–16
objective ends, *see* humanity, as an objective end
objectivity, *see* universalism
obligation, *see* duty
oppression
  acquiescence in, 3, 9–10, 77, 90, 114, 118–22, 130–1, 133, 135, 142–5, 149–50, 154, 158
  definition of, ix, 2–11
  effects of, viii, x–xi, 2–11, 13–14, 17, 20–3, 28, 30–2, 36, 39–49, 50, 54, 56, 69–78, 86, 89, 91–109, 112–15, 115–16, 117, 123–7, 129–30, 132–4, 145–6
  group-specific nature of, ix, 2–6, 8–9, 23–6, 40, 94, 97–8, 119–20, 132, 133–4, 144, 157
  internalized, 9–10, 19, 22, 32, 72, 73, 93–4, 95, 100, 108, 115, 117–20, 123–7, 132–3, 142, 143, 154, 155, 157
  methods of identification, 24–6
  obligation to resist, x–xi, 112–15, 116, 117–18, 121–2, 126–8, 129–35, 140–54, 157, 158, 161, 178–9
    demandingness of obligations of, 103–6, 127–35, 150–4
    historical feminist accounts of, 74–5, 118–20
  psychological, x, 3, 7, 9–11, 18, 50, 62, 71, 72–5, 88, 92–4, 95, 98, 100, 103, 106–9, 112–13, 115, 117–20, 123–7, 132–3, 144, 156–7
  structural and systemic nature of, ix, 3, 6–11, 17, 40, 76–7, 92–4, 97–8, 109, 126–7, 128, 132, 140, 143–6, 148, 150, 151, 153–4, 156–7
ought implies can, 56
  objection from, xi, 128, 131–3, 134, 150–3

paternalism, 19, 32
passions, *see* emotions
perfect duties, 135–8, 183
perfectionism, 29, 43, 46

personality, Kantian, 52
  as conferring dignity, 159, 163, 165–6, 170–1, 173–4, 176–8
  definition of, 86, 162, 163–5, 169, 177
  loss of, 167, 170, 175–6, 178
pluralism
  critiques of liberal, 11, 15, 26–8
  defences of liberal, 28–31, 31–9, 45–9
poststructuralism, 16, 23, 42, 44
power, 4–6, 11, 13, 16, 20–1, 28, 30–1, 92, 94
proceduralism, 29, 31, 46
protest, 113–15, 116

race, ix, 4, 17, 21–3, 23–4, 26, 31, 40, 44, 92–3, 105, 126
radicalism, ix, 2, 13–15, 20–1, 23, 24, 25–6, 41–6, 141
rational nature, viii, ix, 33, 39, 50, 52–6, 56–62, 62–3, 80, 84–6, 110–11, 159–60, 162–6, 169–73, 179–81
  damage to or restrictions on, xi, 2, 72–4, 81, 106–9, 112, 123–6, 126–8, 132–3, 136–7, 145–51, 153–4, 155–6, 159, 183–4
  obligation to protect or respect, xi, 99–100, 112–15, 118, 120–2, 136–9, 141, 144, 146–50, 153–4, 170–2, 177–9, 184–5
  see also humanity
Rawls, John, 20, 22–3, 28–30, 35–6, 37–8, 43, 44, 46, 47, 48, 62, 83
reasonability, 34–6
  vs. rationality, 28–9, 37–8
recognition respect, *see* respect, appraisal vs. recognition
relational autonomy, 16–17, 24, 41–2, 44–5
relative advantage, 5, 39–40, 94
relativism, 22–3, 26–8, 31–2, 37–9
religion, 8, 12, 14, 17, 24–7, 32, 36, 38, 47, 132
resist one's oppression, duty to, *see* imperfect duties, duty to resist

one's oppression; resistance, obligations of
resistance
  activism vs. opting out, 140–1
  internal vs. external, 141–4, 148–50, 154
  obligations of, *see* oppression, obligation to resist
respect, 10, 19, 26, 29, 32, 34–6, 38–9, 58, 60, 62–6, 70, 83, 85, 96–8, 102–4, 140
  appraisal vs. recognition, 162, 163, 168, 169
  see also rational nature, obligation to protect or respect; respect-worthiness, Kantian; self-respect
respect others, duty to, *see* imperfect duties, duty to respect others
respect-worthiness, Kantian, xi, 136, 172–178, 179–80, 183, 185
  as treatment-constraining, 158, 161, 162, 165, 167–9, 169–72, 182
  loss of, 158–61, 162, 167–9, 169–72, 184
rights, group vs. individual, 30–1, 47
risk, objection from, xi, 104, 128, 129–30, 142, 147

Selby, Hubert, 159–60, 180
self, possibility of duties to, 50, 62, 66–8, 73–8, 87, 183
self-deception, 123–4, 144
self-determination, 26
  see also self-government
self-interest, 10, 15, 21, 25, 26, 32, 59–60, 70, 74–8, 82, 100, 117, 119
self-respect, viii, ix, x, 113–15, 116, 117, 141–2, 144, 149
  Kantian duty of, x–xi, 60, 62–6, 68–74, 78–9, 83–4, 87–8, 99, 120–2, 155
  failures of, xi, 68–74, 87, 131, 137, 148, 150, 158, 160–1, 166–78
self-sacrifice, Gendered norms of, x, 50, 73–8, 88, 140
Sen, Amartya, 10, 32–4, 41, 43, 47, 48, 117, 154

sensibility, *see* emotions
servility, 69–72, 74–9, 83, 87–8, 114, 116, 121–2, 137, 155, 158
sexual harassment
  effects on autonomy, *see* autonomy, effects of oppression on
  obligation to resist, x, 89–91, 99–106, 142–3
  street harassment, 89–91, 96
sexual orientation, 17, 105, 126
social ontology, 13, 23, 26
solidarity, 23, 132–4, 141
standpoint theory, 126–7, 156
stereotypes, 8, 92–4, 115, 140, 157
  internalized, 73, 93–4, 95, 125–6
stereotype threat, 73, 88, 93, 115
supererogation, objection from, xi, 128, 133–4

Superson, Anita, xiii, 43, 79, 87, 88, 98, 101, 116, 130–1, 156

Taylor, James Stacey, 106–9, 112–13, 116
tolerance, 27, 29–31, 36–8
transcultural ideals, *see* universalism

universalism ix, 1–2, 13–14, 15, 16, 20–1, 26–39, 43, 57, 63–4, 84
utilitarianism, 12, 46, 116

violence, 9, 39–40, 97, 124

weakness of will, *see* akrasia
Wylie, Alison, 126–7, 156

Young, Iris Marion, 4, 7–8, 20–1, 39, 40, 44, 46

Printed in the USA
CPSIA information can be obtained
at www.ICGtesting.com
CBHW071104280624
10813CB00005B/462